THE QUIET THAT REMAINS

THE QUIET THAT REMAINS

SURVIVAL, SILENCE, AND THE STORY OF A UKRAINIAN FAMILY

BEN SKLIAR-WARD

Otter Stream Press, London, England

First published in the United Kingdom in 2025.

ISBN: 978-1-0682688-2-3

Cover design and artwork by Peishan Li.

Every effort has been made to ensure the accuracy of the information contained in this book. It is based on extensive archival research, personal documents, and historical records. Where gaps or uncertainties exist, they have been acknowledged. Any remaining errors or omissions are the author's own.

All translations from Ukrainian are the author's own, unless otherwise stated.

For the people of Ukraine, past, present, and future.

Не забувай про рідний край
Не забувай про свою рідну землю
А все згадай й добрами
У славі, честі й оповится.

Never forget your native land
Never forget your beloved soil
Recall it all, and through good deeds
It shall be wrapped in glory and honour.

– Wsewolod Skliar, Ukrainian Exile, 1951

CONTENTS

Note on Naming, Terminology, and Translation ix

Map of Central Ukraine, 1939 x

Skliar Family Tree xii

PROLOGUE A Silent Story 1

1. Ukraine and the Long Struggle 4

2 The Cossack Inheritance 11

3. Tracing Fragments: Parish, Memory, and the Skliars of Poltava 27

4. Faith and Endurance: Ivan Skliar (1875–1950) 37

5. Ideology and Survival: The Early Life of Viktor Skliar, 1899–1932.... 59

6. The Holodomor in Kharkiv and Poltava, 1932–1933 82

7. War and Silence: Viktor Skliar in Occupied Ukraine, 1934–1945 95

8. In the Wake of Ruin: Displacement and Exile, 1945–1964 123

9. Silenced by the State: Vadim Skliar in Soviet Ukraine (1924–1985) 140

10. Youth and Resistance: The Formation of Wsewolod Skliar, 1929–1948 155

11. Silence as Legacy: Wsewolod Skliar in Postwar Britain, 1948–1954 181

12. A Chorus of Echoes: Wsewolod Skliar and the Poetry of Witness 196

13. From Slogan to Silence: The Settling of a Life, 1954–1964 208

14. The Quiet That Remains 217

EPILOGUE A Life Remembered: Wsewolod Skliar, 1964–2011 223

AFTERWORD The Unquiet Echo: From Maidan's Hope to War's Defiance, 2011–2025 234

Note on Method and Sources 240

Selected Further Reading 242

APPENDICES

A. Personal Writings of Wsewolod Skliar 245

B. Soviet Directive on Grain Procurement – Kharkiv Region, 1932 262

C. Decalogue of a Ukrainian Nationalist, c. 1943-1945 267

D. Image Credits 278

Acknowledgements 282

About the Author 283

Note on Naming, Terminology, and Translation

This book follows standard transliteration from Ukrainian rather than Russian, except where historical documents or dominant usage require otherwise. For example, *Kyiv* is used in place of *Kiev*, and *Holodomor* rather than *Famine*. Where Russian forms appeared in official contexts – particularly under Soviet rule – they are noted when relevant. Patronymics are included selectively, and only where they aid historical clarity.

Religious and political terms (such as *poslushnik*, *zemstvo*, or *UPA*) are explained at first mention in the main text or in accompanying footnotes.

The book draws extensively on the personal writings of Wsewolod Skliar, whose poems, diary entries, and notes offer insight into the lived experience of displacement, resistance, and cultural endurance. These appear throughout in English translation. Where particularly resonant, the original Ukrainian is also included to preserve the tone, cadence, and cultural specificity of the text. A full list of Ukrainian-language excerpts and their translations appears in Appendices A, B and C.

All translations are by the author unless otherwise noted.

Map of Central Ukraine, 1939

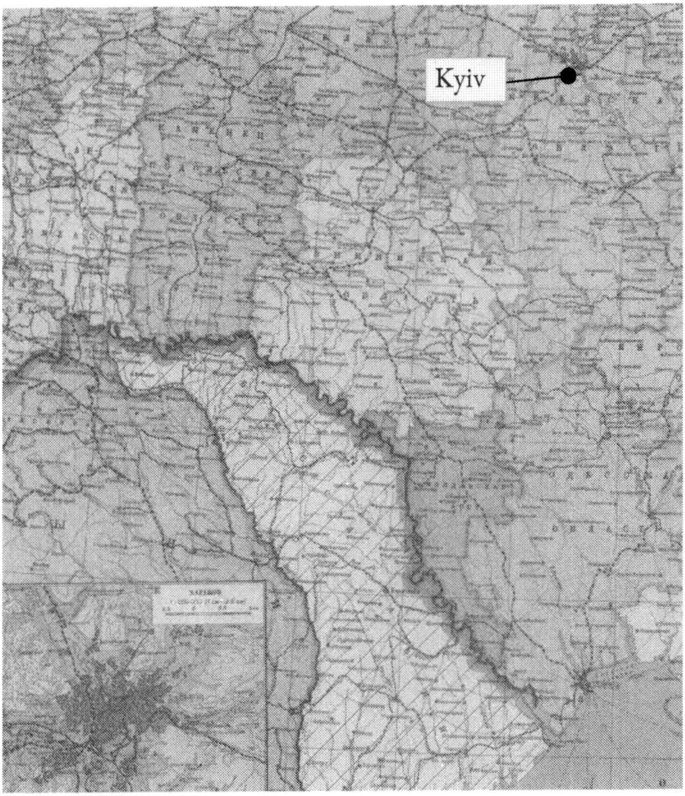

Figure 1: Map of central regions within the Ukrainian Soviet Socialist Republic published in 1939. The annotated locations – Poltava, Kharkiv, and Sakhnovshchyna – form the geographic core of this book's narrative.

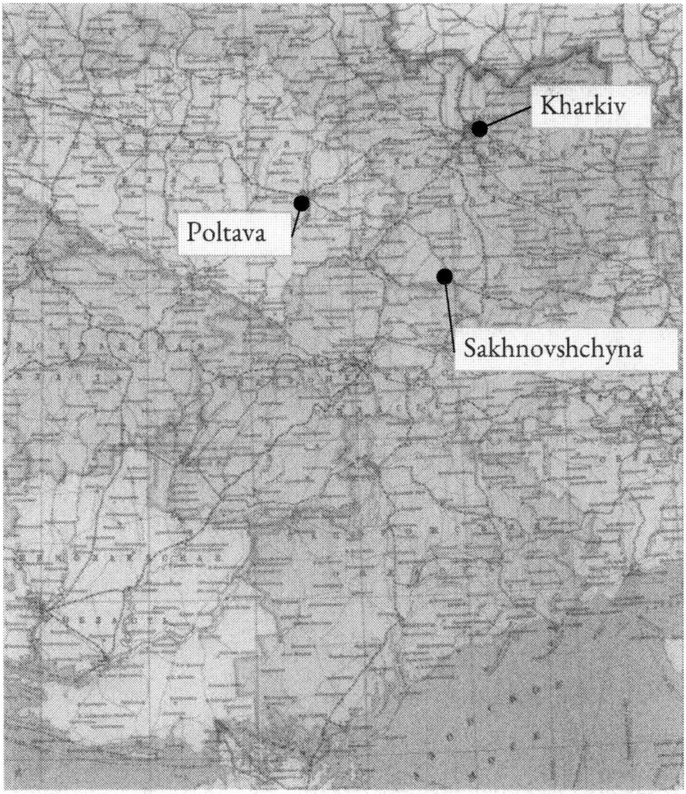
Kharkiv
Poltava
Sakhnovshchyna

Skliar Family Tree

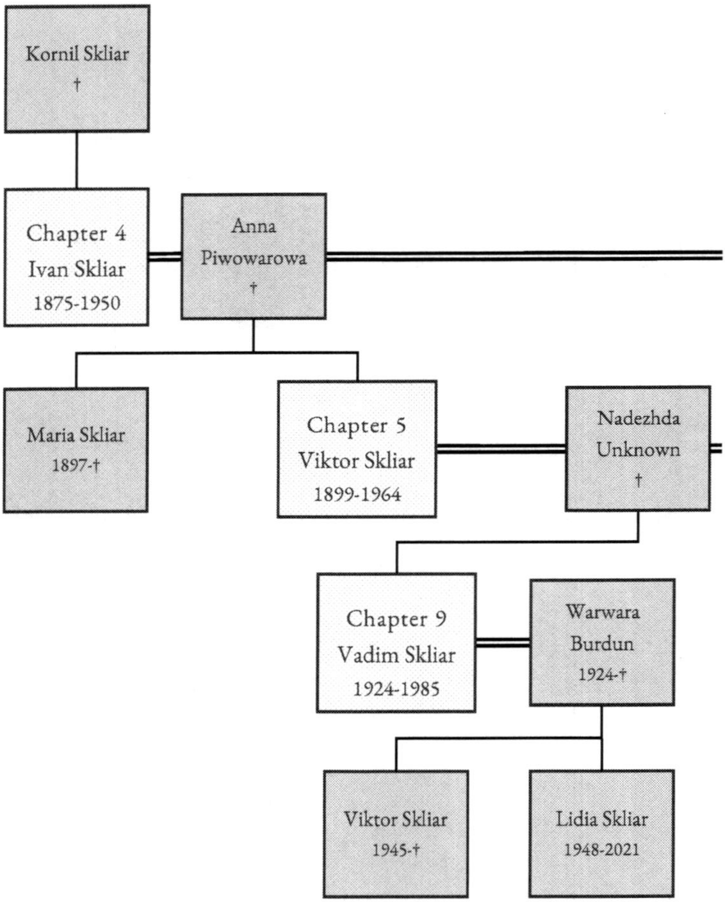

Figure 2: This family tree presents the individuals referenced throughout the book. Those whose lives are explored in detail appear in white, with the chapter of their first major appearance noted above their name. Other figures are included to provide generational and familial context across the century. Dates are shown where known.

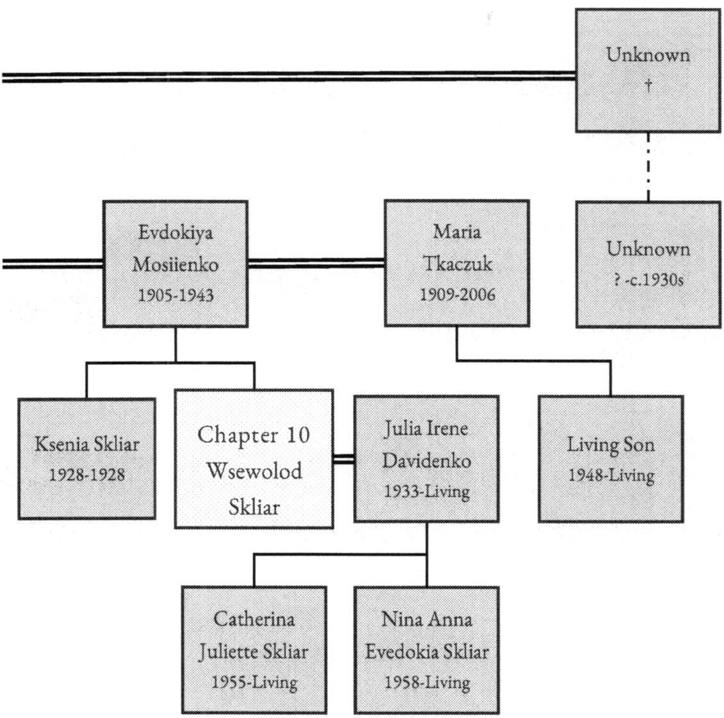
Unknown
†
Evdokiya Mosiienko
1905-1943
Maria Tkaczuk
1909-2006
Unknown
? -c.1930s
Ksenia Skliar
1928-1928
Chapter 10
Wsewolod Skliar
Julia Irene Davidenko
1933-Living
Living Son
1948-Living
Catherina Juliette Skliar
1955-Living
Nina Anna Evedokia Skliar
1958-Living

PROLOGUE

A Silent Story

In 2022, as Russian forces advanced on Kyiv and war returned to Ukrainian streets, the world looked again at a country too often overlooked. Ukraine became visible as a nation fighting for its future – and for a past repeatedly threatened by the same imperial ambitions.

Stories of its present make global news. Yet long before this war, stories of its past survived; passed down in caution, whispered, carried through the everyday.

This is one such story of Ukraine – seen through the lives of the Skliar family – not those who shaped history, but those shaped by it. It begins, as many stories do, with a suitcase. Long forgotten at the back of a cupboard, there were photographs, letters, diaries, a worn leather wallet.

These were not dramatic artefacts. Just the traces of lives lived shaped by displacement and control – names, dates, fragments. The kinds of things that usually disappear.

Figure 3: Viktor Skliar's wallet, carried with him from Soviet Ukraine through Nazi Germany to England. Inside were identity papers, conscription papers, and the passport of his wife, Evdokiya – preserved, but never spoken of.

What emerged was a window into how Ukrainians navigated the twentieth century from the underside: through bureaucratic compliance, adaptation, and cultural persistence. The documents tracked lives shaped by the Holodomor's starvation, Nazi occupation, and post-war exile in Britain – lives that moved in footnotes, under the direction and control of others. Where the risk of being seen or remembered was often greater than the cost of being forgotten. And so people compromised. They survived. But they did not always explain how, or why, or at what cost. They lived in silence.

Many know these patterns – a grandfather's unspoken war, a grandmother's recipes without origin, a language remembered in toasts and curses, not conversation. A past felt, but rarely explained.

The family at this story's centre came from Poltava, once part of the Russian Empire – a place called "Little Russia" on some maps and "nowhere" on others. They were psalmists, bookkeepers, villagers, exiles. Ivan Skliar, who prayed aloud from memory when the prayer books were gone. Evdokiya, whose entire existence persists through a single passport and photo. Viktor, who counted harvests for the Soviets and delivered vegetables for the Germans. Wsewolod, who recorded nationalist poetry from the camp. They were loyal to different governments at different times. They endured. There are no heroes here, and no villains. There is only a struggle for survival.

This book explores what that struggle looked like from below. It asks: what does it mean to be Ukrainian when Ukraine did not exist? What does it mean to pass on a heritage you were never allowed to name? What does it mean to survive without explanation – and what remains when the silence, imposed on a family and a nation for generations, finally begins to lift, demanding that its story be heard?

Ben Skliar-Ward

CHAPTER 1
Ukraine and the Long Struggle

September 1943, Viktor Skliar knew that he could not stay.

His wife, Evdokiya, had been killed months earlier in a Soviet bombing raid. His home was now a place of graves and suspicion. For two years, he had lived and worked under German occupation, coordinating vegetable deliveries for the Nazi occupiers. As the Red Army pushed westward, those who had lived, worked and collaborated under the Germans, like Viktor, faced a choice. Flee, or risk accusations of collaboration and treason.

I have tried to imagine that moment. Not the years before, or the compromises made under occupation, but the morning he decided to go. He would have known what the Soviets did to those they considered traitors. He had worked. His name was on the records. Whatever the reasons, whatever the limits of his choices, he could not count on forgiveness.

And so he packed: he loaded what he could onto a horse-drawn cart: his worn leather wallet, a few papers, some food, and his young son Wsewolod – and put his fate in the hands of Nazi Germany. Their home – a village once tethered to seasons and prayers – had become a ruin without borders. Ahead lay a journey through a shattered

Europe, marked by robbery, hunger, and the slow realisation that they could never return.

* * *

Viktor's escape, though deeply personal, echoed a centuries-old pattern of survival etched into Ukraine's history. It was part of a longer history, repeated across generations of Ukrainians who lived through the collapse of autonomy, the violence of empire, and the struggle to preserve identity in the face of erasure. His journey westward was the latest chapter in a story that had already begun centuries earlier: in fortified villages along the Dnipro, in prayers spoken in forbidden tongues, in the fragile rituals that outlasted conquest.

Ukraine's history is one of interruption. Every time its people began to shape a future, larger forces intervened. Imperial Russia, Soviet rule, Nazi occupation – and now modern Russia – each sought to claim the land and silence its people. Each brought traumas of their own; starvation, repression, war, and exile. Yet within families and communities, Ukrainian life endured through generations. Not always loudly, not without cost – and not without moral ambiguity – often largely in customs and habits.

This account is based on what remains: the contents of a suitcase carried across borders, documents salvaged from upheaval, records in damaged archives, memories preserved in private collections. Parish registers, official gazettes, wartime papers, identity documents, letters, and oral testimony have been used to reconstruct lives that official histories often passed over. But the record is incomplete. Many materials were destroyed in war or lost in flight. Others were shaped by fear, omission, or simply the erosion of time. Where the evidence is uncertain or contradictory, this book acknowledges it. Silence, too, is part of the archive. And so, I began to piece together not just a family tree, but the emotional map of their survival.

* * *

The Skliar name, meaning "glazier" in Ukrainian, once tied the family to artisans who mended village windows. Over time, it carried a prouder echo: a link to Poltava's landowning Cossack lineages, where this story begins.

Their ancestors lived semi-autonomously in fortified villages, where faith, language and self-defence were intertwined. Until the eighteenth century, when the Russian Empire formally imposed direct rule. This was a world where loyalty to the Orthodox Church helped preserve a sense of belonging when political structures collapsed.

By the nineteenth century, Ukraine was firmly under imperial control. The tsarist government banned Ukrainian-language publications, restricted local governance, and placed churches under Moscow's authority. In Poltava, this repression was pervasive. Orthodox priests were monitored, village schools were discouraged from using Ukrainian, and family names were quietly Russified in official records. What survived did so through the persistence of habit: families maintained traditions that spoke to an older, freer Ukraine – in their parish rites, their songs and dances, their language, and their memory. They preserved local dialects, retold folk tales, and observed saints' days that had no place in imperial calendars.

Yet beneath the surface, even as imperial control tightened, a modern Ukrainian consciousness began quietly to take shape. Scholars, historians, and folklorists started exploring and recording Ukraine's rich traditions and language. Despite periodic bans, a Ukrainian-language press emerged, and cultural societies formed cautiously in defiance of official restrictions. This modest cultural revival existed in uneasy tension with imperial realities. Nobles and local elites, while quietly resenting Russian dominance, remained tied to the tsarist hierarchy – dependent for their status and wary of repeating Mazepa's catastrophic mistake. Ukrainian identity, therefore, evolved not separately from empire, but within its constraints: a fragile balance of cultural survival, cautious resistance, and enforced silence.

Around this time, Kornil Skliar appears briefly in a Poltava church gazette – a Cossack, mentioned once and then lost. Beyond that, his life is a void. The State Archives of Poltava, where his story might have lived, lost over 1.5 million documents to wartime destruction.[1] Yet even that fragment suggests continuity – the survival of Cossack memory into a time when such identities were officially discouraged, even prohibited. His son, Ivan Skliar (1875–1950), served as a psalmist, maintaining religious traditions in a world where official Orthodoxy had become a tool of imperial loyalty. While their lives were shaped by the larger movements of history,

[1] The *State Archives of Poltava Region* lost over 1.5 million documents during the Second World War, including parish registers and civil records that likely documented the Skliars' early history. State Archives of Poltava Region, *History of the Archive*, accessed March 2025.

they still held agency. They adapted, compromised, and preserved what they could.

The collapse of the Russian Empire in 1917 brought a brief, chaotic window of possibility. Ukraine declared independence, only to be drawn almost immediately into wars of intervention, civil conflict, and foreign occupation. For families like the Skliars, this period brought both hope and danger. Independence was proclaimed in Kyiv, but power on the ground shifted rapidly between rival governments, each bringing new demands, new taxes, and new risks.

By the early 1920s, Soviet power had taken hold in Ukraine. The initial years of Soviet rule were complex: policies of "Ukrainisation" allowed for a revival of language and culture. But this window soon closed. By the 1930s, under Stalin, Ukraine became the target of brutal campaigns of repression. The Holodomor – the artificial famine of 1932–33 – killed millions. Churches were closed or destroyed; village leaders were arrested or disappeared.

The Skliars lived through this violence. Viktor Skliar (1899–1964), born at the turn of the century, grew up amid the instability of revolution and collectivisation. Like many others, he experienced the betrayal of early Soviet promises: from the protection of Ukrainian culture to its systematic destruction. His wife, Evdokiya Petrova Skliar (1905–1943), raised their children under conditions of fear and scarcity, where even a private conversation in Ukrainian could provoke suspicion.

When Nazi Germany invaded the Soviet Union in 1941, Poltava once again became a battleground. Occupation brought forced labour, deportations, and terror. Survival required constant negotiation with danger. The war shattered communities, tore families apart, and made the choices of survival more precarious than ever. Amid this chaos, Viktor gathered what remained of his family and fled westward as Soviet forces advanced – knowing that return would mean persecution for having survived outside Soviet control.

After the war, Viktor, and his son Wsewolod (1929–2011), lived as displaced persons in Germany, part of the massive, often invisible diaspora created by conflict. Stateless, without the right to return home, they joined the slow, painful movement of Ukrainians across a divided Europe. Eventually, they found their way to Britain, resettling in the council estates of postwar London.

Their story, like many others, was shaped by regimes they did not choose and a future they had to rebuild elsewhere. The quiet endurance – through famine, war, and exile – echoes in Ukraine today, where families once again face invasion and erasure, yet hold fast to language, memory, and hope.

* * *

To understand the traumas of nineteenth and twentieth-century Ukraine, and the world which the Skliars inhabited – Viktor's flight, the suitcase's silent papers – it is necessary to look further back – to Cossack Ukraine, and to the early betrayals that shaped generational mistrust. More than a military frontier, it was a society built on service, faith, and fragile autonomy, where a distinct Ukrainian identity took root under the strain of strategic betrayal and imperial pressure. The destruction of that autonomy – first through broken promises, then by force – marked the beginning of a long pattern: survival amid suppression, loyalty met with erasure.

The traditions, communities, and conflicts of that world left foundations that would endure long after the Cossacks themselves were defeated – shaping how identity, allegiance, and endurance were understood in the centuries that followed.

CHAPTER 2
The Cossack Inheritance

Казав мені один чернець ось так:
"У Києві всьому, всьому зачало:
Та і старий, старий же він козак!
Того ще й не було, те підростало, –
Давно, давно вже Київ панував:

A certain monk once told me this:
"In Kyiv, everything – everything – began.
And he is an old, old Cossack!
What now is, wasn't yet born, it was still growing –
Long, long ago, Kyiv already ruled.

– Amvrosii Metlynsky[2], from *The Underground Church*, 1859

---

[2] Amvrosii Metlynsky (1814–1870) was a Ukrainian Romantic poet, folklorist, and professor associated with the Kharkiv school. Writing under the pseudonym Amaros, he produced elegiac verse steeped in nostalgia and cultural fatalism, mourning the loss of the Cossack past. His melancholic tone later resonated with émigré writers who viewed themselves as the last inheritors of a vanishing Ukraine.

The choices my grandfather's family would later face – who to trust, when to yield, when to run – had been asked before. Ukrainians, and Ukraine, had gambled on survival many times. Treaties and promises crumbled into domination, help turned to conquest. Not because Ukraine lacked strength or loyalty, but because its fate was rarely its own to choose. Again and again, the country was treated not as a subject of history but as a space to be claimed, divided, or denied.

When I think about Viktor in 1941, choosing to work within the Nazi structures rather than resisting or fleeing to the Soviet Union, or my grandfather Wsewolod, who as a teenager scribbled about "*invader-terrorists*" in his diary, fearing the Soviets' return, it feels inherited. The Skliars, like countless families rooted in Poltava's villages, carried a mistrust shaped long before them – forged in a past where survival relied on agreements that fractured, and supposed allies became instruments of domination. It is easy, looking back, to ask why they were afraid. The better question is how could they not have been.

Before there were even Cossacks, there was a frontier – and a way of life bound by faith, autonomy, and survival. What follows is a brief account of how that world rose, and how it was broken – brief, because it has to be.

The Roots of a Frontier Identity (9th–17th century)

For centuries, the lands that would become modern Ukraine lay at the crossroads of empire, trade, and belief. Kyivan Rus' (9th–13th centuries), centred on Kyiv, emerged as a regional power with ties stretching from Constantinople to Scandinavia. In 988, Prince

Volodymyr's conversion to Orthodox Christianity aligned Kyiv with the Byzantine world, anchoring religious traditions that would endure. Even after Mongol invasions shattered Kyivan Rus', and Ukrainian territories were absorbed into the Grand Duchy of Lithuania, the Polish–Lithuanian Commonwealth, and the Crimean Khanate, Orthodox communities endured – preserving faith and custom under mounting political and religious pressure.

Figure 4: *Virgin Orans*, an 11th-century mosaic in Kyiv's Saint Sophia Cathedral, stands as a timeless guardian of Ukraine's spiritual resilience, rooted in Kyivan Rus'.

In the 14th and 15th centuries, new social forms emerged on the steppe frontier. Among them were the Cossacks – military settlers, runaway serfs, and frontier dwellers. By the 16th century, they had forged a distinct identity rooted in autonomy, Orthodox belief, and martial service.

The *Zaporizhian Sich*, a fortified outpost along the Dnieper River, became their stronghold – and a symbol of communal rule. Though loosely tied to the Polish–Lithuanian Commonwealth, the *Sich* evolved from a marginal militia into the heart of a semi-autonomous state with its own political culture: a form of self-governance shaped by custom and command. Authority was exercised through councils rather than courts; land belonged to those who worked it; leadership was earned, not inherited. These norms extended beyond governance. They became habits of rural life – shared obligation, local independence, mutual defence – not codified in law, but embedded in expectation. Families like the Skliars, settled in villages, were part of this world – not as hetmans, but as ordinary villagers who worked the land and preserved the Orthodox traditions that bound Cossack life together.

As Cossack rule deepened, even the name "Ukraine" – once meaning simply *borderland*[3] – began to carry a sense of identity.[4] European cartographers helped fix that idea in the Western imagination. Guillaume Le Vasseur de Beauplan's maps in the mid-1600s introduced the term to European audiences, portraying Ukraine as a coherent inhabited space. But maps were not neutral. Each act of naming implied a claim.

In 1648, an uprising led by Bohdan Khmelnytsky challenged Polish Catholic rule and established the *Cossack Hetmanate*: a semi-autonomous Orthodox polity led by an elected Hetman and backed by its own military and administrative systems. Yet autonomy remained fragile. In 1654, Khmelnytsky concluded the *Pereiaslav Agreement* with Muscovy, seeking protection against renewed

---

[3] In its earliest use, in the 12th-century *Hypatian Chronicle*, "ukraina" described frontiers – lands shaped by conflict and layered loyalties.

[4] For a discussion of the name's etymology and political usage: Hrytsak, Yaroslav. *Ukraine: The Forging of a Nation*. London: Hachette UK, 2023.

Polish aggression – a gamble for survival, born out of perceived necessity in a treacherous geopolitical landscape, that tragically opened the door to Russian interference.[5]

Khmelnytsky turned to Moscow in desperation. Moscow responded with allegiance – then quickly moved to assert control. The language of brotherhood disguised a transfer of power. What was meant as a lifeline became a lever. Though historians continue to debate the precise terms and intentions of the original agreement, in the Ukrainian imagination, *Pereiaslav* became more than a failed alliance. It was the first betrayal – the start of a pattern in which protection masked domination, and trust brought subjugation.

That logic – alliance recast as submission – would return again. It still does.

The Fall of the Hetmanate (18th century)

In the decades that followed, Russian imperial power expanded, and Cossack independence eroded. The *Hetmanate* lost key rights: foreign policy was restricted, Russian garrisons were stationed in Ukrainian towns, and loyalty was increasingly enforced through oaths to the tsar rather than to elected councils. Step by step, the autonomy Khmelnytsky had claimed was hollowed out. These changes came gradually, but their direction was clear. By the early

---

[5] While the *Pereiaslav Agreement* is presented here as a foundational "betrayal" within the Ukrainian national narrative, its historical interpretation is complex and has been subject to extensive scholarly debate. For more nuanced analyses of the agreement and its long-term consequences, see works by historians such as Yaroslav Hrytsak and Zenon Kohut, who explore the varied motivations and shifting political contexts surrounding the treaty.

18th century, the idea of a self-governing Cossack state had been largely overtaken by Muscovite authority.

As political control shifted, so too did language and perception. What had once been a frontier republic came to be treated as a subordinate province. The memory of Cossack self-rule remained, but it now sat uneasily within an imperial order that demanded loyalty and erased distinction.

In 1708, Hetman Ivan Mazepa allied with Charles XII of Sweden in a final, desperate bid for fuller autonomy. It was a gamble, much like Khmelnytsky's decades earlier—an alliance born of perceived necessity in a treacherous geopolitical landscape, not of deep-seated trust. But where Pereiaslav had marked the beginning of an uneasy and increasingly challenged dependence, Mazepa's revolt was a decisive attempt to sever that bond—a move that, while controversial and divisive among the Cossack elite, underscored the intolerable pressures facing the *Hetmanate*.

At the *Battle of Poltava* in 1709, the gamble failed catastrophically. Swedish forces were routed, Mazepa's position collapsed, and Ukraine's political future was sealed under Russian rule. The silence that followed was generational.

If Pereiaslav had sown deep mistrust, Poltava carved it into the bedrock of Ukrainian historical memory. In this reading, Mazepa foresaw the inevitable erosion of *Hetmanate* rights—the tightening grip, the broken promises—and chose radical action to pre-empt complete subjugation. The cost of failure was absolute. After Poltava, there were no more illusions. Autonomy was placed on an irreversible path toward erasure. What followed was not compromise or coexistence, but absorption. Ukraine's fate would now be decided elsewhere.

This absorption created a profound paradox for the remaining Ukrainian elite. They mourned lost autonomy and quietly resented their subjugation, yet their privileges, and even their identities, came to depend on the very tsarist hierarchy that suppressed them. Any thoughts of resistance were tempered by the harsh lessons of the past: overtures to other European powers had come to nothing, and Mazepa's devastating failure stood as a lasting warning. Thus emerged a complex reality—a yearning for self-determination coexisting uneasily with a pragmatic reliance on the empire that denied it.

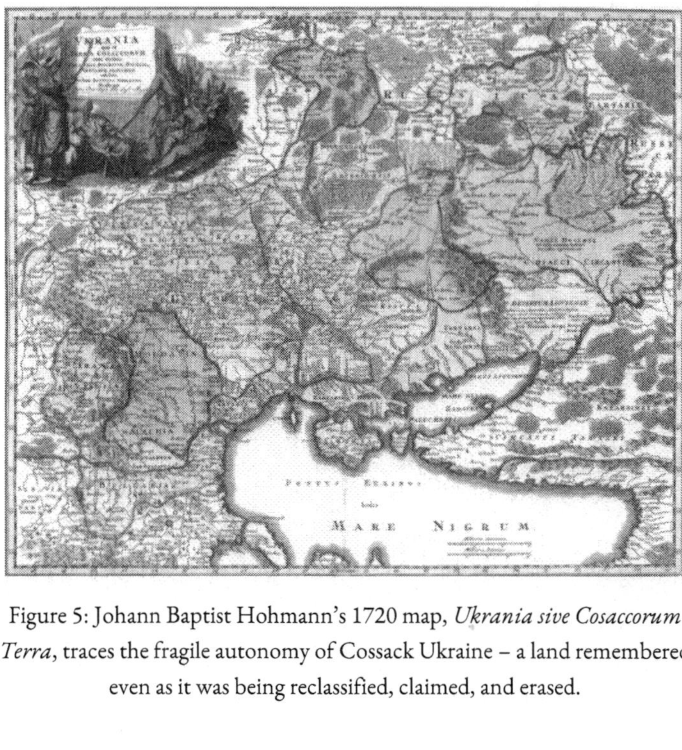

Figure 5: Johann Baptist Hohmann's 1720 map, *Ukrania sive Cosaccorum Terra*, traces the fragile autonomy of Cossack Ukraine – a land remembered even as it was being reclassified, claimed, and erased.

The *Hetmanate* lingered in name for a while longer, but its legacy structures were steadily dismantled. Councils were dissolved, registers closed, local officers replaced by imperial appointees. Authority flowed downward from St Petersburg, not outward from community councils. Serfdom expanded. The Orthodox Church, once a bastion of local identity, was brought under Moscow's control.

By the 1780s, even the formality of autonomy was extinguished. In 1781, the office of Hetman was abolished altogether. The following year, Catherine the Great imposed direct imperial governance across central Ukraine, replacing Cossack jurisdictions with Russian provincial administration. What remained of Cossack self-rule was folded into the bureaucracy of empire. The frontier had been reclassified. Its history, and the freedoms once tied to it, were slowly overwritten – by Imperial Russia's actions.

From Republic to Province (19th century)

By the start of the nineteenth century, the Ukrainian lands east of the Dnipro were fully absorbed into the Russian Empire. The last vestiges of Cossack autonomy had been dismantled. The Hetmanate was gone. The *Sich's* lands were folded into new Russian provinces. Where Cossack hosts had once gathered in council, imperial governors now reported to St Petersburg. The promise of Pereiaslav and the memory of Poltava had resolved into a single truth: Ukraine would not govern itself.

Administrative integration accelerated. Russian became the language of courts, schools, and official correspondence. Orthodox churches were placed under the control of the Russian Synod, ending their local independence. Ukrainian printing was curtailed, particularly in religious and educational contexts. Serfdom, entrenched since the late eighteenth century, deepened the dependence of rural life on landlords and imperial administrators. What had once been a fluid frontier was now a managed province – categorised, taxed, and observed.

As central control tightened, official interest in Ukrainian identity grew. In the 1830s and 1840s, the imperial state began to view Ukrainian language and culture not as local colour, but as a potential threat. The *Brotherhood of Saints Cyril and Methodius* – a small, intellectual group in Kyiv promoting Slavic unity and cultural autonomy – was suppressed in 1847. In 1863, the *Valuev Circular* banned most Ukrainian-language publications. A decade later, the *Ems Ukaz* of 1876 extended the prohibition to nearly all printed and imported Ukrainian material.

This state-sponsored attempt to render Ukrainian culture invisible – to confine its language to the domestic sphere – had a profound impact on communities like Poltava. If Pereiaslav ended political trust, and Poltava crushed hopes of autonomy, this was the third betrayal: an attempt to strip Ukraine not just of power, but of voice. The state no longer feared rebellion. It feared memory – and moved to erase the language that carried it. When Wsewolod insisted his children learn Ukrainian, it wasn't an assertion of identity. It was a correction – a quiet reversal of a prohibition he knew too well, even if no one explained where it had come from.

And yet, the erasure was never total. Beneath the surface of imperial rule, older rhythms endured. In villages across Poltava and beyond, life remained tied to memory more than decree. Land still passed through family lines; feast days followed the old calendar. The local parish, though now subordinate to Moscow, continued to baptise, marry, and bury – marking time in a language that no longer appeared in state texts.

Church registers, stamped with imperial seals, still recorded individuals – like Kornil Skliar – as "Cossack": a designation that no longer conferred rights, but meant something. Even if no one could say exactly what. Perhaps it was pride. Perhaps it was a kind of snobbery – a way of recalling, or inventing, status long after the system that sustained it had disappeared. Or perhaps it marked something quieter: not privilege, but continuity. A way of saying: *we were here, and we remember who we were* – even if no one else does. Even if we're not meant to.

The councils were gone, but habits of shared decision-making persisted. Ukrainians continued to practise a culture the empire sought to forget – not through defiance, but through quiet, habitual repetition.

Much of this continuity was held by women. In the absence of formal institutions, they sustained tradition through practice. They arranged dowries, preserved recipes, embroidered altar cloths, managed land, and taught children the cadences of daily life. Widows could act as household guardians; grandmothers fixed names and events in memory. At feast days and baptisms, women recited prayers the Church no longer officially printed – but had never quite erased. In kitchens and gardens, around tables and cradles, they kept culture alive when the state no longer recognised it, binding family and faith together in small, habitual acts that empire could not reach.

Figure 6: Taras Shevchenko, *Peasant Family* (1843). Domestic life, sustained largely by women, preserved care, ritual, and memory in households, anchoring Ukrainian identity.

Beyond the household, oral tradition carried memory where writing was censored or lost. Stories passed from mouth to mouth – names, sayings, cautionary tales. In village squares and market gatherings, blind minstrels known as *kobzars* performed *dumy* – epic poems of betrayal, endurance, and loss. They sang of fallen Cossack heroes and oppressive foreign rulers, of loyalties tested and lands unjustly taken. In these narratives, a distinctly Ukrainian history was preserved, transmitted from generation to generation, quietly resisting imperial censorship. These were living memory shaped into rhythm, carried aloud precisely because few could read and fewer were permitted to write. Elsewhere, memory took quieter forms: proverbs, blessings, lullabies, and superstitions – fragments of a shared past kept alive in voice when ink had been forbidden. My family kept no kobzar songs, no dumy shared at the table. But sayings persisted – warnings, proverbs, a few phrases I didn't recognise as history until much later.

Central to this unnamed heritage, and fundamental to the very essence of Ukrainian identity, was the Ukrainian language itself. More than a mere medium of communication, it was – and remains – the lifeblood of culture, the carrier of historical memory, and the primary wellspring of its rich poetic tradition.

Memory also moved through the body. Seasonal rituals, harvest customs, and dances carried echoes of older orders. The *hopak* – explosive, squatting, defiant – was once a Cossack martial display; by the nineteenth century, it survived in weddings and festivals as the *prysidannya*[6], no longer military but still unmistakably local. Even everyday gestures – the way bread was broken, blessings made, tables laid – repeated actions that had outlasted the laws that once gave them meaning. In villages across Poltava and beyond, people followed inherited rhythms without always knowing their origins. These were not preserved as history, but lived as habit – cultural muscle memory passed from movement to movement, generation to generation.

In the cities – especially Poltava and Kharkiv – a different form of memory took shape. Writers like Ivan Kotliarevsky and Hryhorii Kvitka-Osnovianenko began to turn the rhythms of village life into literature. Kotliarevsky's *Eneida*, a parody of Virgil's epic recast in

---

[6] The *Prysidannya* is a traditional Ukrainian dance movement, characterised by deep squatting steps and kicks, commonly associated with Cossack dances such as the *hopak*.

Ukrainian vernacular, was playful in tone but radical in implication: it showed that the language of peasants could carry classical weight. Kvitka's sentimental sketches rendered village characters with care, not caricature. These works did not resist empire by manifesto. They reclaimed tone and voice. In a world that insisted Ukrainians were "Little Russians", they asserted a local dignity the state refused to name. What had survived in song, gesture, and story now found printed form – not entirely free, but recognisably their own.

What endured was never just tradition. It was memory shaped by need – repeated, adapted, and often stripped of context. These habits kept a culture alive, but not always intact. The next chapter turns to what was lost, distorted, or silenced in the name of survival.

Memory, Myth, and the Costs of Survival

For many, the Cossack is the enduring image of Ukraine: horseman, rebel, Orthodox believer, defender of the land. Growing up, the Cossack was a distant but constant presence – a flash of heroism in old films, the fierce figures in books, even the name of our first dog. The Cossack dog's name wasn't just whimsy – it was my family's nod to a past we barely understood. While that image stems from real communities rooted in the 16th- and 17th-century steppe, the reality was more complex.

By the eighteenth century, Cossack society had begun to mirror the very hierarchies it once resisted. A powerful officer class, the *starshyna*, accumulated wealth and privileges. Some sought Russian noble status: others pledged loyalty to the tsar. The old ideals of brotherhood, once practised in the councils of the *Sich*, grew more ceremonial than real. In time, the Cossack image was reshaped not only in memory, but in propaganda – deployed by tsars and Soviets alike to serve new narratives of loyalty, rural strength, and imperial unity. There was little space in these retellings for the landless, the serf, the orphaned widow, or the non-Orthodox neighbour.

While the Cossack ideal emphasised freedom and autonomy, the reality for a significant portion of the population – the majority – within the *Hetmanate*, and particularly as its autonomy eroded, was harsh. The expansion of serfdom meant that for peasants, life was characterised by arduous labour, limited rights, and vulnerability to the demands of landowners and the state. The geopolitical turmoil of the era, with its frequent wars and shifting allegiances, often resulted in devastating consequences for the agrarian population, including significant loss of life and economic hardship.

The Orthodox Church, too, carried a double legacy. It remained a centre of village life – baptising, marrying, burying, and marking the seasons – but it was no longer a shield against empire. In 1686, the *Kyiv Metropolia*, the historic heart of Ukrainian Orthodoxy, was formally transferred from Constantinople to the Moscow Patriarchate. From that point forward, sermons, feast days, and parish schools were drawn ever closer into Moscow's orbit. Two hundred years later, Ivan Skliar served as a psalmist – a Ukrainian voice inside a Church that now spoke for Moscow. He was not outside the system. He was its servant – but not in its language.

Figure 7: Ilya Repin's 1893 sketch, *Reply of the Zaporozhian Cossacks*, held in the Kharkiv Art Museum, captures the defiant Cossack myth – bold and theatrical, yet masking a history layered with compromise and loss.

Survival had its cost. It required compromise. Old loyalties were kept alive, but often in muted form – softened by nostalgia, shaped by omission, and clouded by uneasy pride. What reached later generations was not a clean story of resistance or defeat. It was something knottier: a memory formed through both endurance and accommodation. Even in the seventeenth and eighteenth centuries, to survive meant navigating conflicting allegiances, shifting powers, and moral ambiguity. Heroism was rarely pure. The legacy that endured was built as much on silence as on defiance.

* * *

The Cossack past did not disappear. It receded into habit – into the way a parish council met, the way a blessing marked a threshold, the way a family remembered who once worked a field. Where records fell silent, memory moved by other means. It lived in customs, in stories, in names passed down not for pride, but for continuity.

But continuity alone did not protect. The old world left behind more than rituals and proverbs. It passed on something harder: a deep caution, a sense that survival depended not on assertion, but on adaptation. To live as Ukrainian – in language, in memory, in faith – was to navigate what could be shown, what must be hidden, and when silence was safer than truth.

In places like Poltava, that inheritance was ordinary. It was not heroic. It was careful, durable, and often invisible. Families remembered loyalties that no longer had legal standing, preserved identities that were not permitted to name themselves aloud. They did not forget who they were. But they learned to carry that knowledge in ways empire would not notice.

This is the world my grandfather inherited. Not a legacy of open defiance, but one shaped by centuries in which being Ukrainian meant being watchful – mistrustful of allies, wary of promises, attuned to the difference between private memory and public silence. Of all the things passed down, it was language he held most tightly. Ukrainian had been forbidden, marginalised, misnamed. To speak it – and to teach it – was, for him, not just habit, but inheritance. Before the twentieth century began, that fear had already been learned. So had the quiet insistence on continuity.

CHAPTER 3

Tracing Fragments: Parish, Memory, and the Skliars of Poltava

Од козацтва, од гетьманства
Високі могили –
Більш нічого не осталось,
Та й ті розривають;

From the Cossacks, from the hetmans
High graves – Nothing more remain,
And even those are being torn apart;

– Taras Shevchenko[7], from *Haidamaki*, 1838

---

[7] Taras Shevchenko (1814–1861) is widely regarded as the foundational figure of modern Ukrainian literature and national consciousness, and is often referred to as the spiritual father of the nation. Born into serfdom, Shevchenko transcended the profound constraints of his origins to become not only a celebrated poet and painter, but the embodiment of Ukraine's cultural revival and national awakening. His poetry – richly infused with Christian symbolism, historical memory, fierce political critique, and profound empathy for the oppressed – provided an enduring source of inspiration and resilience during periods of intense imperial and later Soviet repression. Works like

The suitcase had always been there, somewhere at the back of a cupboard. For years, it was mentioned but never opened – a kind of placeholder for conversations that were too difficult, or too unfinished, to pursue. It was only after my grandmother moved out of the flat, fifteen years after my grandfather's death, that the box reappeared. In outward appearance, it was unremarkable: battered, worn at the edges, filled with notebooks, documents, photographs, and an old wallet.

I had long suspected it would be ordinary. There were no illusions of discovering medals, declarations, or proofs of heroism. But even so, when I finally opened it, the initial sense of anticlimax was sharp. What lay inside was not revelation, but residue: diaries written in urgent, slanted cursive; brittle official papers; fragments of a life moved through bureaucracy and survival, not through recognition or reward.

Still, something pulled me onward – the sense that meaning clung to these fragments, even if they refused to fall neatly into place. My Ukrainian was basic, but I could piece together names, places, dates. With a dictionary at hand and translation tools close by, the outlines of a story began to form. The first real anchor came with an autobiographical note written by my grandfather in 1949, hidden in a notebook otherwise focused on electrical engineering: a sketch

---

Kobzar, published in 1840, became symbolic cornerstones of Ukrainian identity, encapsulating both the longing for freedom and the moral imperative to resist injustice. Shevchenko's influence extends beyond literature; he remains a central, almost mythical figure in Ukrainian culture, a voice that galvanised generations to remember, resist, and reassert their nationhood.

of his movements through displacement and resettlement after the Second World War. It was a starting point – modest, but certain.

From there, the documents charted a life of exile: registrations with refugee camps, applications for displaced persons' status, employment passes in unfamiliar countries. They painted a vivid picture of uprooting and endurance across the twentieth century. Yet when I tried to go further back, into the life left behind in Ukraine, the trail grew faint. The documents became fewer, the handwriting older. Memory itself seemed to thin out.

The earliest formal records dated from the 1920s: trade union membership cards, church documents, scattered pages from the fragile civic life of Poltava under shifting regimes. There was no tsarist bureaucracy left to consult. No grand Cossack muster rolls. The further I searched, the more apparent it became that the structures of formal memory – the institutions that might have recorded lives like my ancestors' – had themselves broken apart long before the documents reached me. The betrayals – Pereiaslav, Poltava, and the empire's suppression of language – had already done their work. Autonomy was gone. Identity remained, but now under new rules.

Some figures emerged with reasonable clarity. Ivan Skliar – my great-great-grandfather – appeared across multiple records: a psalmist in Orthodox parishes, a participant in village life, a man who stitched together survival across war, revolution, and famine. Through public archives, parish registers, and surviving testimonies, I could trace his education, his postings, his family. His was a life shaped by duty and endurance, rather than by dramatic public acts.

But even here, certainty came with effort. In trying to trace Ivan's father, Kornil Skliar – the Cossack – I encountered one of the more painful lessons of archival work: the cost of partial evidence. A Kornil Skliar appeared in church records – a Cossack, a parish trustee, a local council member (*zemstvo*). For a time, it seemed he fit: a bridge between Cossack memory and imperial administration – the story I maybe wanted to tell. But the trail didn't hold. The names matched; the details did not.[8] There was no choice but to begin again. The Kornil who appears in Ivan's documents remains elusive. Beyond his name, and the faint designation of "Cossack", little else survives. Oral recollections from my grandfather suggest he was a priest or churchman, but the archive is silent. Scholarly integrity demands that the gap remain visible. The frustration of hitting these archival brick walls is a familiar one for historians, but when it's your own ancestor, the silence feels more personal, more acute. In a history built from fragments, invention cannot be allowed to fill what's missing.

More importantly, I learned that absence itself carries meaning. In the modern Ukrainian experience, families like mine did not lose their histories through neglect or indifference, but through a slow attrition: war, repression, displacement, bureaucratic erasure. It is

[8] Reconstructing the life of Kornil Skliar presents a familiar challenge in Ukrainian village history: the fragmentary record. At least six men by that name appear in 19th-century sources from the Poltava region, but without consistent patronymics or parish registers, firm identification remains elusive. He is known only through the patronymic of his son Ivan; no documentation of his own birth, death, or occupation has survived. Largely absent from family memory – as acknowledged by his great-grandson Wsewolod Skliar – suggests an early death, and perhaps the start of a wider rupture in oral transmission brought on by war, repression, and displacement. What remains is not certainty, but structure: memory shaped by loss and adaptation.

not only extraordinary suffering that leaves silences; ordinary endurance does as well. Lives lived in loyalty to village, church, and land often left few traces the empire considered worth recording. Survival was its own form of invisibility.

Beyond the suitcase, I searched public archives – parish registers, ecclesiastical gazettes, refugee records – often finding absence where I hoped for detail. Yet these gaps traced the contours of lives lived at the edges of empire.

Patterns emerged. The Skliars who appear in 19th-century records are no longer tied to regiments or courts, but to parishes. In places like Luchka, Hadyach, Opishnya, and Bilopillia, the name recurs – not among officers or landholders, but among psalmists, church elders, and parish trustees. Their authority sat at the intersection of Cossack inheritance, imperial administration, and Orthodox order – a blur of tradition and structure, of inherited roles recast within new systems. What endured was less a formal status than an ethic of responsibility: to tend the parish, to manage disputes, to preserve what could still be held together.

Figure 8: *The Intercession* (1739-1741), Sulymivka, Poltava, adorns the Church of the Intercession, its vibrant hues embodying the faith that sustained Cossack-era parishes and Skliar lives.

Prokopi Filippov Skliar stands out. In the 1860s, he was elected elder (*starosta*) of the Pokrovskaya Church in Luchka, later serving as chairman of its parish council. His appointment was recorded in the *Poltava Eparchial Gazette* – a faint but firm imprint of communal trust. Prokopi's role was not ceremonial. Parish elders oversaw financial management, charity, and the maintenance of sacred spaces. In a world where higher structures of Ukrainian autonomy had collapsed, it was through roles like his that fragments of self-governance endured.

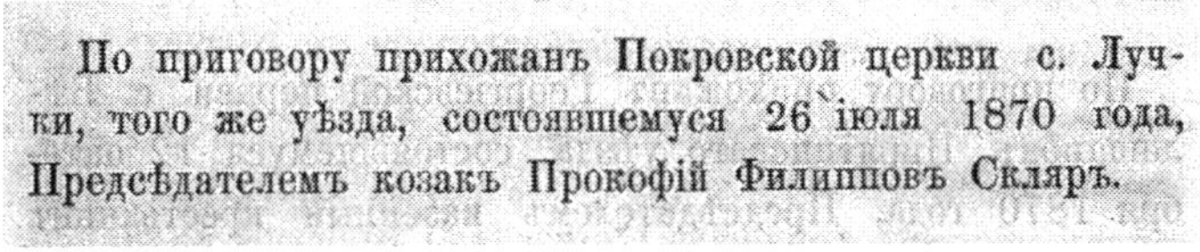

**По приговору прихожанъ Покровской церкви с. Луч-
ки, того же уѣзда, состоявшемуся 26 іюля 1870 года,
Предсѣдателемъ козакъ Прокофій Филипповъ Скляръ.**

Figure 9: An 1870 parish election record from Pokrovskaya Church, Luchka, names Prokopi Filippov Skliar as elder, his "Cossack" title a quiet echo of a fading past.

The life of Prokopi's brother, Pavel Filippov Skliar, embodied the contradictions of his time. He began as an *unter-officer*[9] in the Imperial Army – a Cossack serving an empire that had erased Cossack autonomy – and later became a Ukrainian-speaking psalmist in an Orthodox Church subordinated to Moscow. In villages like Luchka, where formal schooling was limited, the psalmist was not only a liturgical singer but a teacher, a moral guide, a keeper of ritual. Parish records from the 1870s confirm Pavel's steady presence, leading chants, guiding festivals, maintaining registers – small acts of preservation against the slow pressure of imperial assimilation.

Figure 10: Late 19th-century Poltava village life. Thatched homes, garden fences, and barefoot children capture the daily realities of the humble world where the Skliars' faith and memory endured.

[9] An *unter*-officer in the Russian Imperial Army was a non-commissioned officer (NCO), equivalent to corporal or sergeant.

Prokopi's son, Kornil Prokopovych Skliar – not to be confused with Ivan's father – fully entered the secular structures of the Russian Empire, yet continued to identify as a Cossack in church records. In local government documents from Hadyach, Kornil Prokopovych appears as a *zemstvo* representative – part of the district-level councils introduced in the 1860s to manage roads, schooling, taxation, and healthcare. Where earlier generations had served the parish, Kornil served the *zemstvo*: filing reports, managing budgets, working in Russian rather than Ukrainian. His presence marks a shift. Survival now required fluency not only in faith, but in bureaucracy.

Figure 11: *Zemstvo Members Having Lunch* (Grigorij Myasoyedov, 1872). Introduced after 1864, zemstvo councils offered constrained but meaningful spaces for civic engagement. Families like the Skliars navigated these new structures of governance amid shifting imperial pressures.

Some silences, however, could not be bridged. Women, in particular, all but disappear from the records. A mother's name on a baptismal certificate; a dowry agreement; a rare signature on a petition – these are the exceptions. More often, they are absent entirely. Survival was a collective achievement, but it was recorded selectively. The gap is not just archival. It is structural, and its presence haunts every page. Where written records fall silent, I turned to oral testimony, much of it preserved by women. My grandmother, joined to the Skliars through marriage and rooted in Galicia's Ukrainian heritage, shared fragmented stories of Ukraine's past – tales of resilience, Cossack autonomy, and kinship. These memories, often richer than the suitcase's brittle papers, offered glimpses of a world empire tried to erase – preserved not fully, but enough to be remembered.

What the suitcase revealed, and what the archives confirmed, was not a story of rupture or glory. It was something quieter: persistence shaped by constraint. The Skliars survived not through rebellion, but through adaptation. They became psalmists, parish trustees, *zemstvo* clerks, teachers. They worked within the structures that remained. They endured.

This chapter does not resolve the record. It defines its edges. The documents, the omissions, the inconsistencies – these are not gaps around the history. They are the history. They show how identity was managed, erased, and reassembled. They speak not only to one family's path through empire and displacement, but to a broader Ukrainian condition: endurance without certainty, survival with moral ambiguity.

* * *

The fragments do not end the story. The story now turns to Ivan Skliar – born around 1875, at the edge of a world already shifting. He came of age in a village shaped by parish duty, imperial oversight, and names that still bore the residue of Cossack status.

The promises made at Pereiaslav, the defeat at Poltava, the silencing of Ukrainian language under the empire – all of these lay behind him, not as history recounted, but as conditions inherited. His is the first life that can be followed in full: through registers, records, and routines that survived. Not a figure of rebellion or renown, but of continuity – someone who carried forward a way of living when little else remained.

CHAPTER 4

Faith and Endurance: Ivan Skliar (1875–1950)

О, плачте, ви, хто сльози ма в очах,
О, плачте над руїнами святині!
Нехай побачу я ще в тих сльозах,
Що в вас душа ще досі не в руїні.

Oh weep, you who still carry tears in your eyes –
Weep for the ruins of the sanctuary.
Let me see in your weeping
That your soul has not yet crumbled to ruin.

– Volodymyr Samiylenko[10], from *Above the Ruins*, 1891

---

[10] Volodymyr Samiylenko (1864–1925) was a Ukrainian poet, satirist, and civic intellectual known for his refined verse and moral clarity. Writing under the Russian Empire, he combined classical forms with a quiet nationalism, addressing themes of false piety, ethical decay, and passive complicity. His legacy endures as a voice of sober patriotism and inner renewal.

I did not grow up with the Orthodox Church – or any church. Until I began tracing Ivan Skliar, my great-great-grandfather, I had never stepped into a service except as an outsider. I stood at the back, caught by the glow of icons, the scent of beeswax, the low chant rising like a pulse. The word "psalmist" felt distant, ceremonial. I did not know it was a life, woven into the habits of a village structured around faith.

At the turn of the twentieth century, Ukraine remained stateless. Cultural expression was tightly policed; political autonomy long extinguished. Yet in rural villages, the Orthodox parish continued to hold space for identity – even within the very acts of worship. Although the Church was salaried by the empire and formally loyal to the tsar, parish life often quietly diverged from imperial prescription. While state-backed Orthodoxy emphasised figures like St George, symbol of imperial might and patron saint of empire, Ukrainian communities maintained a particular devotion to saints like St Nicholas (*Mykolai*), rooted deeply in local custom and popular reverence. Psalms were sung in familiar cadence; feast days celebrated in embroidered *vyshyvanky*[11], ancestral prayers, and traditions specific to local memory. The parish preserved, quietly, persistently – from within – what the state would not.

Among its stewards stood the psalmist: a lay figure, neither fully priest nor ordinary parishioner. He led chants, assisted in liturgy, and maintained the rhythms of parish life. Trained in Russian,

---

[11] *Vyshyvanka* refers to a traditional Ukrainian embroidered shirt, often handmade and richly patterned. While historically worn for ritual and festive occasions, it has also become a powerful cultural symbol – signifying national identity, continuity, and resistance, especially in times of political repression.

often serving in Ukrainian, he existed between categories – embedded in the village, appointed by the Church. In homes where books were rare, his voice carried scripture, instruction, and memory. His authority was practical and moral.

For families like the Skliars, parish service had long replaced older forms of leadership. Where earlier generations had been elders, record-keepers, and parish trustees, Ivan's work followed the same ethic – only now within a narrower world. The village church was no longer a remnant of autonomy. It was the last place where continuity could still be practised aloud.

Figure 12: Vasily Polenov's Orthodox church interior (c. 1880s) evokes the sacred spaces where Ivan Skliar led chants, preserving Ukrainian identity in Poltava's parishes.

One such figure was Ivan Skliar. Born in the 1870s, he trained in monastery and ministry school, then served for decades in the parishes of rural Poltava. His life was not exceptional – and that is what makes it valuable. In tracing his path, we see how faith, literacy, and routine held together the remnants of a world already under pressure. He left no writing, no sermons. Everything I know of his life comes from registers, postings, salaries – the kind of details that say little and suggest much. Ivan's story begins in steadiness. But it does not end there.

Service and Stability: Psalmist Life in Poltava, 1875–1914

Ivan Skliar's path was not unusual. He was born to a Cossack family rooted in parish life; his father, Kornil likely served in similar clerical or lay religious roles.[12]

Like many Ukrainian boys from devout rural households in the late 19th century, Ivan entered religious service young. By 1890 – aged around fifteen – he had begun a clerical journey that would place him at the heart of village life, carrying forward a system built on memory, duty, and belief.

His education began at the *Opishnya Two-Class Ministry School*, a modest but rigorous institution within the imperial education network. These schools were designed to produce functionaries of the Church and state, offering training in Russian, scripture, arithmetic, Church Slavonic, and moral instruction. Though ideologically conservative, they gave many rural children their first access to formal schooling – and their only route to clerical careers.

---

[12] Later family recollections described Kornil as a priest, but it is more plausible that Kornil served in a lay capacity – perhaps as a psalmist, trustee, or elder – within the Orthodox parish system. These roles were often recalled generically as "priest" in oral history, reflecting authority and religious function more than formal title.

From there, Ivan entered the Exaltation of the Cross Monastery in Poltava as a *poslushnik*, or novice. This stage was not primarily theological. It was practical and ascetic – rooted in discipline and daily routine. *Poslushniki* worked in gardens, swept courtyards, rang bells, served meals, and rose before dawn for morning prayers. They lived within monastic order but without vows, absorbing the habits and rhythms of Orthodox life. For boys like Ivan, it was a formative apprenticeship – not to priesthood, but to the moral authority of the village psalmist.

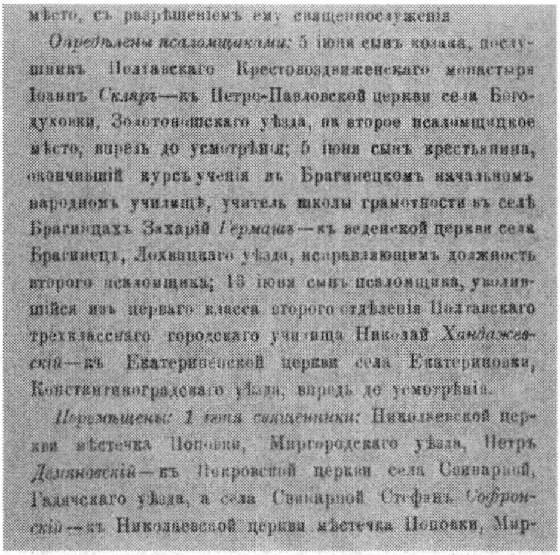

мѣсто, съ разрѣшеніемъ ему священнослуженія

Опредѣлены псаломщиками: 5 іюня сынъ козака, послушникъ Полтавскаго Крестовоздвиженскаго монастыря Іоаннъ *Скляръ*—къ Петро-Павловской церкви села Богодуховки, Золотоношскаго уѣзда, на второе псаломщицкое мѣсто, впредь до усмотрѣнія; 5 іюня сынъ крестьянина, окончившій курсъ ученія въ Брагинецкомъ начальномъ народномъ училищѣ, учитель школы грамотности въ селѣ Брагинцахъ Захарій *Германъ*—къ веденской церкви села Брагинецъ, Лохвицкаго уѣзда, исправляющимъ должность второго псаломщика; 13 іюня сынъ псаломщика, уволившійся изъ перваго класса второго отдѣленія Полтавскаго трехкласснаго городскаго училища Николай *Хандажевскій*—къ Екатерининской церкви села Екатериновки, Константиноградскаго уѣзда, впредь до усмотрѣнія.

Перемѣщены: 1 іюня священники: Николаевской церкви мѣстечка Поповки, Миргородскаго уѣзда, Петръ *Дамяновскій*—къ Покровской церкви села Свинарной, Гадячскаго уѣзда, а села Свинарной Стефанъ *Софронскій*—къ Николаевской церкви мѣстечка Поповки, Мир-

Figure 13: An 1890 Poltava Eparchial Gazette notice records Ivan Skliar's appointment as psalmist at Bohodukhivka; his "Kozaka" heritage a faint echo of Cossack memory.

In 1890, aged about fifteen, Ivan began as psalmist at Bohodukhivka's Church of Saints Peter and Paul, followed by brief posts in Chernobay and Mykhailivka[13] – typical early assignments

[13] *Poltava Eparchial Gazette* (*Полтавские епархиальные ведомости*), issues no. 13, 19, and 23 (1890). Poltava: 1863–1917.

that allowed church authorities to assess temperament and adaptability.

Figure 14: Ivan Skliar's early ecclesiastical appointments (1890–1912). This map shows the locations of Bohodukhivka, Zolotonosha (A); Chernobay (B); and Mykhailivka (C), Konstantinograd. These villages across central Ukraine were where Ivan served during his early religious career. Also shown are Opishnya (D), where he studied, and Dar-Nadezhda I, where he would later serve long-term.

By 1912, Ivan had taken up a long-term post in the village of Dar-Nadezhda. The Nikolaevskaya Church there – constructed in 1871 – was a wooden building with a bell tower and parish house, typical of rural ecclesiastical architecture. Its reach was substantial: over 5,200 parishioners across sixteen villages, two affiliated church schools, and 112 *desyatinas* of land (about 122 hectares).[14] Ivan served as senior psalmist alongside a clerical team that included two

[14] A *desyatina* (*десятина*) was a unit of land area in the Russian Empire, roughly equal to 1.09 hectares or 2.7 acres. It was commonly used in agricultural and church landholding records.

priests (Father Ivan Terletsky and Father Stepan Illyashevych), a junior psalmist (Fedor Lysenko), and a lay elder (Semen Soloha).

Salaries were modest: the senior priest received 106 I per year, the junior ninety-four; Ivan, as senior psalmist, earned thirty-six. By modern standards, these were not generous incomes. A rural teacher might earn 120 I; a village policeman, closer to 150. But the figures do not tell the full story. Clerical posts often came with housing, land access, and informal income – from record-keeping, letter-writing, or gifts for sacraments. For psalmists like Ivan, the role offered security, literacy, and standing in a world with few such opportunities for Ukrainian villagers.[15]

Nikolaevskaya Church was both a place of devotion and a local hub for administration, education, and cultural life. Ivan's role expanded accordingly. As senior psalmist, he oversaw parish books, coordinated feast days, supported literacy, and acted as an intermediary between clergy and lay families. These were not ceremonial extras. They preserved communal rhythm and buffered village custom against state intrusion.

[15] *Clerical Register of the Poltava Diocese* (*Справочная клировая книга по Полтавской епархии на 1912 год*), digitised on HistPol, accessed March 2025.

Figure 15: A c. 1900 photograph of Sakhnovshchyna, near Ivan Skliar's Dar-Nadezhda parish, captures the village rhythms he sustained as psalmist.

Liturgical practice followed shared forms but bore local inflection. Psalms, icons, and embroidered cloths connected homes to the church calendar, embedding memory in gesture and repetition. Ivan's work helped transmit belief and obligation – often without a written word. The language he sang in, the rites he kept – these were not acts of defiance, but nor were they entirely safe. In carrying forward older rhythms under imperial terms, Ivan rehearsed a national dilemma his father had likely already faced, and his son and grandson would later live more acutely: how to endure, and how much to let go.

Like many psalmists, Ivan married and raised a family within the orbit of parish life. His first wife, Anna Piwowarowa, though almost entirely unrecorded, likely sustained the moral and material fabric of their home.[16] As the wife of a psalmist in rural Ukraine, she managed a household that was both private and public – a site of hospitality, instruction, and informal counsel. Clerical homes like theirs were regularly visited by neighbours seeking blessings, literacy help, or advice on feast days. Anna would have prepared for name days, tended the family's icons, and taught psalms by rote before her children ever entered a classroom. She may have embroidered *rushnyky*[17] for church use or marked fasts with particular foods – rituals traditionally passed quietly from mother to daughter.

Though Orthodox liturgy denied her a formal voice, she held the rhythm of its seasons through action. In a world where trust, custom, and reputation carried weight, her labour underpinned her husband's standing – and shaped the early identity of her children, long before politics or ideology intervened.

---

[16] Anna Piwowarowa appears only on Viktor Skliar's 1945 Displaced Persons Identity Card, listed as his mother. The document, completed in postwar Germany, contains falsehoods (birth year, birthplace, occupation) to evade Soviet repatriation, casting doubt on Anna's name. The surname Piwowar, meaning brewer, is, however, common in Poltava around the period. For example, entire households are recorded in Holodomor memorial books. If Anna was Ivan's first wife, she may have died young after bearing children, leaving no further trace.

[17] *Rushnyky* are traditional Ukrainian ritual cloths, often hand-embroidered, used in both domestic and religious contexts. They are typically draped over icons, used in wedding and funeral rites, or hung in homes as protective and symbolic objects. The patterns and colours vary by region, with motifs often conveying blessings, continuity, or ancestral memory.

Figure 16: Ukrainian women from the Poltava region, c. 1914. Dressed in richly embroidered blouses and layered beadwork, these young women reflect the strength of prewar village traditions. Clothing and ornament served not only aesthetic purposes but embodied regional identity and spiritual symbolism – forms of cultural continuity preserved through generations. This image evokes the domestic world women like Anna Piwowarowa sustained – woven with memory, ritual, and community.

Anna had at least two children: Maria Ivanivna Skliar (born 1897) and Viktor Ivanovych Skliar (born 1899).

Maria, the elder, would go on to embody many of the values Anna instilled. Educated at the *Poltava Eparchial Women's School* – an institution founded to train clergy daughters in scripture, arithmetic, and needlework – she graduated in 1913 and became a teacher in Sakhnovshchyna. Her role was more than occupational. As Wsewolod later recalled, she was a composed and upright presence: a moral anchor whose quiet perseverance carried older rhythms into the Soviet era. Within her classroom, she sustained fragments of cultural memory – Ukrainian verse, Orthodox gestures, an ethos of dignity – despite the demands of ideological conformity. Married to Ivan Astashenko, Maria carried forward her mother's legacy in a different key: not through liturgy, but through pedagogy.

Maria and Ivan raised two children, Antonina and Anatoli. During the war, they lived for a time with their uncle Viktor and cousin Wsewolod. Wsewolod later recalled their closeness in childhood – a small but enduring source of kinship and care amid the wider collapse of everyday life. Maria's ability to provide structure and continuity – through teaching, caregiving, and familial presence – quietly mirrored the resilience shown by many Ukrainian women whose labour sustained both households and communities through years of uncertainty.

Anna is believed to have died young, with Ivan remarrying soon after. The family lived near the church; their household was part of a clerical estate where stability depended not only on salary, but on fidelity to ritual and standing in the eyes of the community.

By 1914, life in Dar-Nadezhda followed a steady rhythm. The seasons turned, feast days were kept, and the parish remained a fixed point in village life. Ivan's household was stable, his role secure. But that order was fragile. Across the empire, pressures were mounting: strikes in the cities, unrest in the countryside, warnings of a war that had not yet come. In places like Dar-Nadezhda, the horizon still felt distant. But change was coming fast – and when it arrived, it would reach even the quietest parishes.

War's Shadow: Poltava and Ivan's Parish, 1914–1917

When war broke out in 1914, Ukraine had no state, no army of its own, and no voice in the decisions that sent its people to the front. Divided between empires, Ukrainians fought on both sides of the Eastern Front: for Russia in the east, and for Austria-Hungary in the west. The war was not framed as theirs, yet its toll fell heavily on Ukrainian people and Ukrainian lands – over half a million Ukrainian military and civilian losses.[18] Villages were emptied by conscription, grain requisitioned, churches burdened with refugees, and communities drawn into a conflict they could neither shape nor escape. What began as a distant campaign quickly reached the village – not as battles, but as a fracture in the social and political order – one that would soon open into revolution.

In central Ukraine, Poltava contributed heavily to the imperial war effort. Thousands were drafted; requisitions intensified; field hospitals spread across the countryside. Though far from the front, the region experienced quiet upheaval. By 1916, food shortages were deepening. Prices doubled. Wounded soldiers arrived from Galicia and Poland. Displaced families were housed in church estates and village homes. In places like Dar-Nadezhda, where Ivan Skliar served, the Church became more than a spiritual presence. It was a kind of social anchor. Its services offered structure. Its calendar marked time. Its psalms held memory.

---

[18] Erlikman, Vadim. *Poteri narodonaseleniia v XX veke: spravochnik*. Moscow, 2004, 34.

As a psalmist in his early forties, Ivan was likely exempt from conscription. Imperial law typically spared church-workers, especially in rural parishes, where their roles were considered essential to morale and cohesion. Some younger clergy were later mobilised as chaplains, but Ivan's age, post, and the absence of records all suggest he remained in Dar-Nadezhda. His son Viktor, fifteen in 1914, was still studying at the Poltava Theological Seminary and too young to be called up. Their wartime service, like that of many clergy, was measured not in combat, but in continuity.

And that continuity became a form of burden. Across Poltava, psalmists like Ivan shouldered new pressures: funerals for local conscripts, prayers for the wounded, quiet acts of care for families housing the displaced. The imperial state demanded loyalty, and the Church answered in Russian. But inside village parishes, older rhythms persisted – Ukrainian hymns, family rites, local prayers. In homes stretched thin by absence and grief, these rituals gave shape to the strain.

The war also brought tremors that would later widen into collapse. Nationalist pamphlets circulated through underground groups such as *Prosvita*[19]. Ideas of autonomy, once whispered, began to gather weight. In Dar-Nadezhda, it is unlikely Ivan engaged directly – his service lay elsewhere. But he would have heard the shifts: the changed tone of sermons, the rumours from Kharkiv and Kyiv, the tension that reached even quiet villages. By 1917, the Tsar had

---

[19] *Prosvita* ("Enlightenment") was a Ukrainian cultural society promoting language, education, and national identity. Though founded in Galicia, its influence spread eastward, including to Poltava, through underground networks in the early 20th century.

fallen. The centre had cracked. And Ivan's world, already strained, stood on the edge of something larger than war.

From Liturgy to Silence: Church Under Siege, 1917–1940

The world Ivan Skliar had helped sustain did not vanish overnight. But from 1917 onward, Orthodox religious life in Ukraine was no longer merely endangered – it was targeted. What began as political transformation hardened into ideological erasure. Across the countryside, bells fell silent. Icons were torn from walls, parish doors nailed shut.

In the early revolutionary years, there were glimmers of reform. In 1921, a new *Ukrainian Autocephalous Orthodox Church* (*UAOC*) was proclaimed – seeking independence from Moscow and a return to native tradition.[20] It drew support from clergy, intellectuals, and many rural believers. But it lacked state protection. By the decade's end, its leaders had been arrested or executed, its parishes closed or absorbed, by state decree. That silence soon widened.

However, in villages like Dar-Nadezhda, the silence did not arrive all at once. In 1929, long after the collapse of the tsarist order, Ivan's grandson Wsewolod was baptised in Dar-Nadezhda – by Father Terletsky, who had served alongside Ivan since at least 1912. That small act – quiet and inconspicuous – suggested that some lines of

---

[20] The UAOC was an attempt to create an independent, Ukrainian-language church that would reflect local traditions rather than Russian control. Though initially supported by elements of the intelligentsia and rural clergy, it faced persecution almost from inception and was dismantled by Soviet authorities by the end of the decade.

tradition had not yet broken and that the parish system still held, at least in part – embedded deeply enough in daily life to survive even amid formal collapse.

With the UAOC dismantled, the official Church came under attack as a relic of the old imperial order. Clergy were denounced as class enemies. Parish land was seized. Even psalmists – un-ordained, often poorly paid – were categorised as "religious functionaries" and treated with suspicion. Their roles carried forward memory and tradition. And to the Soviet leadership, memory and tradition were dangerous.

Repression intensified with Stalin's consolidation of power. Parish life retreated indoors. Icons reappeared behind cupboard doors. Psalters were hidden. Services were whispered behind curtains or held at dawn. Baptisms moved to kitchens. Funerals became hurried, stripped of liturgy. In many villages, even these gestures ceased. Similar to Cossack traditions a century earlier, faith persisted in less formal rituals: voice, habit, and timekeeping. Much of this domestic continuity was sustained by women, whose labour rarely entered the record. While clergy were arrested and churches dismantled, women maintained fasts, repeated blessings, and taught hymns by memory when books and buildings were gone.

This was not passive adaptation. It was quiet resistance. Psalms were no longer sung in choirs, but in fragments – a chant at harvest, a proverb murmured at a wake. In some homes, lines from Shevchenko's Psalms and the Book of Psalms blurred into each other – half-prayer, half-poem, remembered by heart when printed texts had vanished. The psalmist's voice, reduced to a murmur, still carried the past: a feast marked in silence, a verse spoken at a graveside. Not rebellion, but refusal – to forget, to relinquish meaning, to surrender the truth beneath it.

In 1931, Ivan Pylypenko – a priest living in Dar-Nadezhda – was arrested for "anti-Soviet agitation". He was sentenced to three years' exile in the Northern Territory. A village priest, Ukrainian, born in Runivshchyna, educated, but non-partisan. His story gives shape to the risk Ivan lived with, and the thin margin on which survival depended.

Figure 17: The Destruction of St. Michael's Golden-Domed Monastery, Kyiv (1935–1937). One of Ukraine's most revered Orthodox sites, St. Michael's was demolished as part of Soviet efforts to eradicate religious influence and Ukrainian heritage. Its destruction marked the violent rupture of centuries of spiritual and cultural tradition.

Ivan's exact movements and actions during this period remain undocumented. But his survival in Dar-Nadezhda – when thousands of church-workers were imprisoned, exiled, or executed – places him among the few who endured. By the mid-1930s, over 90 percent of Orthodox churches in Ukraine had been closed, looted, or destroyed. Some were repurposed as barns, clubs, or depots; others were levelled entirely. One of them was Trinity Church in Opishnya, where Ivan had trained as a novice. Its bricks were torn down and used for pavements. Workers died dismantling its walls. Iconoclasm was both material and symbolic: frescoes whitewashed, altars looted, psalm books destroyed. Across Ukraine, sacred architecture was stripped away brick-by-brick. Yet the traditions those buildings carried did not vanish overnight. In homes and memory, their rhythms remained.

The violence intensified under Stalin's Great Purge. More than 100,000 clergy, psalmists, and lay workers were arrested across the Soviet Union. In Ukraine, many were executed in pits at Bykivnia, Sandarmokh, and other NKVD[21] sites. Entire parish staffs disappeared. Liturgy was almost entirely replaced by silence.

---

[21] The *People's Commissariat for Internal Affairs* (*Narodnyi Komissariat Vnutrennikh Del*). The NKVD were the Soviet secret police agency responsible for political repression, mass deportations, and extrajudicial executions.

Figure 18: Trinity Church, Opishnya, c. 1920. A former training ground for Ivan Skliar, the church stood as a centre of spiritual and communal life in Poltava region. Its demolition in the early 1930s reflects the scale and intent of Stalinist religious repression – a campaign against institutions, and memory itself.

Fragments of Ivan's later years linger in household memory. His grandson Wsewolod, born in 1929, later recalled visiting a large house with land in the 1930s. There were no sermons, no open catechism – but traces of the sacred remained: a calendar still observed, prayers whispered behind drawn curtains, a quiet reverence that shaped the day. Wsewolod described his grandfather simply as "a priest" – a child's impression, formed more by presence than by office, but powerful nonetheless. He also remembered his half-brother Vadim living in the house during those years, sharing in its subdued routines. In a land of silence and suspicion, Ivan's customs and quiet authority anchored the household – passing on meaning that could no longer be spoken aloud.

Piecing together Ivan's life from archives and Wsewolod's recollections, I've wrestled with how he survived the purges when so many others did not. Most psalmists vanished. Ivan did not. Part of me wants to believe he simply kept his head down, stayed useful, avoided notice. But that feels too neat – and Stalin's Ukraine rarely allowed for tidy endings.[22] Wsewolod remembered a large house with land in Dar-Nadezhda – unusual for a psalmist by the late 1930s. It hints at something harder to name: perhaps a quiet understanding with local officials, perhaps protection, perhaps silence when others were taken. I cannot know. But I do not believe survival came without cost. Under a regime that punished memory, endurance required choices – some of them uneasy. I do not excuse those choices. But I will not judge what I cannot see clearly. What matters is that something endured: a voice, a presence, a trace of meaning passed on, even if it could no longer be named.

In the decade that followed, that rhythm continued – quieter still, but not entirely broken.

Faith in Private: The Last Decade, 1941-1950

Orthodox policy shifted again in the 1940s. After the Nazi invasion in 1941, the Soviet state briefly eased restrictions on religious practice, allowing some churches to reopen and clerical figures to

---

[22] Survival among lower-ranking clergy during the Stalinist repressions often depended on circumstances beyond their control. Some clergy survived by avoiding visibility, adapting rituals to domestic settings, or quietly ceasing public roles. Others were spared arbitrarily. In many cases, the line between collaboration, endurance and evasion was blurry – marked less by ideological choice than by timing, discretion, and local relationships.

re-emerge – especially in rural areas. Services resumed in limited fashion, though always under surveillance. Ivan would have witnessed this change. He may even have resumed occasional duties, though this remains undocumented. Like many others, he may have offered blessings, supported church services, or contributed quiet observance at home. But the respite was partial and short-lived.

Figure 19: Ivan Skliar with his second wife, alongside Viktor and Maria – children from his first marriage; c.1905. A rare portrait of family stability before Soviet repression.

In 1943, Stalin authorised the re-establishment of the Moscow Patriarchate as a state-sanctioned Church. In theory, certain rites were permitted to resume. In practice, fear and monitoring continued to shape what could be practised, and how. By the late 1940s, religious instruction remained banned, clergy were watched, and psalmists – never formally protected – remained exposed to renewed suspicion.

Ivan, by then in his seventies, did not vanish from village life. He may have continued to assist others – writing letters, marking saints' days, helping neighbours maintain old observances. Though formal parish structures had collapsed, his home still carried echoes of a clerical past.

He is believed to have died around 1950. No obituary survives. His death went unmarked in bulletins – because by then, there were none. But in oral memory, he remained: not as a figure of grandeur, but as the last psalmist within the Skliar family. His vocation, once public and prescribed, had become entirely domestic – sustained through routine, presence, and the quiet continuation of a role that could no longer be named aloud.

* * *

Ivan Skliar's life was shaped by faith, service, and quiet endurance. He left behind only formal records – no writings, no monuments, no sermons. What endured was the pattern of his life: liturgy performed under scrutiny, customs maintained in private, identity carried forward without declaration. His role became smaller over time, but he remained by adjusting. In a system that punished memory, survival depended on silence.

That silence became the legacy. For his children and grandchildren, Ivan was not a storyteller but a reference point – a man who kept his footing as institutions collapsed, who continued to observe when observation itself became suspect. What he preserved was not resistance, but continuity: a form of Ukrainian identity compatible with fear.

But survival altered what could be passed on. Faith retreated indoors. Language was guarded. Public memory narrowed to private gesture. The Orthodox Church Ivan served no longer belonged to the community; it belonged to the state. His vocation, once public, ended in caution.

Viktor, his son, inherited that caution. He would carry it into a different century – shaped not by liturgical calendars, but by war, occupation, and famine. What follows is not a continuation of Ivan's world, but its reckoning: the moment when the costs of endurance could no longer be deferred.

CHAPTER 5

Ideology and Survival:

The Early Life of Viktor Skliar, 1899–1932

І кождий з нас те знав, що слави нам не буде,
Ні пам'яті в людей за сей кривавий труд,
Що аж тоді підуть по сій дорозі люди,
Як ми проб'єм її та вирівняєм всюди,
Як наші кості тут під нею зогниють.

Yet each of us knew well he should no glory reap,
Nor would man's memory requite our toilsome pain,
That long before our seed along that road would sweep,
Ere we could break a path and make it smooth and plain,
Our bleaching bones would lie beside it in a heap.

– Ivan Franko[23], from *The Stonecutters (Kameniari)*, 1878

[23] Ivan Franko (1856–1916) was a Ukrainian writer, scholar, and political thinker. A polymath from Galicia, he combined socialist and nationalist ideals, publishing extensively on history, class, and cultural identity. His novel *Zakhar Berkut*, later found in Wsewolod's reading list, promoted collective endurance and became a touchstone in exile. Translation by Percival Cundy, 1948.

I used to see Viktor Skliar's life as simple: a disappointment, his drinking and silence leaving pain. Family stories told it that way. But the suitcase's contents, archives, and Wsewolod's testimony revealed a deeper complexity.

He was born into a devout Orthodox household in Dar-Nadezhda. His father was a psalmist; his childhood steeped in ritual, language, and memory. But the world he inherited was already breaking. Viktor trained for the Church, only to be swept up in revolution. He fought for Ukrainian independence, then served the Soviets in the Red Army. Later, as a grain bookkeeper, he worked within a system that would soon turn on its own people. Even his personal life leaves uncomfortable questions: family memory hints at coercion in his first marriage, though no record confirms or resolves it.

I can't pass judgement: survival demanded impossible choices. The first half of the 20th century hit Ukraine with relentless force. War, famine, shifting borders, and state terror tore through ordinary lives. Yet, not all chose alike.

This chapter does not seek to excuse or indict.

Viktor Skliar came of age as Ukraine itself was violently torn apart and remade. His early life mirrors the nation's trajectory: from a brief flicker of independent hope through the brutal consolidation of a new, unforgiving Soviet order, a period that would test every Ukrainian's capacity for ideological navigation and sheer survival.

Foundations of Faith, 1899–1917

Viktor Skliar was born on 28 June 1899[24] in Dar-Nadezhda – a village parish in the Sakhnovshchyna district of Poltava guberniya. His father, Ivan Skliar, was a psalmist, and the household was known locally for its education, religiosity, and strong sense of cultural identity. Wsewolod, Viktor's son, would later describe himself as "*the son of a cultured family*" raised under Soviet rule by a "*deeply Ukrainian father*" who instilled in him "*the spirit of Ukrainian nationalism*".[25]

At the time of Viktor's birth, Dar-Nadezhda was a modest but active parish centre. Nearby Sakhnovshchyna – a rapidly growing railway town – had become the region's administrative and economic hub.[26] While religious life remained anchored in Dar-Nadezhda, daily life increasingly revolved around Sakhnovshchyna's emerging opportunities. Viktor would later relocate there, likely between 1919 and 1924, as he entered

[24] In a 2008 recollection, Wsewolod Skliar confirmed that while Viktor's UK passport listed his birth year as 1895, this was a deliberate fabrication, consistent with other falsified details he provided upon his arrival in the UK – both for himself and for Wsewolod. These alterations were necessary to facilitate employment opportunities, as displaced persons often faced bureaucratic obstacles when seeking work and residency in post-war Britain.

[25] This recollection, like many from survivor families, reflects both remembered reality and retrospective construction. Such terms often conflate local standing, moral character, and cultural aspiration – especially when filtered through the lens of displacement. These quotations are drawn from *Appendix A: Autobiographical Note, c. 1949.*

[26] Fomicheva, M. P., and V. F. Svidchenko. "Sakhnovshchyna, Sakhnovshchynskyi Raion, Kharkivska Oblast." In *Istorii mist i sil Ukrainskoi RSR* (Histories of the Cities and Villages of the Ukrainian SSR), originally published 1967. Accessed March 2025.

adulthood and started a family.[27] Ivan remained behind. It was there, in 1929, that his grandson Wsewolod was baptised.

Between 1911 and 1916, Viktor studied at the *Poltava Theological Seminary* – an Orthodox institution designed to prepare priests and psalmists. His enrolment reflected the path expected of him: a continuation of the clerical roles held by his father and grandfather. The seminary offered students from modest rural families a rare route to education, literacy, and status. But it also served the Russian imperial project. Its aim was not only to train clergy, but to instil loyalty to the Tsar and promote Russian language and culture. Since the 1860s, Russian policy had worked to erase the public life of Ukrainian language and custom. By the time Viktor entered the seminary, Ukrainian print was Almost entirely restricted, parishes were forced into imperial alignment, and identity was something practised quietly, not proclaimed.

[27] Viktor's German-issued identity document (1943) lists his birthplace as Dar-Nadezhda, while his residence from at least the 1920s onward is recorded as Sakhnovshchyna. This shift corresponds with family recollections and baptismal records, suggesting a generational transition in residence – from Ivan's continued life in Dar-Nadezhda to Viktor's move closer to the railway and grain economy of Sakhnovshchyna.

Figure 20: *Poltava Theological Seminary*, c. 1905. Where Viktor Skliar studied from 1911. The seminary trained clergy but also became a quiet centre of Ukrainian cultural awakening.

For Ukrainian students, the experience could be both empowering and alienating – offering sacred instruction while downplaying their native identity and discouraging Ukrainian-language expression. Among its graduates was Symon Petliura, the future leader of the *Ukrainian People's Republic*. While there is no evidence that Viktor was politically active during his time at the seminary, the dissonance he absorbed – between service and suppression, between ritual and identity – would later resurface in his choices. The seminary formed him. But it also placed him near a growing fracture: where inherited duty met a rising sense of national difference.

Viktor's academic path was uneven. He advanced each year but not without difficulty. He failed dictation, repeated a full year, and retook exams in geography and arithmetic.[28] Like many seminarians from rural backgrounds, he struggled within the rigid, centralised system. Yet even unfinished, the education left its mark: liturgical fluency, a grounding in sacred order, and the moral vocabulary of duty. These years shaped his understanding of belief and responsibility – long after the world he had trained for had collapsed.

By 1914, as war gripped the empire and his father's parish world came under increasing strain, Viktor remained cloistered within seminary walls – learning rites already threatened by the violence outside. In 1917, the Russian Revolution and the collapse of imperial authority brought his studies to an end. The clerical path he had trained for was shattered. Thousands of seminarians – Viktor among them – were left adrift. Some were conscripted, others returned home, uncertain of what future remained.

What followed was not reinvention, but improvisation. Into the vacuum left by empire came ideology. The frameworks of belief and duty that had shaped Viktor's youth were replaced by new demands for loyalty – demands that would ask him to choose, and then choose again.

---

[28] Seminary classes were divided into ranked categories based on academic performance. "Category 1" denoted high achievers; "Category 2" indicated standard progression without honours; "Category 3" was used for students at risk of failing or repeating a year. Viktor was listed in Category 2 for most years but fell to Category 3 in 1913 and repeated the course in 1915. In 1912, he failed dictation; in 1916, he retook geography and arithmetic. These patterns were not uncommon, especially among students from poor or rural backgrounds, for whom the seminary's academic and disciplinary demands could be overwhelming.

Revolution, Survival, and Soviet Rule, 1917–1921

The collapse of the Russian Empire in 1917 upended Viktor Skliar's world. Across Ukraine, the old order gave way not to stability, but to a dizzying cycle of regimes – each promising liberation, each extracting loyalty. In the space of just four years, Viktor served two of them.

In 1919, like many young Ukrainian men of his generation, he joined the pro-independence Ukrainian Army under Symon Petliura, who had become head of the *Ukrainian People's Republic*[29]. Formed in 1917 following the collapse of tsarist rule, the UPR was a fledgling attempt at Ukrainian statehood – a democratic republic that sought to establish national sovereignty amid the chaos of civil war. For men like Viktor, shaped by Orthodox discipline and decades of cultural repression, it was a chance – however fragile – to reclaim something long denied: a state that recognised their language, their customs, their past. The ideals he fought for were not new. They were inherited.

Petliura's forces fought on multiple fronts – against the Bolsheviks, the White Army, and, increasingly, one another. Their aim was clear: a sovereign Ukrainian state, free from Russian rule. But the

---

[29] The *Ukrainian People's Republic* (UNR/UPR) was declared in November 1917, following the collapse of tsarist authority. Initially part of a federative plan with Russia, it proclaimed full independence in January 1918. The republic faced immediate opposition from Bolshevik forces, White Russian armies, and Polish territorial ambitions. Despite attempts at international diplomacy and shifting alliances, it was militarily defeated by 1921. The idea of Ukrainian sovereignty, however, endured in exile and memory.

means were fractured, the allies unreliable, the cause increasingly desperate.

Viktor's path into the nationalist movement was shaped by background and by conviction. After years of learning in Russian, praying under Moscow's oversight, and watching Ukrainian expression pushed to the margins, joining the *UPR* may have felt less like a rebellion and more like a correction – an attempt to claim, if only briefly, the voice his father's generation had been forced to lower. His son Wsewolod later recalled that Viktor held firm political views in favour of Ukrainian independence – views that placed him in direct opposition to the emerging Soviet order. Like Petliura, he came from Cossack ancestry. Like Petliura, he studied at the *Poltava Theological Seminary*, though neither man completed their studies. Both were formed by a mix of religious instruction and national awakening, in a time when faith and identity were closely bound. Their shared trajectory – steeped in Orthodox tradition but turned toward political defiance – reflects a generation that grew up under empire, but refused to accept its permanence.

It was not a clean war. The Ukrainian countryside, where Viktor likely saw action, became a contested theatre of violence and vengeance. Villages changed hands multiple times in a month. Armed detachments – *Petliurites*[30], Reds, Whites, *Makhnovists*[31] –

---

[30] Followers of Symon Petliura.

[31] The Makhnovists were an anarchist revolutionary army led by Nestor Makhno, active primarily in southern Ukraine from 1918 to 1921. They promoted stateless peasant

swept through, demanding supplies, men, silence. Each army came dressed in its own ideals; each carried out looting, conscription, and, often, retribution. For soldiers like Viktor, the line between defender and target blurred.

By late 1919, with the nationalist cause faltering, Viktor was conscripted into the Red Army's Sakhnovshchyna command. Like many former supporters of the Ukrainian cause, he now found himself serving its conquerors. There was little choice. The Red Army, consolidating power across Ukraine, absorbed thousands of young men through forced mobilisation. For someone with seminary education and clerical skills, the likely path was bureaucratic. Viktor served as a clerical private – a low-ranking role that required literacy but little trust. His recruitment did not signal conversion, but adaptation: a decision to survive in a world where allegiance could no longer be freely chosen. He never spoke of his conscription – not to his son, not in writing. When called up again during the Second World War, he refused to serve. The silence that surrounds 1919 speaks not only to trauma, but to the difficulty of reconciling loyalty, survival, and the shifting demands of power. Did he justify the shift to himself? Did he regret it? Was it a choice, a response to the excesses of Petliura-affiliated forces? There are no answers. But what is clear is that his journey mirrors that of a generation whose ideals were no match for the tide of empire.

---

self-rule and opposed both Bolshevik and White forces. Though briefly allied with the Red Army, they were ultimately suppressed by the Soviets. Their movement drew strong rural support but left few stable records, contributing to their marginalisation in official histories.

In 1920, a year after Viktor's conscription, Poltava itself erupted in armed revolt. Led by underground elements loyal to the *Ukrainian People's Republic*, the uprising briefly seized the city before being violently suppressed by Bolshevik forces. Hundreds were executed in the aftermath. Many more disappeared into prison camps or mass graves. While Viktor's involvement, if any, is undocumented, the uprising underscores the volatility of the region – and the scale of resistance that endured even as Soviet power tightened its grip.

The violence of that year offers a possible context for a more personal loss. Family testimony, passed down by Viktor's son Wsewolod and preserved by his descendants, holds that Viktor was not the only member of the Skliar family to fight for the nationalist cause. A brother – unnamed in surviving records – is said to have joined Petliura's army and been executed. No documentary trace of this figure has been found, and the identity of Ivan Skliar's second wife, and any children she may have had, remains unknown. Church records for the period are missing. But given the scale of the reprisals that followed uprisings across central Ukraine, the story fits a wider pattern. In a civil war that split families and scattered allegiances, archival erasure became its own kind of loss. The absence of proof is not proof of absence – it is a consequence of rupture, and a legacy passed down not as fact, but as feeling. What survives is memory – fragmented, partial, and marked by silence.

In 1921, as Bolshevik control hardened, Viktor was transferred to the *First Category Reserve*[32]. Petliura's army had been defeated; the

---

[32] In the Soviet military system, the *First Category Reserve* referred to men who had completed active service but remained eligible for recall. These individuals were typically under 35 years old and could be called back in the event of mobilisation.

future belonged to the victors. When Viktor returned to civilian life, he did so quietly. There were no stories, no justifications. He, like Ukraine, had survived – but not unbroken.

The war left more than political fracture. It also unleashed terror on communities that had long lived side by side. Petliura's name would later become inseparable from the pogroms that devastated Jewish life across Ukraine. What, if anything, Viktor witnessed is unknown. There are no records. He never spoke of it. But silence, too, leaves its trace – and the neighbours who once shared the land with him were no longer there.

A Broken World: Pogroms and Silence, 1917–1921

The years of revolution and civil war brought devastation to nearly every corner of Ukraine. For the Jewish population, they brought terror. Between 1918 and 1921, over a thousand pogroms swept through Ukrainian towns and villages, killing tens of thousands of Jews. The violence was chaotic and decentralised – carried out by Bolshevik units, White officers, independent warlords, and, frequently, forces aligned with the *Ukrainian People's Republic*. While no side held a monopoly on atrocity, the UPR bore particular responsibility: its forces were responsible for nearly half of all pogroms during the civil war period, whether through direct action or failure to control units acting in its name.[33]

---

[33] Historian Oleg Budnitskii estimates that forces of the Ukrainian People's Republic were responsible for approximately 50% of pogroms committed during the civil war. Budnitskii, Oleg. *Russian Jews Between the Reds and the Whites, 1917–1920*. Philadelphia: University of Pennsylvania Press, 2012, 217.

The scale of destruction was especially acute in central and eastern Ukraine. In the Poltava region alone, dozens of communities saw looting, assault, and massacre. Market towns near Sakhnovshchyna – such as Zinkiv, Khorol, and Myrhorod – suffered repeated attacks. Jewish homes were burned. Synagogues desecrated. Survivors fled westward or into silence. Some of the worst atrocities were carried out by loosely affiliated Petliurite units, often acting without central command. Petliura himself denounced the violence, but the condemnations did not stop it.

The Skliar family left no record of involvement, and it is unknown whether Viktor witnessed any pogrom directly. He never spoke of them. But he wore the uniform of an army under whose name such acts were committed. His silence may reflect ignorance, distance, shame – or simply the boundaries of what could be acknowledged after defeat.

Family memory, passed down through Wsewolod, speaks of pride in Viktor's service. But it omits the darker legacy of those years. Ukrainian nationalism emerged from the ruins of empire with both aspiration and violence at its core. Any reckoning with that history must hold both. The dream of sovereignty coexisted with complicity. Between them lay the lives of the murdered, too often left unremembered.

This book cannot fill in what Viktor did or did not see. But it can mark the absence. Jewish and Ukrainian lives overlapped in the marketplaces and train stations of Poltava. They diverged, tragically, in 1919. That divergence – of fate, of memory, of mourning – remains part of the historical record, even when it leaves no trace in the family one. Viktor's own silence after 1919 reflected a different kind of reckoning: not violence, but a quiet, compromised domesticity.

After the Guns Fell Quiet, 1921–1924

By 1923, Viktor married Nadezhda[34] from Kharkiv, a union strained by ideological and personal tensions. Oral testimonies offer conflicting accounts of the marriage's nature. Wsewolod, Viktor's son, described it as arranged, formalised around 1923. Lidia, Vadim's daughter and Nadezhda's granddaughter, claimed Nadezhda, aged thirteen, was raped by Viktor, with the marriage, in her account, formalising the act. Neither account is verified by documents. The truth remains uncertain—but the allegation, even unproven, marks a serious rupture in Viktor's early life, and reflects the wider silence surrounding trauma and coercion in that era.[35]

Viktor and Nadezhda had one child together: Vadim Skliar, born on 12 February 1924 in Sakhnovshchyna. After the divorce, he

---

[34] Nadezhda's maiden name does not appear in surviving records. She is listed in found archival material under two married surnames: Skliar (from her first marriage to Viktor) and Averka (from her second marriage).

[35] Lidia's testimony, drawn from Vadim and Nadezhda, carries weight, yet Wsewolod's, via Viktor, reflects family memory's complexity.

In early Soviet and wartime Ukraine, sexual violence was rarely recorded in official documents – and even more rarely remembered in public testimony. Social shame, institutional silence, and postwar reconstitution often erased these experiences from the historical record. In the context of displacement, where marriages were sometimes arranged to formalise or conceal coercion, the line between consent and survival could become blurred. What endures is often not the act, but its omission. Testimonies like Lidia's, though unverifiable through documents, reflect a broader truth: that rape, pregnancy, and forced union were part of the social fabric – and that their legacies were shaped as much by omission as by fact.

remained with his grandfather, Ivan, who raised him through the 1940s.

Wsewolod recalled that Viktor had begun drinking in his youth – possibly as early as eleven – a common enough pattern in Cossack culture, where alcohol was deeply embedded in social life.[36] By the 1920s, amid war, revolution, and cultural collapse, his drinking deepened into dependency, likely an escape from upheaval. Many young men faced similar struggles under Soviet repression's toll. For Viktor, alcohol became a refuge – a way to blunt the dislocation of war, revolution, and eroded belief. But it also shadowed his life. The accusations surrounding his first marriage to Nadezhda – troubling and unresolved – emerged within this period, further complicating his already fragile moral legacy.

These personal fractures unfolded against a wider backdrop of cultural turbulence. While Viktor struggled to find stability in the wake of violence, the Soviet regime began experimenting with a new approach: *korenizatsiya*. It was an era of cautious revival, when the Ukrainian language returned to classrooms and public life – but only under the shadow of ideological control. For a man like Viktor, whose identity was shaped by Orthodoxy, quiet patriotism, and inherited restraint, the changing political winds offered little reassurance.

[36] In many parts of Ukraine, especially among Cossack-descended and peasant communities, the consumption of *horilka* (vodka) was deeply embedded in cultural tradition – appearing in songs, feast days, and village rituals. While communal drinking had long been normalised, Viktor's dependency appears to have exceeded custom. According to family recollection, it had already become habitual by adolescence.

The Rise and Fall of Korenizatsiya, 1924–1933

In the 1920s, the Soviet regime launched a policy known as *korenizatsiya* – "indigenisation" – aimed at winning over non-Russian nationalities by promoting native languages and cultures. For a brief moment, it seemed the state might allow what empire had tried to erase. In Ukraine, Ukrainian-language schools opened, local officials used the vernacular, and cultural life re-emerged – though always within strict ideological bounds.

But the space for expression was fragile. By the early 1930s, the Soviet leadership reversed course. Ukrainian publications were shut down, officials purged, and public life re-Russified. What had been encouraged now marked one out for suspicion. Language itself became a liability. A culture that had been sanctioned once more became subversive. And the habit of silence – long practised, long passed down – returned as the safest inheritance.

In this climate, Viktor's marriage, however it began, proved unsustainable. His family – shaped by Orthodox tradition and Ukrainian sentiment – clashed with Nadezhda's, who aligned more closely with the Soviet order. Her Party ties pushed Viktor into a world where faith and nationalism were suspect, testing his ability to adapt. Their ideological and generational divide soon became irreconcilable.

The Soviet Family Code of 1918 had already secularised marriage and permitted civil divorce, radically altering personal life. For families rooted in Orthodox values these reforms were deeply unsettling. Divorce, once rare and stigmatised, became more accessible, though still emotionally fraught. In mixed marriages like

Viktor and Nadezhda's, the tension between tradition and ideology often played out painfully at home.

On 4 May 1925, the couple formally divorced in Sakhnovshchyna, recorded as entry No. 3 in the district's journal of civil acts. Their split reflected not only personal estrangement, but the broader fractures running through Ukrainian life – between belief and conformity, tradition and ideology.

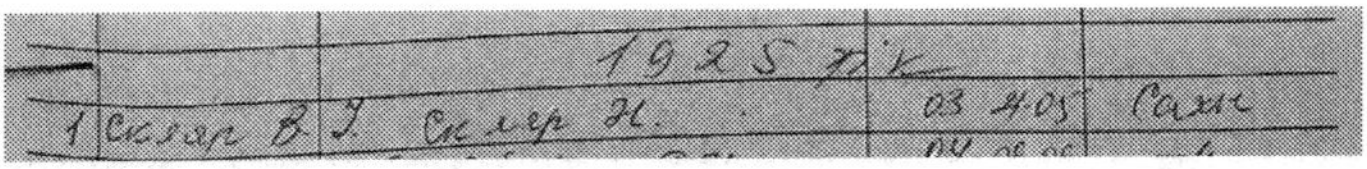

Figure 21: Entry from the Sakhnovshchyna civil register recording Viktor and Nadezhda Skliar's divorce on 4 May 1925. A formal severing within a rapidly shifting social order.

Viktor would not have taken divorce lightly. The Church had treated marriage as a sacrament, dissoluble only under rare and often scandalous circumstances. By contrast, the Soviet civil code reduced it to an administrative procedure. For Viktor, whose education was clerical and whose father was a psalmist, the act of divorce under Soviet law marked a disjunction: between the moral frameworks he had inherited and the ideological structures he now inhabited. Whether he saw it as necessity, failure, or simply the outcome of irreconcilable lives, it reflected a broader shift – from sacred order to bureaucratic authority – that had already reshaped much of Ukrainian life.

This shift is also reflected in Viktor's employment. In 1924, he began work in the grain industry as a bookkeeper in Kharkiv, and joined the trade union the same year. By then, unions had become instruments of state control – overseeing labour discipline, allocating entitlements, and reinforcing ideological conformity.

Grain accounting, once a matter of local trade, had become central to Soviet planning and control. Where once he had been prepared for a role rooted in sacred order, he now served a system governed by quotas and compliance. The grain office replaced the parish; ledgers replaced liturgy. It was stable employment, but it marked another step into a world where authority was no longer moral, but bureaucratic.

Figure 22: Nadezhda with her sons Viktor and Vadim, October 1946. Posed and unsmiling, the portrait bears the marks of Soviet formality, yet the repetition of names suggests a thread uncut, even as her life moved forward.

Nadezhda remarried a regional official, taking the surname Averka, and became a headmistress in Michotka, likely in Voronezh Oblast. She named her two sons Viktor and Vadim, a puzzling echo of her first husband and son, its meaning unclear – perhaps remembrance, coincidence, or reinvention.[37] Her story, marked by fracture and adaptation, threads quietly through the Skliar narrative.

By 1927, Viktor had remarried; this time to Evdokiya Petrova Mosiienko[38], born in 1905 in Oleksandrivka, a village in Sakhnovshchyna district. She belonged to a generation of women raised between revolution and restoration, expected to uphold tradition even as it fractured. As the wife of a grain bookkeeper, she occupied a role that was at once domestic and political. While not formally involved in Party or administrative life, women like Evdokiya played a critical interpretive role in everyday survival. They navigated what could still be said aloud, what traditions could be kept discreetly, and how to manage family routines under new ideological scrutiny. In a household tied to grain procurement – a politically sensitive sector – even hosting guests, observing feast days, or deciding what language to speak at home became quiet acts of judgement. Their labour was cultural and adaptive: maintaining stability in a world where the rules kept changing.

[37] Nadezhda's naming of her sons after her first husband and son lacks documented explanation, leaving open questions of intent amidst her traumatic past and Soviet context.

[38] The spelling of her surname in Ukrainian is likely "*Мосієнко*" based on records of residents in Sakhnovshchyna. One record from 1945 suggests her maiden name was Bondarenko. This is unlikely to be correct as the record contains other inaccuracies and was intentionally altered to minimise the risk of repatriation to the Soviet Union.

Figure 23: A *korovai* from Sakhnovshchyna, decorated with traditional dough birds and floral motifs. Prepared collectively by women, the *korovai* was more than bread: it was a ceremony of survival, blessing, and continuity. In villages like Sakhnovshchyna, such acts held a family's meaning when institutions failed to.

Their wedding, likely held in Sakhnovshchyna, may have been marked by the baking of a *korovai* – the ceremonial bread that once anchored village celebrations. Made from a single piece of dough and adorned with birds, braids, and floral motifs, the *korovai* symbolised prosperity and communal blessing. In Sakhnovshchyna, where the tradition was especially strong, its preparation was a collective act: women gathered to bake, neighbours sang, and families honoured the bond publicly – even when life remained precarious. Such a ritual marked not just a marriage, but a fragile continuity – a holding-together of meaning in an unsteady world.

Together, they had two children:

- Ksenia Skliar, who died of malaria at three months old.[39]
- Wsewolod Skliar, born April 2, 1929.

Ksenia's death, though tragic, was not uncommon in the 1920s. Malaria was widespread in Ukraine, particularly in the aftermath of World War I and the Russian Civil War. By 1923, reported malaria cases had surged to over 350,000, particularly affecting regions such as Kharkiv, Odessa, and Ekaterinoslav.[40] The spread of the disease was exacerbated by population displacement, deteriorating living conditions, and the collapse of healthcare infrastructure.

During these years, Viktor and Evdokiya built a quiet but precarious life in Sakhnovshchyna. Viktor continued working as a bookkeeper in the grain industry, remaining in the profession through at least 1940 – employed by cooperative enterprises. In the Soviet context, these were not independent associations, but state-regulated bodies tasked with meeting central quotas and managing local economic functions under Party oversight. They offered little autonomy but played a key role in implementing the economic demands of central government at a local level.

---

[39] A review of the indexes, for birth records, for the Sakhnovshchyna district between 1925 and 1928 reveals no entries for Ksenia Skliar. This could suggest the family were elsewhere when she was born, that record-keeping was poor, or that records have not survived. Vadim Skliar's birth was not officially registered until 1937, indicating that delays or omissions in local recordkeeping were potentially not uncommon during this time.

[40] Jewish Telegraphic Agency. "Terrible Plague of Malaria in the Ukraine." *Daily News Bulletin, Cable and Telegraphic Despatches*, August 21, 1924.

Figure 24: *Bread Is Our Strength* (1931). This Soviet propaganda poster, produced at the height of the First Five-Year Plan, exhorts citizens to harvest grain in service of the state, proclaiming "Bread is our strength – interventionists face the grave". It glorified agricultural labour and cast grain as a weapon in the ideological struggle. Viktor Skliar's work as a grain accountant unfolded in the shadow of this mobilisation, where spreadsheets became instruments of control and survival.

Grain was the Soviet state's lifeblood, and by the early 1930s, agricultural labour had been reimagined as ideological warfare. Propaganda celebrated grain as a weapon of strength, but for local administrators like Viktor, the reality was harsher. His ledgers documented receipts, shortfalls, and confiscations – often coded under euphemisms like *spetsraskhody* ("special expenditures") that masked the violence of forced seizures. The system demanded mathematical precision, political loyalty, and ideological blindness – yet punished honesty with charges of sabotage. Some clerks inflated harvest figures to shield neighbours; others falsified deliveries to survive audits. Every entry became a negotiation: between survival and complicity, caution and betrayal.

Evdokiya's quiet strength anchored their home as Viktor faced the grain industry's pressures, her care a bulwark against collapse. However, beneath the appearance of order, Viktor's own life began to fracture. A daughter dead, a marriage lost, and the slow erosion of the ideals he had once carried. The deeper losses were already unfolding, even before famine would expose them fully.

* * *

By the early 1930s, Viktor Skliar occupied a position that had little to do with the one he had been trained for. He had not entered the Church, as his father had. Instead, he had joined a failed war for Ukrainian independence. For a time, he had believed in the possibility of a different future – one shaped by language, culture, and national self-rule. That belief did not survive the civil war. Petliura's army collapsed. The Red Army advanced. Viktor was conscripted by the state he had tried to resist. He never spoke of it again.

What followed was not allegiance, but adjustment. He worked in the grain sector. He joined the trade union. He remarried. The choices narrowed. A brief window of cultural recognition had opened in the 1920s. By the end of the decade, it had closed. Ukrainian language and memory were again reclassified as risk. Viktor's literacy gave him work. His silence kept him alive. Whether this was a moral compromise or a form of resistance depends on where one draws the line between complicity and endurance. He never said.

His path traced the trajectory of a country forced to absorb defeat, adapt to surveillance, and relearn caution. What began as national aspiration became a private inheritance: service had become clerical, faith had become private, identity had become quiet. The promise of independence collapsed into repression; open expression into quiet transmission. Across Ukraine, loyalties once held in public now passed in silence from parent to child – language kept alive behind closed doors, history remembered without explanation. Viktor did not resist. But he preserved.

The next rupture would not be military. It would be deliberate, systemic, and enacted through hunger. And this time, it would reach into every village.

CHAPTER 6
The Holodomor in Kharkiv and Poltava, 1932–1933

Figure 25: *Black Square* by Kazimir Malevich (1915). Created by Kyiv-born artist Kazimir Malevich, Black Square marked a radical break with representational art – and with the old order. Malevich called it "the zero of form": a void of continuity, certainty, and meaning. For Ukrainians, that void was not abstract. It was lived – etched into bodies, memory, and silence. In this chapter, where evidence grows sparse and memory grows heavy, Black Square stands as a symbol: not of what can be seen, but of what has been lost.

History often divides itself cleanly in hindsight. But for those who lived through it, catastrophe announced itself through subtle shifts: an empty shelf, a neighbour's arrest, a meal skipped then not replaced. The famine that followed was not sudden. It arrived through requisition orders, silent officials, and the careful recalibration of fear.

For Ukrainians, this was not the first betrayal. Promises had been made before – at Pereiaslav, at Poltava, under *korenizatsiya* – and broken. What made the famine different was its intimacy. It reached into homes, into fields, into the body itself.

This chapter does not present the Holodomor as a statistical event or a national trauma in abstraction. It anchors the famine in one place – Sakhnovshchyna – and follows its consequences through the limited and often evasive traces left behind. However, what happened in Sakhnovshchyna was not exceptional; it happened across Ukraine.

For Viktor and Evdokiya Skliar, the famine's cruelty lay not only in hunger but in the moral corrosion it demanded. Grain became currency. Ledgers became weapons. Silence became protection. Whether they resisted, complied, or simply endured is unknown.[41] What can be said is this: they survived. And in Stalin's Ukraine, survival was never neutral.

---

[41] Viktor's precise role in the grain apparatus is not documented beyond basic employment records. The moral ambiguities described here reflect the documented structure of grain administration across Soviet Ukraine, not his personal actions, which remain unrecorded.

State Terror in Sakhnovshchyna

Between 1932 and 1933, Ukraine experienced one of the most devastating man-made famines in history – the Holodomor[42], deliberately engineered by Soviet policies under Joseph Stalin. Poltava and Kharkiv, historically some of Ukraine's richest agricultural heartlands, became paradoxically some of the regions most ravaged by starvation.

Stalin's aggressive collectivisation campaign (1928–32) imposed impossible grain quotas, stripping villages like Sakhnovshchyna (now in Kharkiv province) of their harvests.[43] Once a modest trading town, Sakhnovshchyna was forcibly restructured into a node within the procurement system: no longer feeding communities, but fulfilling quotas.

By June 1932, internal party correspondence acknowledged the food crisis.[44] A confidential memorandum from the Kharkiv

---

[42] The scholarly consensus recognises the Holodomor as a genocide. While debate persisted in earlier decades – particularly over whether the famine was ethnically targeted or primarily economic – contemporary research confirms that the famine was engineered through coercive grain requisitions, internal border closures, and the suppression of aid. Its impact disproportionately and deliberately targeted Ukrainians. Though a small minority of historians continue to argue over terminology, these are now semantic or politically motivated distinctions. This book unequivocally adopts the position that the Holodomor constituted genocide – experienced as such by its victims, and documented as such by its perpetrators.

[43] Formerly of Poltava province; transferred to Kharkiv province 9 February 1932.

[44] Kharkiv Regional Party Committee. "*Memorandum to the Central Committee of the Communist Party of Ukraine on the Extremely Tense Food Situation in Certain Districts of the Region*", No. 69, June 1932. PPA IIP at the Central Committee of the

Regional Party Committee to the Central Committee recorded verified cases of starvation across dozens of districts – thirteen of them in Sakhnovshchyna alone. Officials warned that famine was undermining field labour, posing a "*direct threat of disruption*" to the agricultural season.

The response was not relief, but repression. On 7 November 1932, the Kharkiv Regional Committee issued a top-secret directive demanding a "*decisive breakthrough in grain procurement*".[45] Sakhnovshchyna and neighbouring Balakliia were singled out as delinquent. Non-compliance was framed as sabotage orchestrated by "*organised kulak elements*"[46] and aided by "*village communists who had become de facto agents of sabotage*". Emergency measures followed:

The directive authorised commissions to enter the districts and impose emergency measures:

- Identify and prosecute village communists accused of aiding grain procurement sabotage; expel them from the party and try them as class traitors.

Communist Party of Ukraine, F. 1, Op. 1, Spr. 2073, Arch. 44–48. Published in *Голод 1932–1933 років на Україні: очима істориків, мовою документів*, ed. R. Ya. Pyrih (Kyiv: Politvydav Ukrainy, 1990), 190–193.

[45] Bureau of the Kharkiv Regional Committee of the Communist Party of Ukraine. Minutes on Measures to Eliminate the Disruption of Grain Procurement in Sakhnovshchyna and Balakliya Districts, November 7, 1932. State Archives of Kharkiv Region. See *Appendix B: Soviet Directive on Grain Procurement – Kharkiv Region, 1932* for a full transcription and translation.

[46] *Kulak elements* refers to peasants labelled as "wealthy" or resistant to collectivisation, often targeted for repression.

- Seize goods and halt credit to kolkhozes and farmers who failed to meet grain quotas; redistribute supplies to compliant districts.
- Conduct at least ten rapid court trials within five days through travelling *oblast courts*[47]; publish verdicts as public deterrents.

The policy was escalated further on 14 November, when the same committee ordered a halt to all industrial goods to underperforming districts.[48] Sakhnovshchyna appeared on a watchlist: warned that if targets were not met, it too would be cut off. The directive authorised not only the suspension of supplies but the confiscation of goods already delivered – a shift from punishing individuals to economically strangling entire communities.

Though the directive did not explicitly invoke *chorna doshka*[49] – the so-called "black boards" – it mirrored their logic. These lists were a mechanism of collective punishment: entire villages or collectives

---

[47] Oblast Court (*обласуд*) refers to the regional-level court in the Soviet judicial hierarchy. Such courts had authority over criminal, administrative, and civil matters, and could be deployed on a mobile basis to enforce state policy – particularly during the grain requisitions and political purges of the early 1930s.

[48] Bureau of the Kharkiv Regional Committee of the Communist Party of Ukraine. "*Resolution on the Termination of the Delivery of Goods to the Village and the Procedure for Further Supply of Industrial Goods to Districts and Villages That Fulfil the Grain Procurement Plan*", No. 104, 14 November 1932. PPA IIP at the Central Committee of the Communist Party of Ukraine, F. 2, Op. 1, Spr. 11, Arch. 87–88. Published in *Голод 1932–1933 років на Україні: очима істориків, мовою документів*, ed. R. Ya. Pyrih (Kyiv: Politvydav Ukrainy, 1990), 248–250.

[49] The *black-board* was a Soviet punitive measure used to isolate and punish entire villages for failure to meet grain quotas. Communities placed on the list were denied food, supplies, and trade access, effectively leading to mass starvation.

deemed non-compliant were publicly named, sealed off, deprived of supplies, and subjected to intensified repression. The November 1932 directive authorised nearly identical measures. Commissions could seize goods, prosecute "*individual farmers who wilfully defaulted*", and purge kolkhozes of "*hostile and alien elements*" – especially those of kulak origin. In practice, the lists functioned as *black boards* in all but name.

Travelling sessions of the Oblast Court soon arrived, led by Comrades Belyaev and Haylit. Their mandate: prosecute quickly, sentence visibly, and suppress resistance. A confidential memorandum to the Central Committee later that December paints a grim picture of the district under pressure.[50] Written by K.V. Sukhomlyn, Deputy Chairman of the Ukrainian SSR's Council of People's Commissars, it described Sakhnovshchyna as paralysed by hunger, sabotage charges, and state violence. Party purges, mass searches, and staged prosecutions unfolded against a backdrop of decaying collective farms and strategic grain seizures.

In collective farms such as "March 8" and "Spark of Communism", communists themselves were accused of hiding grain, leaking information, and orchestrating "diabolical" sabotage: livestock poisoned, bread left to spoil, and grain scattered or lost. Threshing machines broke down or underperformed, sometimes due to

---

[50] K.V. Sukhomlyn, Deputy Chairman of the Council of People's Commissars of the Ukrainian SSR. "*Memorandum to the Central Committee of the Communist Party of Ukraine on the State of Grain Procurement in the Kharkiv Region*", No. 130, 29 December 1932. PPA IIP at the Central Committee of the Communist Party of Ukraine, F. 1, Op. 1, Spr. 2040, Arch. 95–102. Published *in Голод 1932–1933 років на Україні: очима істориків, мовою документів*, ed. R. Ya. Pyrih (Kyiv: Politvydav Ukrainy, 1990), 301–306.

deliberate wrecking. Grain lay in fields while famine deepened. The crisis, Sukhomlyn concluded, was not just logistical — it revealed "a breakdown in both policy and morality", sustained by scapegoating and fear.

Such directives were not exceptional. Hundreds like them were issued across Soviet Ukraine in late 1932, revealing the famine's deliberate coordination and its role in political subjugation. In Sakhnovshchyna, the impact was devastating. Goods were seized, courts arrived, and silence followed.

Figure 26: Postcard issued in 1948 by the Ukrainian Youth Association in Germany, marking the 15th anniversary of the Holodomor. Stalin devours grain atop a pile of corpses. The caption reads: "*8,000,000 victims of hunger in Ukraine*". Wsewolod Skliar preserved similar images in exile.

Although direct archival material is limited, Sakhnovshchyna is believed to have been among the hardest hit. Of the 130,000 death records from 1932 – 33 preserved in Kharkiv oblast, few cite "*hunger*" as the cause – a deliberate omission. Most confirmed deaths occurred among children and the elderly. In one 1933 record, a kolkhoz worker from the *Zirka Collective* collapsed at a bread-distribution point in Kharkiv; the official cause of death was recorded only as "*unknown*".[51]

Survivors' voices, preserved in oral accounts, reveal Sakhnovshchyna's stark toll.

Eyewitness Testimonies from Sakhnovshchyna

A deeply affecting testimony comes from Lidiya Kostiantynivna Zavorotnia (née Proskurnia), born in 1925 and a lifelong resident of Sakhnovshchyna.[52] She recalled how her family, once thirteen strong, lost almost everything during collectivisation – their horse, cow, carriage – and later, many of their lives. Her father brought home small amounts of milk from his job as a farm watchman, but hunger claimed her parents, her sister, and her sister's family. She described in haunting detail how bodies went unburied, some

[51] During the Holodomor, Soviet authorities prohibited doctors from citing "hunger" or "starvation" as causes of death, instructing them to use euphemisms such as "exhaustion", "digestive disorder", or "unknown". This concealment was systematic. In Kharkiv oblast alone – where Sakhnovshchyna is located – the *National Book of Memory of the Victims of the Holodomor* records over 130,000 deaths during the famine years. Very few list "hunger," reflecting official efforts to obscure the scale and nature of the catastrophe.
Sources: Holodomor Museum, *The History of the Holodomor*, accessed March 2025; *National Book of Memory of the Victims of the Holodomor of 1932–1933 in Ukraine: Kharkiv Oblast* (Kyiv: Ukrainian Institute of National Memory, 2008); Ukrinform, "Holodomor: What Memorials Tell Us," accessed March 2025.

[52] *"Some were thrown into the well, some into the cellar".* Testimony of Lidiia Kostiantynivna Zavorotnia (née Proskurnia, b. 1925). *Holodomor Era Oral Testimony Archive*. Accessed March 2025.

thrown into wells and cellars by brigade leaders, and how entire communities vanished. Only three households remained in her hamlet by the end of the famine.

Her account contains some of the most difficult memories of the Holodomor: arbitrary death, social disintegration, and the murder and partial cannibalism of a child. The woman responsible, she said, was later released and remained in the village. Lidiya's voice does not seek dramatisation – only to record the stark horror of what she saw. Her words are a searing reminder that the Holodomor's violence reached deeply into daily life in villages like Sakhnovshchyna.

Another survivor, Anastasiya Vasylivna Sydash, born in 1924 near Sakhnovshchyna, recalled how Soviet requisitions stripped families of food, leading to immense suffering.[53] She vividly described the moment in 1933, after the new grain harvest, when her father returned from the collective farm with sacks of grain, ground them into flour at a local windmill, and her mother baked fresh bread. Anastasiya remembered the fragrant bread placed on a cabbage leaf, and how her father gathered his five children around the table to mark the moment. "*My children*", he said, "*you will forget how beans smelled, how baked beets smelled, but you should never forget the smell of today's bread*". In that moment, her father passed on more than gratitude. He passed on a message: that survival had meaning, but it came with memory – and memory had to be guarded.

---

[53] Testimony of Anastasiya Vasylivna Sydash (b. 1924), recorded as part of the Holodomor Mass Burial Site Registry. *Holodomor Memorial Map Archive*. Accessed March 2025.

She also recalled the emotional devastation of losing their family cow, Bilashka, and how fear dominated village life. Adults spoke in whispers, sending children out of the room during serious conversations, particularly about collectivisation or those deported to Solovki – a notorious prison camp that became a symbol of repression and disappearance. Anastasiya later expressed frustration at Holodomor denial, identifying Soviet policies – dekulakisation (the forced removal and dispossession of wealthier peasants) and collectivisation – as the primary causes of the famine.

Viktor and Evdokiya Skliar: Enduring Famine

There is no surviving record of how the Holodomor affected the Skliars in detail. But geography and employment speak plainly. Viktor was working as a bookkeeper in the grain milling sector in Sakhnovshchyna at the height of Stalin's famine. He would have seen the consequences, if not been drawn into the machinery itself. Whether he altered records, witnessed arrests, or faced threats remains unknown. But the pressure to cooperate – or at least remain silent – would have been immense.

His wife, Evdokiya Petrova Mosiienko, left even fewer traces. Like many rural women, her history was undocumented, but her role was critical. Famine resistance took place in kitchens. Rationing scarce food, watering soup, bartering cloth for flour, shielding her young son – these were likely her daily negotiations. Soviet policies targeted the village, but women managed the home, making ethical choices in private that were tactical as well as maternal. Their quiet ingenuity was often the difference between endurance and collapse.

That endurance, in turn, was cultural as well as physical. In kitchens stripped of icons and songs, women like Evdokiya held onto fragments: a private feast day, a candle lit unseen, lullabies whispered from older worlds. In places like Oleksandrivka – Evdokiya's home-town – and Sakhnovshchyna, women were the keepers of memory – not as nostalgia, but as necessity. They remembered which proverb belonged to which crisis, which ancestor had carried which psalm, and how to shape dough into meaning. If her wedding had indeed been marked by the *korovai*, it is not impossible she passed its symbolism to her son, even if she never baked it again. These gestures were how history, and identity, endured.

Viktor, for his part, may have endured a different contradiction, carried by many Ukrainians: working inside the very system that enforced hunger, yet carrying, later in life, a quiet but unwavering loyalty to the idea of Ukraine. Perhaps he found a way to serve without betrayal. Perhaps he justified what he witnessed. Perhaps the contradiction was simply endured.

Neither left a written account. But silence itself tells a story: memory was passed not in full sentences but in gesture, euphemism, and avoidance. Trauma was carried not just in what was said, but in what was deliberately left unsaid. For Viktor, the famine left lasting marks. He became cautious, sceptical, slow to speak. He distrusted authority, avoided overt politics, and remained quietly watchful – traits common among Holodomor survivors, many of whom developed a deep suspicion of state promises and an instinct to move quietly when danger returned.

For decades, Soviet authorities denied the famine had ever happened. Journalists were barred, records altered, open discussion criminalised. Memory went underground – guarded in fragments, kept in private. Only in the late 20th century did serious efforts to recover the truth begin, often led by diaspora communities and post-independence Ukraine. In such conditions, memory did not simply preserve grief – it preserved truth.

The legacy of the Holodomor was not just historical. It shaped how Ukrainians lived, the caution they passed down, and the silences they maintained. Its impact did not end with the famine. It echoed through every decision that followed.

* * *

The Holodomor ended, but nothing returned.

Across Ukraine, the silence it imposed remained. The churches were empty. The language had changed. Families no longer asked questions. Hunger had passed, but the lesson held: nothing was safe from the state – not food, not truth, not memory.

Viktor Skliar left no account of what he saw. He had worked in the grain system while his country starved. Whether he followed orders, stayed quiet, or found ways to help is unknown. But he survived. And survival came at a cost.

The Holodomor did not teach fear. That had been taught before – by betrayal, invasion, and collapse. What it taught was submission. It made fear a condition of life.

Viktor lived through it. But not unchanged. His silence deepened. His caution hardened. Whatever belief remained, it no longer sought expression.

The famine was over. But it had done its work.

What came next would not ask what Viktor believed – but what he was willing to endure.

CHAPTER 7

War and Silence: Viktor Skliar in Occupied Ukraine, 1934–1945

О горе тим, що вроджені в темниці!
Що глянули на світ в тюремнеє вікно.
Тюрма – се коло злої чарівниці,
Ніколи не розіб'ється воно.

O grief to those born in the darkness of prison!
Who first saw the world through a cell window.
A prison is the circle of a wicked sorceress –
It shall never be broken.

– Lesia Ukrainka[54], from *A Moment of Despair*, 1896

---

[54] Lesia Ukrainka (1871–1913), born Larysa Kosach, was a Ukrainian poet, playwright, and cultural icon. Writing in the face of chronic illness and political repression, she forged a literary voice of intense moral clarity. Her work, often rooted in classical and folkloric motifs, transformed personal suffering into spiritual defiance. A central figure in Ukrainian modernism, she remains a symbol of resilience and uncompromising inner strength across generations.

After finishing the last two chapters, I needed a break.

I had spent weeks tracing Viktor's early adulthood – famine, forced labour, the collapse of everything he had been trained to believe in. I thought the second half of his life might offer something different. Some recovery. A redemptive turn. I was wrong. What came next was harder still: war, loss, exile, and a long descent into silence. There is no rescue arc here. Only the slow erosion of a man shaped by systems that gave nothing back.

Still, it isn't simple. Viktor collaborates. He disappears from one child's life. He rewrites his past to survive. These are not comfortable facts. But neither do they fall cleanly into guilt or innocence. Like many Ukrainians caught between Stalin and Hitler, his choices were made in a world where morality had been pushed to the margins – where doing what was needed often meant doing what could not be explained later. And beneath those choices ran something deeper still: a fear shaped not only by famine, but by history. A fear inherited from past betrayals, reinforced by every new regime. His story doesn't ask for sympathy. But it does ask not to be judged too quickly.

* * *

By 1934, Viktor Skliar had already lived through three collapses. The Orthodox world of his childhood had been dismantled; the *Ukrainian People's Republic* he fought for had been defeated; and then came the Holodomor. The Soviet state that replaced imperial Russia brought famine, dispossession, and silence. What remained was routine – rituals sustained not by faith, but by fear.

The years that followed offered no reprieve. Stalin's repressions deepened. The war that many feared – and few could name – drew closer. In villages like Sakhnovshchyna, memory remained private and survival provisional. Viktor continued to work, now more watchful than ever. His identity – once shaped by liturgy and national cause – became quieter, harder to define. His convictions are harder to trace. His fears, clearer.

This chapter follows Viktor through the next decade: from the tightening grip of the Stalinist state, through Nazi occupation, forced labour, and the loss of his family. These are not stages of a linear story, but fragments of a fractured one. The lines between agency and coercion blur. Institutions that once anchored life – church, family, homeland – fall away. In their place, Viktor moved through bureaucracies, border zones, and the grey spaces of survival.

Here, the narrative reopens in 1934 – not at a turning point, but in a deepening silence. War has not yet arrived. But the decisions it will demand are already taking shape.

Stalinist Repression and War's Approach, 1934–1941

After the Holodomor, life in Soviet Ukraine did not return to normal – it became quieter, darker, and more closely watched. The famine had shattered communities. What followed was a different kind of violence: the silence of enforced conformity. Between 1934 and 1939, the Soviet state tightened its grip through surveillance, arrests, and ideological purges.

The *Great Terror* (1936–1938) was not a wave but a storm: fast-moving, disorienting, indiscriminate. Under Stalin's orders, the

NKVD drew up arrest quotas by region – fixed numbers of *enemies* to be found and eliminated. In Ukraine, suspected nationalists, clergy, *kulaks*[55], and former members of the intelligentsia were especially targeted. A denunciation from a neighbour, a past association, or the wrong surname could be fatal. Torture was routine. Confessions were extracted, trials were brief or non-existent, and sentences – often execution – were carried out swiftly.

In the Ukrainian SSR[56], tens of thousands were arrested or disappeared into the gulag. At Bykivnia, outside Kyiv, forests were filled with the bodies of the shot. Whole professions were gutted: teachers, archivists, priests, librarians, agronomists. The very memory of Ukraine's cultural autonomy faced complete erasure. Ukrainian-language schools were shuttered or Russified, any remaining churches repurposed as storehouses or clubs. Even silence could be dangerous. As the Russian poet, Osip Mandelstam, wrote, "*Only in Russia is poetry respected – it gets people killed*".

Repression was not only vertical – arrests from above – but lateral: carried out through forced displacement, mass surveillance, and the deliberate fragmentation of suspect populations. In early 1935, families from western Ukrainian districts such as Polonskyi, Shepetivskyi, and Pluzhnianskyi were forcibly deported under NKVD orders. Labelled as *kulaks*, Petliurites, or "bandit elements", they were loaded into trains bound for the east. On 26 and 28 February, and again on 1 and 2 March, *deportation echelons* –

---

[55] Kulak; a peasant classified by Soviet authorities as relatively wealthy or resistant to collectivisation.

[56] The Ukrainian SSR (Ukrainian Soviet Socialist Republic) was the official name of Soviet-controlled Ukraine from 1922 to 1991.

specially designated train convoys used by the NKVD for forced resettlement – were unloaded at Sakhnovshchyna and Kyshevka stations in Kharkiv oblast, where NKVD and border officials met the arrivals and processed them for resettlement.[57] The deportees included ethnic Ukrainians, Poles, Jews, and Germans – entire households deemed politically unreliable or resistant to collectivisation. Sakhnovshchyna, far from peripheral, continued to be a node in the machinery of Soviet control: a site of sorting, processing, and quiet erasure.

In this atmosphere, Viktor Skliar – now in his mid-thirties – continued to work as a bookkeeper in the grain industry, a role that offered little visibility. No direct records survive from these years, but his continued employment suggests he avoided attention. Like many, he may have survived by keeping his head down, saying little, and following the line. His father, Ivan Skliar – a psalmist– would have been living under even greater suspicion.

In August 1939, Nazi Germany and the Soviet Union signed the *Molotov–Ribbentrop Pact*[58], agreeing in secret protocols to divide Eastern Europe into spheres of influence. Weeks later, they invaded Poland, carving up its territory between them. For Ukrainians

---

[57] V.H. Baidych, "*Депортація (переселення) селян з території Вінницької області в березні 1935-го – червні 1936 року (на прикладі Полонського, Шепетівського та Плужнянського районів)*" [*Deportation (Resettlement) of Peasants from the Territory of Vinnytsia Oblast in March 1935 – June 1936 (Using the Example of Polonskyi, Shepetivskyi, and Pluzhnianskyi Districts)*], *Podilska Starovyna* 1, no. 7 (2021): 66.

[58] The *Molotov-Ribbentrop Pact* was a non-aggression treaty between Nazi Germany and the Soviet Union, signed on 23 August 1939. Its secret protocols divided Eastern Europe into zones of influence. Western Ukraine, then part of Poland, was annexed by the USSR under this agreement.

under Soviet rule, borders held, but repression deepened: nationalist leaders were arrested, churches closed, and land seized.[59] In 1940, Soviet expansion into the Baltics and Bessarabia only intensified the climate of fear. The trauma of famine, layered with renewed surveillance, bred quiet forms of dissent – not open protest, but silence, guarded speech, and withdrawal. In places like Poltava, the mood was not open panic, but a quieter, deeper fear. The memory of famine persisted. People knew what Moscow's promises meant. They spoke less, trusted less, and waited – not for hope, but for whatever would come next.

Figure 27: Viktor Skliar's Soviet military ID, issued 11 November 1940, recording his registration for army service in Kharkiv as a private in the accounting corps. While the document confirms his processing, family

[59] The term "liberation" was commonly used in Soviet propaganda to justify territorial annexations. In reality, these actions involved military occupation, political repression, and the imposition of Soviet rule over populations with distinct national identities.

testimony suggests he did not proceed into active service. The later Displaced Persons tag hints at the exile to come.

In November 1940, Viktor received an official mobilisation summons, ordering him to report in Kharkiv for military duty. The slip assigned him to the army's accounting corps – a clerical role consistent with his civilian work. He reported, was processed, and issued a military ID booklet confirming his registration. But whether he ever served beyond that point is unclear. His son, Wsewolod, later recalled that Viktor did not "accept" the call-up, suggesting he avoided further orders, quietly slipping out of the system. In Poltava, such evasions were common, if dangerous. For men like Viktor, it may have felt less like open defiance and more like a final refusal to place their lives fully in Soviet hands. The paperwork remained. But whatever belief he still carried, it no longer sought uniform or command.

Sometimes I try to imagine what Viktor felt when that slip arrived. In 1919, he had been conscripted after fighting for Ukraine's independence – an uneasy compromise, perhaps, but made in the chaos of civil war. By 1940, the choice would have felt starker. This was the state that had starved his village, erased his language, and turned grain into a weapon. I cannot know his exact calculation. But I suspect the summons was not just an order, but a reminder – for him, and for millions of Ukrainians called up that year – that there was no safe place outside the system that had already betrayed them.

Nazi Occupation of Kharkiv and Poltava, 1941–1943

On 22 June 1941, Nazi Germany launched *Operation Barbarossa*, a full-scale invasion of the Soviet Union that turned Eastern Europe into one of the bloodiest theatres of the Second World War. German forces advanced rapidly, overwhelming Soviet defences and seizing large swaths of Ukrainian territory.

As the Germans advanced through the summer of 1941, Viktor would have watched with the same cautious dread felt across Poltava. The Soviet state that had starved his village, erased his language, and conscripted him twice now demanded loyalty once more, even as its forces faltered. There was no euphoria at the prospect of German arrival – only apprehension at what came next. In those months, the fear was both of the front itself and of the reckoning it would bring. For those who had endured the Holodomor and survived Stalin's purges, survival had taught them one thing: whatever followed, it would not be kind.

By late September, Poltava had fallen, followed by Kharkiv on 24 October.[60] These cities – strategically vital and symbolically charged – fell under brutal occupation. In Poltava, mass executions, arbitrary arrests, and the targeting of Ukrainian nationalists, Jews, and Soviet officials became routine. Thousands were murdered at

[60] *The First Battle of Kharkiv* (October 1941) marked the city's initial capture by Nazi Germany during *Operation Barbarossa*. The occupation was swift and brutal, with widespread executions, repression, and destruction targeting civilians, Jewish populations, and Soviet personnel.

nearby sites such as Matviyivka[61], but the most systematic and devastating violence was reserved for Ukraine's Jewish population.

The Holocaust and Ukrainian Memory

The war brought suffering to all Ukrainians – but for Ukraine's Jews, it brought annihilation. Between 1941 and 1944, Ukraine became one of the major killing grounds of the Holocaust. Over a million Jews were murdered on Ukrainian soil – many in mass shootings carried out by German *Einsatzgruppen*, often with the assistance of local collaborators. In Poltava, Kharkiv, and surrounding districts, entire communities were wiped out. Victims were marched to forest clearings, ravines, or open pits and executed – often within sight, and sometimes knowledge, of their neighbours.

In Sakhnovshchyna, most of the Jewish population had fled by the time the Germans arrived in early November 1941. Those who remained – at least two families – were murdered that month in the town's central park. On 16 November 1941, German troops and local auxiliaries executed more than fifteen civilians, including non-Jews, in a separate action nearby. Later, partisans were also shot or hanged in public. Witnesses recalled neighbours warning one another in advance, and children seeing their fathers taken away.

---

[61] Matviyivka, near Poltava, was one of several mass execution sites used by Nazi forces in Ukraine, where political prisoners, Jews, and civilians were murdered during the occupation.

The site of the shootings was later marked by a memorial, but many of the victims remained unnamed.[62]

The relationship between Ukrainians and Jews during the war defies simplification. Some Ukrainians risked their lives to shelter Jews. Others participated in or facilitated persecution, motivated by ideology, fear, antisemitism, or the brutal arithmetic of survival. In the early stages of occupation, nationalist organisations and local militias were involved in pogroms and in staffing German-controlled auxiliary police forces. These actions remain the subject of serious historical debate and carry an enduring moral weight.

Ukrainians, too, suffered mass violence, forced labour, and deportation. Many were sent to camps; millions were displaced. But the genocide of Ukraine's Jews was unique in scope, intent, and irreversibility. It was not a by-product of war, but a policy of extermination. While both communities were victims of the Nazi regime, their experiences were not the same. Recognising that difference is essential to any honest reckoning with the period.

This book, focused on Ukrainian family memory, follows the Skliars through exile, famine, and repression. But it cannot tell their story without acknowledging the erasure of others alongside them. The roads Viktor and Wsewolod travelled once passed Jewish

---

[62] Testimony and archival research confirm that on 16 November 1941, German soldiers and local auxiliaries executed over fifteen civilians in Sakhnovshchyna. Two Jewish families had been shot earlier that month in the town park. Further executions of partisans followed in 1942. These events have been documented by Yahad – In Unum, an international research organisation investigating Holocaust mass graves and eyewitness testimony in Eastern Europe. See: *Yahad – In Unum. Sakhnovshchyna, Kharkiv Region, Archival Case File. Yahad – In Unum Village Dossier Collection, Paris, 2021. Accessed March 2025.*

homes, schools, and synagogues that are no longer there. That absence is not only a historical fact – it is a presence that shadows every village lane and family archive. In recording one survival, we must also remember what could not survive. As the occupation deepened, Viktor's own survival became entangled in the moral grey zones that defined life under Nazi rule.

The Grey Zone of Survival, 1941–1943

For Viktor, the German occupation brought no clear choice. The Soviets had brutalised Ukraine, but the Germans arrived not as liberators, but as a new power demanding labour, obedience, and silence. By the autumn of 1941, survival shaped every calculation. The state that had starved his village, erased his language, and twice conscripted him was gone – but its memory remained vivid. Like many Ukrainians, Viktor entered the German system not out of allegiance, but out of fear: of Soviet return, of hunger, of what would happen if he stood outside any system at all. Taking work under the Germans was not a decision of principle. It was the continuation of what the Soviet years had taught him: keep your head down, accept what work was offered, and endure.[63]

Viktor's work at the Fruit and Vegetable Distribution Centre in Sakhnovshchyna began in mid-1941, while the region was still under Soviet control. His later Nazi-issued permit, stamped

---

[63] Postwar Soviet tribunals made little distinction between voluntary and coerced wartime labour, resulting in thousands of convictions for "collaboration" regardless of circumstance. Yet scholars have shown that local employment under occupation was rarely ideological. In most cases, Ukrainians accepted administrative or logistical roles to avoid deportation, starvation, or reprisals.

September 1943, recorded his employment as starting on 3 June 1941 – a date that made bureaucratic sense to the occupiers, even if the Germans had not yet arrived. Perhaps he had been assigned the role by Soviet authorities, and the Germans simply imposed their system over it. Or perhaps the date was later inserted for administrative neatness.[64] The paperwork did not care.

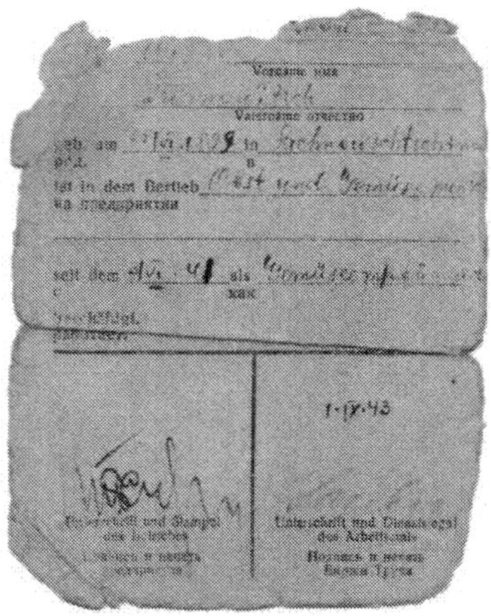

Figure 28: Viktor's forced labour ID, stamped September 1, 1943, for a Nazi-run Fruit and Vegetable Centre. This fragile paper bound him to survival in a regime that saw him as disposable.

[64] This document, issued in Nazi-occupied Ukraine, records Viktor's employment at the Fruit and Vegetable Distribution Centre from 3 June 1941. The area was still under Soviet control until early autumn, raising questions about the recorded start date. It is possible the date was retroactively formalised after the Germans took over administration, or reflects an earlier Soviet-assigned role absorbed by the new authorities. While the document does not explicitly state that Viktor's employment was forced, the coercive structures of Nazi labour policy – particularly for Ukrainians classified as *Ostarbeiter* or local auxiliary workers – left little room for refusal.

By 1943, his position had become part of the *Zwangsarbeit* (forced labour) system, supporting the Nazi war economy with little room for refusal or resistance. His duties – receiving vegetables for German administrators – were now embedded in a regime that saw Ukrainians as disposable. The faded stamp on his permit captured the cold logic of occupation: what mattered was that he worked. For whom, and when, was secondary.

Viktor's coerced labour sustained a Nazi system, but for him it was survival, not complicity. His deep anti-Soviet sentiment – hinted at in Wsewolod's later accounts and confirmed by his eventual flight – suggests he saw the Germans as the lesser threat. In choosing between two occupying tyrannies, he followed a tragic pattern familiar to millions of Ukrainians in World War II: navigating an impossible moral labyrinth where collaboration and survival became almost indistinguishable.

Perhaps he questioned the cost. His silence offers no answer.

Across eastern and central Ukraine, where Soviet rule had shaped life for over two decades, few resisted openly. Some collaborated – out of ideology, necessity, or the fragile hope of autonomy. Others joined underground cells, or withdrew into silence. Beneath that quiet, defiance endured. For many, the memory of Russification, collectivisation, and famine shaped every decision. What looked like passivity was often a learned calculus of survival, forged from past betrayals.

Through 1941 and 1942, Viktor remained in Sakhnovshchyna, navigating worsening conditions as German control solidified in Poltava and Kharkiv. Some initially viewed the Nazis with ambivalence, recalling the trauma of the Holodomor. But disillusionment soon followed. Food requisitions, Jewish killings, and forced labour intensified. Civilians faced curfews, surveillance, and mandatory work assignments. Partisan sabotage brought brutal reprisals. Even churches, once safe spaces, became targets. In this shifting landscape, survival demanded caution, adaptability, and a sharp awareness of power.

Figure 29: Evdokiya Petrova Skliar's Soviet passport, issued 10 June 1941. It records her birth in Oleksandrivka, Poltava region, and her social status as a peasant. A 1942 stamp under occupation suggests continued mobility during wartime upheaval.

Meanwhile, Evdokiya – Viktor's wife – was issued a Soviet passport in June 1941, an unusual document for a rural woman. It recorded her as Ukrainian by nationality and *peasant*[65] by social status. Later stamps show that she travelled under occupation, moving between

---

[65] While internal passports became mandatory for urban residents in the 1930s, rural women often lacked such documents unless they had employment or travel needs outside their village.

Poltava, Kharkiv, and Dnipro. Why she moved is unclear: perhaps to evacuate relatives, collect supplies, or navigate some other survival need.

That her name appears at all is striking. Most rural women left few formal traces beyond marriage or death records. Yet through 1942, Evdokiya's Soviet passport remained in active use – overlaid with German stamps and registrations as the occupation authorities absorbed Soviet bureaucratic structures rather than dismantling them entirely. She moved through checkpoints, carried papers, and navigated systems of surveillance that blurred old and new regimes. Whatever the reason for her journeys, they carried risk – but she moved under her own name, and under watch.

In May 1942, Soviet forces briefly retook Sakhnovshchyna.[66] German recapture brought swift revenge. Houses were burned, civilians executed – including, according to one witness, a girl torn apart by birch trees.[67] By early 1943, as the tide turned at Stalingrad, the Red Army retook Kharkiv, only to lose it again weeks later in the Third Battle of Kharkiv.[68] The city was left in ruins. Poltava, still under German control, endured relentless bombings, scattering

---

[66] The *Second Battle of Kharkiv* (May 1942) was a Soviet offensive aimed at retaking the city. Although initially successful, it ended in a disastrous encirclement of Red Army forces. The German counteroffensive led to tens of thousands of Soviet casualties and paved the way for further Nazi advances into Eastern Ukraine. Survivor testimony reports mass executions and atrocities committed during the reprisal.

[67] Testimony of Mirrah Kogan, recorded in Odessa, 2003. Interview by Natalia Fomina. *Centropa Archive*. Accessed March 2025.

[68] The *Third Battle of Kharkiv* (March 1943) was a major counteroffensive by German forces following the Soviet capture of the city. The Germans briefly retook the city, causing extensive destruction and civilian casualties.

families and shattering homes like Viktor's. The shifting frontlines pushed survival beyond endurance. There was no refuge. Only movement, calculation, and the hope that the next assault might pass by.

Figure 30: Soviet airmen beside a Sukhoi SU-2 Bomber, winter 1941 – 42. Used in raids on Kharkiv, including the March 1943 bombardment that killed Evdokiya Skliar and her family in Poltava.

In March 1943, a Soviet air raid struck Viktor's home. Evdokiya, his second wife, her two sisters – one of them Wsewolod's godmother – and two young children were killed.[69] Viktor and Wsewolod survived only because they had been working in nearby fields. Vadim, Viktor's son from his first marriage, was away at boarding school in Opishnya.

[69] Their names are undocumented.

With Evdokiya's death, the last structure of care collapsed. She had held together ritual, routine, and relationship – all under a regime that denied their worth. Her death was not only a private tragedy. It marked the disappearance of a quiet, unrecognised resilience that had made survival possible.

The loss was total. But it was not yet the end. The fragile structures Viktor had clung to – faith, family, home – were gone. Silence, once protective, had become unbearable.

Figure 31: Evdokiya Mosiienko. The only known photograph of her, carried by Wsewolod into exile – a quiet testament to her endurance through famine and war.

I have tried to imagine that day. I cannot. I do not know what Viktor thought as he stood before the ruins, or what Wsewolod remembered, or whether guilt threaded through survival. Maybe he blamed the Soviets. Maybe himself. Why were the men in the fields, and not the women? Was it luck, habit, or the small decisions that decide everything?

All I know is that after that day, Wsewolod carried a single photograph of his mother across a continent, into exile. I think he needed that photograph – not just as memory, but as proof. Proof that she had existed, that he came from somewhere, that something had been loved and lost and still mattered. That photo now sits on my bookshelf: a testament to endurance. Nothing else remained.

Viktor stayed. For months, he remained in Sakhnovshchyna, under occupation, in a home emptied of meaning. The Red Army was approaching, but he did not yet move. To leave meant one kind of risk; to stay, another. What came next would be no choice at all. But in March 1943, the moment of decision had not yet come.

Flight and the Fracture of Home, Sep.–Nov. 1943

Viktor likely remained in Sakhnovshchyna until early September 1943. His German-issued identity card, stamped on the 1st, confirmed his role at the Fruit and Vegetable Distribution Centre. But by mid-September, the Red Army was closing in. Sakhnovshchyna fell back under Soviet control between 16 and 18 September, leaving little doubt about the fate of those who had worked under German occupation.

Sometime between 1 and 16 September, as the front closed in, Viktor made his decision. He fled.

Viktor's decision was not political. It was survival. The Red Army's return meant retribution, not liberation. He had endured famine, conscription, and the bombing that killed his wife – and he knew the state made no distinction between coerced labour and collaboration. The memory of the Holodomor, of persecution, of betrayal, remained vivid. Staying would mean arrest, execution, or exile to the gulag. Fleeing offered no safety, only another system of exploitation. But for Viktor, it was the only choice left in a world where every structure he had once trusted – church, family, nation – had collapsed.

His flight fitted the wider pattern. Across Ukraine, families like the Skliars joined a vast, desperate movement westward. By 1944, perhaps as many as 500,000 Ukrainians were pushing into Central Europe, carrying little more than forged papers or a cart of belongings.[70] It was not hope that drove them, but fear – of Soviet vengeance, German brutality, and what might come after. The journey was fraught with risk: advancing Soviet troops, German suspicion, random violence, and constant bombardment. Many never made it.

For Viktor and Wsewolod, it was a final rupture. This was the last time they would see any other family members – including Viktor's eldest son, Vadim.[71] From that point forward, they lived in different histories. One in exile, one in silence. Their home had become a borderless ruin.

This was more than a private tragedy. It was a collapse of historical belonging itself – part of a wider fate shared by Eastern Europeans displaced by overlapping regimes that left no room for ambiguity, no right to neutrality. Their choices were not about freedom. They

---

[70] Popowycz, Jennifer L. *World War II, Displacement, and the Making of the Postwar Ukrainian Diaspora, 1939–1951.* PhD diss., Louisiana State University, 2022, 1.

[71] Vadim was separately displaced to Germany during the war but was later forcibly repatriated to Soviet-controlled Ukraine. More details on Vadim's story and his fate under Soviet rule are covered in *Chapter 9.*

were about survival in a world where the categories imposed upon them – collaborator, refugee, loyalist – recognised no complexity.

In an autobiographical note written in 1949, Wsewolod recorded, simply: *"In 1943, we were forced to evacuate from our native land to foreign soil, and to live our lives as God willed. We travelled a great distance from our homeland, turning to our kin in Halychyna"*.[72] Their westward departure was arranged by Viktor's employer, who secured passage as part of a group headed towards Germany. They left by horse and cart, carrying little beyond a few papers and what they could load.

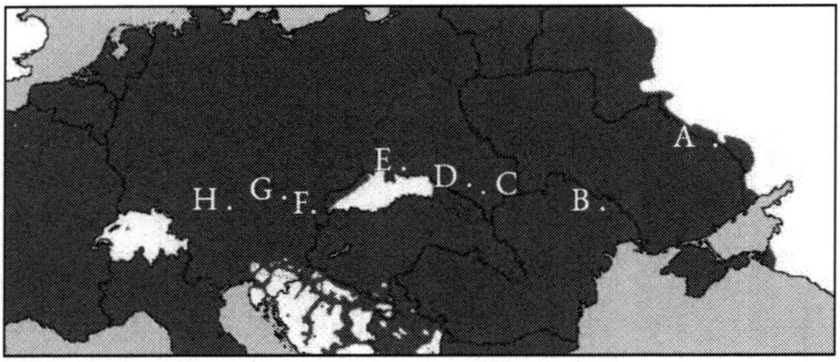

Figure 32: Viktor and Wsewolod's 1943–1945 flight from Ukraine to Bavaria. Each marker shows a step through war's chaos. Their journey reflects not just personal loss, but a nation's desperate search for survival. Labels correspond to entries in Table 1.

[72] This, and subsequent quotations are drawn from *Autobiographical Note,* c. 1949, reproduced in *Appendix A*.

	Date	Location	Wartime Authority	Present Country
A	Until around October 1943	Sakhnovshchyna	*Reichskommissariat Ukraine*– Nazi Germany	Ukraine
B	Around November 1943	Transnistria	Romanian-occupied territory	Moldova / Ukraine
C	By April 1944 to July 1944	Drohobych	*Distrikt Galizien*, General Government – Nazi Germany	Ukraine
D		Sambir	*Distrikt Galizien*, General Government – Nazi Germany	Ukraine
E	31 July 1944	Nowy Sącz	Poland, General Government – Nazi Germany	Poland
F	26 October 1944	Vienna	Nazi Germany	Austria
G	By 3 January 1945 until at least March 1945	Gmünd and Heidenreichstein	Nazi Germany	Austria
H	Around July 1945	Landshut	U.S. Zone of Occupation	Germany

Table 1: Key locations in Viktor Skliar's wartime journey. This table reconstructs Viktor's westward flight between 1943 and 1945 – tracing his movement through collapsing regimes, from Nazi-occupied Ukraine to the American Zone in Bavaria.

The journey was long and difficult. Travelling by cart and on foot, they moved through a landscape fractured by war, where roads were dangerous and bombings constant. Early in the journey, their pet dog, Bantyk, was run over by their own carriage – a small but enduring loss that Wsewolod remembered more clearly than the larger devastations that followed. Hunger and violence became routine. The dog was personal.

In Transnistria – the borderlands between Ukraine and Romania – they were robbed overnight, losing what little they had except the cart and horse. They continued westward, moving without security or destination, caught in the wider dislocation of a continent in collapse.

Through War's Borderlands, Nov. 1943–Oct. 1944

By April 1944, Viktor was documented in Drohobych, a historically Ukrainian town under Nazi occupation. Identity records suggest he also passed through Sambir, a known centre of nationalist activity, though the sequence is unclear. Their westward route, via Transnistria, had already taken them more than 1,200 kilometres (approximately 750 miles) – a journey made by cart and on foot, across frontlines and through fractured lands.

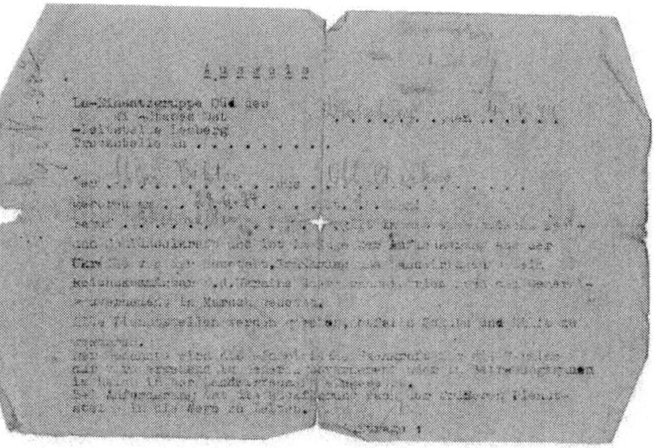

Figure 33: Viktor Skliar's identification document, issued by the German Occupational Administration in Drohobych, 4 April 1944. It lists him as a bookkeeper under Reich supervision – a fragile artefact of a life reduced to paperwork, stamps, and oversight.[73]

In Sambir, a centre of nationalist resistance, Viktor found himself once more navigating blurred lines between conviction, caution, and survival. The town was a hub for the *Ukrainian Insurgent Army* (*UPA*), which by 1944 fought both Nazi and Soviet forces using guerrilla tactics. Their struggle for Ukrainian independence carried both fierce idealism and enduring controversy – their name linked to both national liberation and interethnic violence,

[73] This document, issued by the German Occupational Administration in Drohobych, records Viktor Skliar as a relocated bookkeeper classified as a "domestic specialist for Ukraine". It notes that he had been transferred via Transnistria and was under the authority of the Reich Commissar for Ukraine. He was to be employed temporarily in the General Government or supporting zones of the Reich, with instructions to facilitate his return if required. The bureaucratic language reflects how forced labour was codified as skilled deployment and how mobility was tightly controlled by the Nazi state.

including the massacres of Polish civilians in regions like Volhynia and Eastern Galicia.[74] Nazi tolerance for nationalist units was already eroding. Reprisals, arrests, and crackdowns intensified as frontlines shifted.

There is no surviving record of Viktor's role in Sambir. It is plausible he offered support – practical, moral, or incidental – as many did in those volatile circumstances, including his son. But whether his actions were driven by conviction or the logic of proximity remains unknowable.

His past offers clues, but no certainties. Viktor had once fought for Ukrainian independence under Petliura. His nationalism was not an invention of occupation, but an inheritance, tempered by the hard experience of repression, famine, and state service. By the 1940s, any idealism that remained was cautious, quiet, shaped by a life that had demanded constant compromise. If he assisted the UPA, it was likely less a declaration, more a negotiation: a way to survive while holding onto fragments of belief. For Viktor, wartime Ukraine offered few clean choices. His life does not reveal indecision, but an enduring pattern – adapting, without surrendering entirely.

---

[74] The legacy of the Organisation of Ukrainian Nationalists (OUN) and the Ukrainian Insurgent Army (UPA) remains deeply contested. While these groups fought for Ukrainian independence and engaged in resistance against both Nazi and Soviet forces, their actions also included violence against civilians, particularly during the ethnic cleansings in Volhynia and Eastern Galicia. This book does not attempt to adjudicate that legacy, but acknowledges its complexity. In the context of this chapter, what matters is not a definitive judgment of the movement, but the fact that individuals like Viktor and Wsewolod were drawn into its orbit – sometimes by belief, sometimes by proximity, and often by the absence of any viable alternative.

By mid-1944, they reached Nowy Sącz in occupied Poland, where the *Ukrainian Relief Committee* helped refugees pass westward. On 31 July, Viktor received an evacuation permit for travel through Slovakia – a paper trail of retreat. The journey from Drohobych to Nowy Sącz, some 180 kilometres (110 miles), would have taken days, crossing still-hostile, still-occupied lands. A later fragment of the permit suggests it was checked or reissued during further transit.

Into Forced Labour, Oct. 1944–May 1945

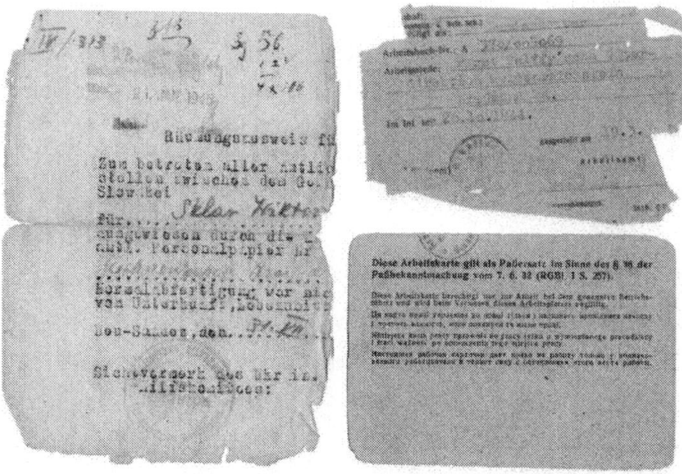

Figure 34: Viktor's transit and labour documents, from Nowy Sącz to Vienna, 1944–1945, stamped with Nazi oversight. These tattered papers were his lifeline, navigating a world of displacement.

Viktor's next steps took him through Strasshof, near Vienna – one of the largest transit camps in Nazi-occupied Austria. The journey from Nowy Sącz to Vienna spanned over 370 kilometres (230 miles), likely covered by foot, rail, and forced requisition. While no surviving records confirm precisely when Viktor arrived, his

German work permit suggests he passed through the camp in late October 1944.[75] Stamped with the Nazi eagle, its faded ink felt to me like the cold signature of a regime that turned people into numbers. The bureaucracy did not care where he had come from, only that he could be moved, processed, and put to work.

Strasshof an der Nordbahn functioned as a redistribution hub for Eastern European forced labourers – Ukrainians, Poles, and Soviets alike. Thousands passed through its gates, processed into agriculture, construction, arms production, or worse. Some never left at all, sent onward to labour camps or death. For Viktor, passage through Strasshof offered no safety, only continued transit – into another layer of bureaucracy, another system of exploitation.

By early January 1945, records place Viktor and Wsewolod in Gmünd, Lower Austria. A *Ukrainian Relief Committee* certificate and financial receipt confirm their presence there on 3 January 1945. Gmünd, like much of Lower Austria, was collapsing: German troops retreating, refugees flooding in, civil authority crumbling. Trade collapsed into barter. Law into bribery. For displaced persons like Viktor, there was no stability – only the grim economy of the margins.

---

[75] A surviving fragment of an undated document references "Strasshof", suggesting that Viktor passed through the transit camp near Vienna. While the exact date of his stay remains uncertain, the proposed timing aligns with his documented arrival in Austria on 26 October 1944. Strasshof served as a key transit hub for forced labourers being redistributed across the Reich, making it a probable waypoint before his placement in Gmünd and Heidenreichstein. The fragmentary nature of the document prevents precise confirmation, but its existence reinforces the likelihood that he was processed through Strasshof during this period.

On 21 January, their evacuation permit from Nowy Sącz was stamped again in Gmünd – the small bureaucratic proof of a journey still in motion.

By 19 March, Viktor was formally assigned to the *Fürst Pálffy Estate* in Heidenreichstein, twenty kilometres west. The estate supported Nazi war production through agriculture, quarrying, and cement work. Wsewolod later recalled that they worked in the quarry – a role far removed from Viktor's past as a bookkeeper. His background may have offered him administrative tasks alongside the physical labour, but neither brought safety or autonomy. Oversight was strict, the conditions harsh, and any illusions of status or privilege had long since vanished. In such places, where labour erased identity, Ukrainians like Viktor clung to old songs. Folk melodies reworked with new words. Banned nationalist anthems, hummed softly under breath.[76]

By April 1945, the war neared its end. American troops entered Gmünd on the 12th, though it is unclear if Viktor and Wsewolod were still there. They do not reappear in surviving records until 31 July 1945, when Viktor was registered as a displaced person in Eugenbach, near Landshut, in the American zone of occupation. This gap suggests they spent the intervening months moving

---

[76] Songs like *Oh, the Red Viburnum in the Meadow* (*Ой у лузі червона калина)* circulated widely among Ukrainians in exile, displaced persons camps, and partisan networks during and after the war. Originally composed during the First World War by Stepan Charnetsky and revived by the Sich Riflemen, it became a symbol of national endurance. In the 1940s, it was quietly sung by labourers, insurgents, and émigrés – an act not of overt protest, but of cultural survival. In this context, song became a means of remaining spiritually intact amid displacement and repression.

westward again – navigating the ruins of a collapsed Nazi regime, and an already fractured post-war Europe.

Their status had changed. From forced labourers under a dying dictatorship, they had become displaced persons in a shattered continent. Their journey westward – marked by hardship, hunger, and danger – had not ended. It had only entered a new phase: of waiting, of paperwork, of refusal to return to a homeland now locked behind the Iron Curtain.

The war's end did not bring freedom. Like millions of others, Viktor emerged into a Europe of camp registries, ration queues, and geopolitical uncertainty. The frontlines had passed, but there was still nowhere to go.

* * *

For Viktor, the war's end was not a moment of release, but a shift in the kind of fear he faced. The frontline receded, but no safe ground emerged. He had survived two regimes, lost almost everything – yet the hardest part was still ahead: to navigate a world where his very identity was a liability, and where the old fear – of Moscow, of what it meant to be Ukrainian under Russian rule – had not faded, but deepened.

His story, ending in the shadow of Nazi collapse and the dread of Soviet return, was Ukraine's story in miniature: a land ravaged, its people scattered, and the brutal respite from one oppressor only heralding the resurgence of another. The fear of Moscow, etched into Viktor's life by the Holodomor, war, and exile, was not a wartime aberration. It was the inheritance of centuries – a fear that would outlive the frontlines, shaping what remained of his family's fractured future.

CHAPTER 8

In the Wake of Ruin: Displacement and Exile, 1945–1964

Хоч плачуть, долоні стискають,
Ненависть палає в очах –
До неба сто рук витягають,
А небо – сповилось в імлах...

Though they weep, their fists are clenched,
Hatred burning in their eyes –
A hundred hands reach toward the heavens,
But the sky is shrouded in mist...

– Sydir Tverdokhlib[77], from *The Mountains*, 1908

---

[77] Sydir Tverdokhlib (1886–1922) was a Ukrainian poet, translator, and nationalist intellectual associated with Galician modernism. His work blended Symbolist aesthetics with political urgency, exploring themes of struggle, exile, and spiritual despair. A supporter of Ukrainian independence, he was assassinated at 36 under murky political circumstances. Though less widely remembered than his contemporaries, his verse remains a haunting testament to a generation marked by cultural revival and historical rupture.

The war was over. The map of Europe had been redrawn. But for millions of displaced persons – including Viktor Skliar – the end of fighting brought no clear future.

The camps came first. Not prisons, not quite shelters – they were waystations of paperwork, waiting, and quiet dread. Viktor was registered as a displaced person in the American zone of occupation on 31 July 1945. The forms did not ask what he had survived. They asked where he would go next. For men like him, that was a dangerous question.

The Soviet Union wanted them back. Through threats, propaganda, and Allied acquiescence, repatriation campaigns swept Ukrainians onto trains eastward. Few were given the chance to explain why they had fled. Fewer still trusted the promises that awaited them.

For men like Viktor, who had lived under German rule, worn Nazi-issued work permits, and fled west, return was no option. It was a death sentence waiting. So they remained in the camps – caught in a system that saw them as displaced, as files to be processed, but never as people with a country they could safely call home.

For Viktor, war's end offered no release. The threat of arrest gave way to the fear of return. The frontlines had receded, but the danger had not. He had survived two regimes and lost nearly everything – and yet, the hardest part still lay ahead: how to remain unseen in a Europe where his very identity had become a risk.

* * *

After the war, nearly three million Ukrainians found themselves stranded across Europe, most in Germany and Austria. They included former forced labourers, concentration camp survivors, and civilians uprooted by Nazi occupation and the Soviet advance.[78]

For them, the war's end brought no freedom. The Soviet Union, determined to reclaim its citizens, launched an aggressive campaign of repatriation. Under agreements reached at Yalta[79], the Western Allies permitted Soviet agents into the camps, where threats, propaganda, and force were used to compel return. Trains ran eastward; many never reached home.

By late 1945, the vast majority – over two million – had already been sent back. Most had no choice. But a hard core remained. By 1946, only around 200,000 Ukrainians were still in the Western zones – those who had evaded the net, or whose origins lay outside the postwar Soviet border.[80] For them, return meant arrest, exile, or worse. To stay meant entering a new kind of waiting – under the

---

[78] For a detailed analysis of the treatment of Ukrainian refugees by the Western Allies and the Soviet Union, see Elliott, Mark R. *The Grand Alliance and Ukrainian Refugees*. New York: Palgrave Macmillan, 2000.

[79] The *Yalta Conference* (February 1945) committed the Allied powers to the repatriation of all Soviet citizens. This policy, known as "forced repatriation" or *Operation Keelhaul*, led to the return of many unwilling individuals to the USSR, often with severe consequences.

[80] While fear of persecution was a primary reason many Ukrainians refused repatriation, it was not the only one. For some, the experience of occupation, forced labour, and exile catalysed a lasting shift in identity. Years spent outside the USSR – exposed to Ukrainian nationalist ideas, émigré networks, or simply the freedom to speak their language – transformed political consciousness. What began as a strategy of survival sometimes hardened into a refusal of Soviet belonging altogether. In this way, exile did not merely protect national identity; it reshaped and, for some, created it.

uncertain protection of the Allied-run *Displaced Persons* (*DP*)[81] camps.

I have often wondered what Viktor felt on that first day inside the camp system. Relief, perhaps, that it was an American zone – not Soviet. Fear, because nothing was settled. Maybe even a flicker of hope. Or perhaps it already felt like the start of a different kind of prison: no barbed wire this time, just forms, silence, and the knowledge that home was gone.

Figure 35: Communal dormitory in a Displaced Persons camp, Wittlich, Germany, 18 April 1945. Forty-eight individuals shared this space, their lives organised around makeshift partitions, basic furnishings, and the routines of postwar survival. Though stark and overcrowded, such interiors became sites of adaptation, mutual care, and cultural continuity.

[81]*Displaced Persons* was used officially after the Second World War to describe refugees living in camps under Allied supervision.

The camps, first under the *United Nations Relief and Rehabilitation Administration* (*UNRRA*)[82], later the *International Refugee Organisation* (*IRO*)[83], offered temporary safety but little comfort. Bureaucracy was dense, conditions harsh, futures uncertain. Yet for many, including the Skliars, the camps became more than holding zones. In Eugenbach, Ergolding, and Ganacker, they joined thousands of others who refused to return, choosing instead the uncertain path of exile. Return meant erasure. Departure offered the faint hope of continuation.

Camp Culture and Community

Life in the Ukrainian DP camps was not only about displacement. It was also about reconstruction – of routine, of memory, of identity. Wherever possible, people organised. Schools opened in corners of barracks; blackboards were nailed to makeshift walls. Children studied in Ukrainian. History was taught from memory – often selective, sometimes mythologised.

---

[82] The *United Nations Relief and Rehabilitation Administration* (*UNRRA*), founded in 1943, was the first major international agency responsible for the care of displaced persons after World War II. It operated hundreds of DP camps across Europe until 1947, providing food, shelter, and basic medical care while managing the initial stages of postwar refugee registration.

[83] The *International Refugee Organization* (*IRO*), created in 1946, succeeded UNRRA as the lead body managing displaced persons. Unlike its predecessor, the IRO also handled long-term resettlement, vetting candidates for emigration and documenting widespread identity alterations by refugees seeking to avoid forced repatriation.

Women were central to this cultural labour.[84] They taught catechism, embroidered ritual cloths, led choirs, and revived folk customs. In Regensburg's Oselia camp, they organised youth groups and Sunday schools. In Delmenhorst, Whitsun Day processions were held in traditional dress. Ukrainian Christmas was celebrated in schoolhouses and barracks, with handmade decorations and carols. These were deliberate acts – part memory, part resistance, part refusal to let rupture become erasure.

Religious life endured in improvised spaces. Chapels were fashioned from storerooms; services held in the open air. Holidays became both sacred rites and affirmations of continuity. Baptisms took place beside bunk beds. Candlelight flickered against unpainted walls. The rituals marked an insistence on survival, even though they couldn't restore what had been lost.

Culture, too, found space to grow. Choirs formed. Theatre groups rehearsed. Newspapers were typed and passed hand to hand. Women shaped much of this world, often through unpaid and overlooked labour. Transnational Ukrainian women's groups framed maternal care as civic duty, allowing women to claim visibility as guardians of continuity and architects of diaspora life.

---

[84] Popowycz, Jennifer L. *World War II, Displacement, and the Making of the Postwar Ukrainian Diaspora, 1939–1951*. PhD diss., Louisiana State University, 2022, chap. 5, "The 'Good Ukrainians': Cultural Nationalism in Ukrainian Displaced Persons Camps, 1945–1951.

Popowycz documents how cultural and religious traditions – led in large part by women – helped re-establish a collective sense of Ukrainian identity in exile. From organising embroidered ritual cloths for makeshift chapels, to staging performances of Lesia Ukrainka's *The Song of the Forest*, women played an essential, though often unrecognised, role in constructing diasporic continuity.

Though labelled "social" or "recreational" in official records, their work was structural: it helped define postwar Ukrainian identity in exile.

But these cultural spaces were not free from tension. Factions emerged. Old rivalries resurfaced. The camps reflected the broader fractures of the émigré world – political, generational, personal. For some, these institutions were lifelines. For others, they felt like substitutes for a homeland that could no longer be returned to.

Yet despite shortages and uncertainty, a kind of rhythm took hold. In small acts – lessons taught from memory, holidays marked with improvised rites – a fragile culture persisted behind wire. Not unified. Not untouched by conflict. But enduring, all the same.

Many of the institutions that would later define Ukrainian life in exile began here. Behind barbed wire and beneath United Nations flags, a foundation was laid – not by consensus, but by necessity.

From Eugenbach to Ganacker: A Life in Transit

Between 1945 and 1948, Viktor moved through several DP camps in Bavaria, each a temporary refuge in a life of exile. He was first registered at Eugenbach, a provisional housing site in the Landshut network, from June to September 1945, before relocating to Camp Ergolding, northeast of Landshut. Ergolding, under American administration, temporarily housed over 330 Ukrainians. By late 1946, he moved again – to Ganacker, a larger rural camp and an early hub of Ukrainian cultural life.[85] A travel permit from August 1947 confirms a temporary return visit to Ergolding, likely to maintain ties.

During this period, Viktor took small but deliberate steps to rebuild a life in exile. He received an identity card from the *Ukrainian Committee for Niederbayern-Oberpfalz* and a travel exemption from the German Military Government. The latter allowed him to move with two horses and a wagon – nominally to visit his mother.[86] Whether fact or pretext, the papers show a man asserting agency, positioning himself visibly within the Ukrainian nationalist cause in exile.

Yet the fractures continued. In 1948, Viktor had a son with Maria Tkaczuk, a fellow displaced person – a fact unknown to the family

---

[85] "*The four largest concentrations of Ukrainian refugees in Bavaria and, indeed, in all of West Germany were at Aschaffenburg (over 5,000 in 4 camps), München (over 5,000 in 3 camps and a transit camp), Regensburg (over 4,000 in 1 camp alone), and the town of Mittenwald near Garmisch (over 4,000 in 3 camps)... Landshut (over 800)... and Ganacker (over 700)*". Also: "*Ukrainian population in UNRRA/IRO camps (American Zone): Ergolding – 195 (1946-1947), 337 (Aug 1946), 102 (May 1947); Ganacker – 707 (1946-1947), 553 (May 1947), 736 (Dec 1947)*".
"*Ukrainskyi Istoryk: Zhurnal istorii i ukrainoznavstva*," vol. XXIII, nos. 3–4 (91–92), 1986. Accessed March 2025.

[86] The exemption, issued in Landshut on 31 August 1945, allows "Skljar Vladimir" to travel from Camp Eugenbach to "Auremberg" with two horses and a wagon, stating "his mother is living there, he wants to remain there". It was preserved among Viktor's personal papers and likely refers to him, not to his son Vadim (also sometimes recorded as Vladimir), who was not in Landshut at the time. Viktor, a widower since 1943, had no known surviving mother, making it probable that the claim was fabricated – a common tactic among displaced persons seeking to avoid repatriation or justify internal travel. "Auremberg" does not match any known location and was likely a misspelling of Augsburg or Nuremberg. The inconsistencies are typical of the bureaucratic fluidity and improvisation of the immediate postwar period.

until decades later. Their son was born in Deggendorf, Bavaria, representing both continuity and rupture. After Viktor's departure for England, he and Maria lost contact. Viktor would never meet his son – a permanent separation that echoed the many losses already carried.

Like thousands of others, Viktor repeatedly refused repatriation to the USSR. It was not passive. It was a deliberate act of survival. Under the terms of the *Yalta Agreement*, the Western Allies had agreed to Soviet repatriation demands. For Ukrainians who had lived under German occupation, return meant arrest, exile, or worse. The Soviet state made little distinction between coerced labour and collaboration. Those who stayed in the DP camps understood this. Refusing to return was a calculated rejection of Moscow's reach – one born of memory, fear, and the lessons of the Holodomor.

To avoid this fate, Viktor, like many, modified his records. His birthplace, originally listed as Dar-Nadezhda, Ukraine, was changed to Dubrivka, Poland, to present himself as a Polish national rather than a Soviet subject. At the time, those born in Soviet territory were routinely handed over to Soviet authorities. Those born in interwar Poland stood a better chance of being classified as non-repatriable. These small acts of documentary reinvention were often the only defence against a regime that offered no clemency – a regime whose reach was extended by Western compliance.[87]

---

[87] The forced repatriation of Soviet citizens, including Ukrainians, was authorised under the 1945 *Yalta Agreement* and carried out by British and American authorities.

Stateless on Paper: Identity and Belonging in Exile

In the aftermath of World War II, survival was no longer just about food, shelter, or safety. For millions of displaced persons – especially Ukrainians – the difference between exile and forced repatriation hinged on something else entirely: paperwork.

Basing on authentical informations we
state that
Mr. Sklar Viktor
calling farmer
born the 28. 6. 1895
in
now living in
is a member of the Ukrainian Committee for Niederbayern-Oberpfalz
in Regensburg.
Regensburg 30.8. 1945
For the Ukrainian Committee
in Regensburg

Figure 36: Viktor's 1945 *Ukrainian Committee* card, listing a false birthplace to evade Soviet repatriation. Its deliberate errors reveal a man rewriting his identity to survive.

By late 1945, both Viktor and Wsewolod Skliar were registered as displaced persons in Bavaria. Like many others, they faced not only

---

Hundreds of thousands were returned to Soviet control, often against their will. Many faced arrest, exile, or execution upon arrival. The most notorious phase of this policy – codenamed Operation Keelhaul – has since been widely condemned. See Bethell, Nicholas. *The Last Secret: The Delivery to Stalin of Over Two Million Russians by Britain and the United States*. London: Andre Deutsch, 1974.

the trauma of recent years, but the immediate need to reinvent themselves on paper. Their documents from this period reveal subtle but deliberate inconsistencies – adjustments to names, dates, places, and family ties – each a tactical choice made in the shadow of geopolitical threat.

Some of these shifts were small. Viktor's birth year, correctly 1899, appears as 1895 in several postwar records – likely to place him outside the prime age bracket for forced labour while still qualifying for resettlement quotas. Wsewolod's date of birth fluctuated even more – listed variously as 1928, 1929, and 1930. At different moments, being older meant eligibility for work or military exemption; being younger offered protection as a minor. The adjustments were intentional, not accidental.

More significant were the changes to their recorded birthplaces and residences. In reality, Viktor and Wsewolod were born in eastern Ukraine – Viktor in Dar-Nadezhda, and Wsewolod in nearby Martynova. By 1945, both were recorded as having been born in Dubrivka, Poland, with prewar residence listed as Sambor, a town in western Ukraine that had been part of interwar Poland. The shift was deliberate, designed to disassociate them from Soviet Ukraine. In the eyes of Allied authorities, those born in territories now claimed by the USSR were automatically Soviet citizens, and thus eligible – or obligated – for repatriation under Yalta agreements. By contrast, those born in interwar Poland could sometimes claim Polish nationality or argue they had never held Soviet citizenship at all. The difference was existential: one label could mean resettlement in the West; the other, interrogation, prison, or deportation.

Other details were also altered. Wsewolod's mother, Evdokiya, appears as "Bondarenko" in several documents – a name found nowhere else in family records. Elsewhere she is always remembered as Evdokiya Mosiienko. The substitution may have been designed to obscure her identity, which – tied to a Soviet passport and known place of death in occupied Ukraine – could have triggered suspicion. Viktor's mother is recorded as "Anna Piwowarowa", another name without precedent in the family archive. Whether these changes were fabrications or clerical errors, the aim was clear: to create plausible distance between their present selves and any paper trail that might tie them back to Soviet Ukraine.

What emerges is not simply a story of desperation, but of a system with no tolerance for ambiguity. The postwar state – Soviet, American, or international – demanded fixed categories: citizen or traitor, refugee or returnee. But people like Viktor and Wsewolod lived in the grey zones. Their lives, provisional and precarious, had to be rewritten to fit forms built for simpler fates. This, too, is part of the legacy of displacement: that survival often depended less on what you had endured, and more on how credibly you could narrate yourself inside someone else's system.

In these shifting names and numbers is not deception, but defensive improvisation. Stateless persons became paper cartographers, redrawing the borders of their identities according to the politics of the moment. These were not fraudulent acts in the criminal sense. They were existential acts – attempts to outmanoeuvre bureaucratic machinery that recognised neither nuance nor context.[88]

Such alterations were widespread in the DP camps. In 1946, the IRO noted that many Ukrainians had "adapted" their documents to avoid forced return. Birthplaces near borders were nudged across lines; Soviet cities became Polish villages; mothers became aunts or disappeared altogether. DP registration cards were not just bureaucratic forms – they were passports to survival, the medium through which memories were edited and futures negotiated.

That Viktor and Wsewolod's documents contain multiple versions of themselves is not an error. It is a truth about the age in which they lived. They chose ambiguity as protection. Their fragmented paper trail tells us not only what they feared, but what they understood: that Moscow's reach extended far beyond Ukraine's borders, and that to be Ukrainian in 1945 was not only a matter of heritage, but a condition of profound vulnerability.

Some of these improvisations were also pragmatic. Wsewolod's 1948 identity certificate, issued by the Office of the Military

[88] The fact that displaced persons often altered their personal documents raises important questions for historians. These records – forms, birth dates, place names – are both archival evidence and intentional distortion. As such, they demand a dual reading: as testimony to lived experience, and as artefacts of self-protection. For Viktor and Wsewolod, strategic misrepresentation was a tool of survival. But for those interpreting their lives decades later, such distortions complicate the archive itself. What appears stable (a name, a birthplace) may in fact be tactical. This does not discredit the record – but it obliges us to read it not as neutral data, but as a form of authored evasion. In this sense, DP files are not only bureaucratic residue, but autobiographical texts – composed under duress, shaped by fear, and revealing both what was risked and what had to be concealed.

Governor, US Zone of Germany, lists his occupation as "coal mining" – likely a fabrication to align with British labour recruitment priorities. The United Kingdom's European Volunteer Workers scheme prioritised men for mining and agriculture, and many DPs adjusted their professions accordingly. Viktor listed himself as an agricultural labourer, though he had been a bookkeeper. In these bureaucratic adaptations, precision gave way to pragmatism. It was survival, not deceit.

In a final irony, the records that helped save them from forced return are now some of the only traces of who they were at that moment. Their real biographies had to be obscured to be preserved.

Labour and Loneliness in England, 1948–1964

In March 1948, Viktor and Wsewolod arrived in Harwich under the *European Volunteer Worker* scheme, with Viktor assigned to menial farm labour in Cambridgeshire. For Viktor, once a bookkeeper, the work was not only unfamiliar – it severed the last ties to the identity he had once known. His skills no longer mattered. The contrast was practical, but also psychological: a man of records and ledgers reduced to physical toil.

Beyond this, the trail of his life becomes harder to follow. A clipping from the *Bognor Regis Observer*, June 1949, offers a rare glimpse – Viktor, at North Mundham Hostel, winning a prize in a cricket club competition. A flicker of belonging? Or a moment that went nowhere? There are no stories that follow.

In London, the pattern set in: sweeping streets, later cleaning at St. Charles Hospital – a building where Wsewolod also worked, though their paths rarely crossed. They lived in the same house, but not together. Viktor retreated upstairs, into routines of habit and isolation.[89] He was still seen at Ukrainian community gatherings in the early 1950s, but even there, the connections thinned. Drink became his companion. Once, he stole the savings Wsewolod had set aside for his newborn daughter. His place within the family shrank to the margins – present, but no longer a participant.

Did he think of Vadim, the son left behind in Soviet Ukraine? Did he hum old songs walking home from the pub? I cannot know.

He no longer spoke of the country he had fled, or the lives he had lost. His routines became his world – not just from habit, but perhaps from exhaustion, or from the knowledge that, in Britain, the roles he once understood – Ukrainian, bookkeeper, father – no longer counted. I don't know if drink numbed his pain or simply filled the space left by meaning. Perhaps it began in custom, hardened in exile, and settled into silence.

Viktor Skliar died on 31 March 1964 – a man who crossed regimes, borders, and roles, only to find himself adrift in a place that gave him no name, no resolution. His life does not resolve into ideology. It traces the toll of living under three regimes, and the silence that survival imposed.

---

[89] The pattern of emotional withdrawal and silence among displaced men – particularly those who experienced multiple ruptures in home, belief, and political belonging – is well documented. In Ukrainian postwar communities, silence often became a learned behaviour: a way to avoid Soviet suspicion, manage intergenerational fracture, or cope with unprocessed trauma. This silence is frequently mistaken for stoicism or moral clarity. But it can also signify dislocation, psychological fatigue, or a loss of voice. In family narratives, the absence of commentary is easily reinterpreted as quiet strength.

Figure 37: Viktor with Wsewolod and granddaughters, 1959, a rare moment of connection in exile. Behind the smiles lies a silence shaped by war and loss.

* * *

That silence did not die with him. It settled in the family he left behind, carried in the fragments his granddaughters recall: a figure at the margins, present but unreachable, a man shaped by losses too fractured to voice. His silence became theirs, too – an inheritance of unspoken pasts, of histories unfinished, of questions no one dared to ask.

But that quiet was more than personal. It echoed a broader Ukrainian condition – of betrayals endured, identities erased, survival paid for in silence. Viktor's life reflects not only a family's fracture, but a national one: of a people who learned that to speak was dangerous, and to endure was to endure quietly. His silence, passed down without words, became part of the exile his descendants inherited – a fragment of Ukraine's unfinished story, still carried in the shadows he left behind.

When Viktor died in 1964, that fracture was already embodied in his two sons. Vadim, reabsorbed into the Soviet system, lived a life of silence and conformity. Wsewolod, exiled in the West, wrestled with memory and a lost homeland. Their divergent paths did not merely mirror Europe's Cold War divide; they mirrored the wreckage of Viktor's own choices – the impossible decisions of a generation for whom survival had long replaced wholeness.

I have tried to make sense of him. Careful yet reckless. Present, but held at a distance. He does not explain himself. The fragments that remain – forms, photographs, a grave – carry no confession. He left behind two sons, divided not only by geography but by the history that shaped them. They never saw each other again.

The next chapter turns to Vadim – the son who stayed – and the system that claimed him.

CHAPTER 9
Silenced by the State: Vadim Skliar in Soviet Ukraine (1924–1985)

О! Нас давно не видно на кону.
Закохані у тишину робітні,
Ми стали скромні, стали непомітні,
Скупі на жест і мову запальну.

Oh! We've long been absent from the stage.
In love with silence in our workroom's shade,
We've grown more modest, quietly self-made,
Restrained in speech, and gesture, and in rage.

– Mykola Zerov[90], from *Creative Silence*, 1932

---

[90] Mykola Zerov (1890–1937) was a poet, translator, and leading figure of the Neoclassicist school in 1920s Ukraine. Advocating cultural depth over agitprop, he resisted Soviet demands for ideological conformity. Executed during Stalin's *Great Terror*, he became a symbol of artistic integrity and intellectual refusal.

While his father and brother fled westward, Vadim Skliar remained – not by choice, but by circumstance. His path illuminates a less visible history of Ukrainian survival: not through escape, but through endurance within a system that demanded forgetting. One son became a displaced person in the West. The other was pulled into the machinery of Soviet reintegration.

Vadim's life was shaped by constraint. Repatriated under duress, reclassified by a state that distrusted him, he navigated postwar life through quiet adaptation. Like millions absorbed back into the Soviet fold, he found a place – never fully trusted, never entirely erased. The record is thin, but its silences trace another form of survival: difficult to document, easy to overlook, essential to understanding what it meant to live under a regime that erased as much as it ruled.

For those returned to Soviet Ukraine, the war's end brought no liberation. It marked the beginning of a different captivity. Labelled "traitors" simply for surviving outside Soviet control, repatriated citizens were met not with welcome, but with interrogation, forced labour, and lifelong surveillance. Vadim's return was no homecoming. It was a reinsertion into a system that branded him suspect. His silence, imposed by fear, became both shield and sentence – a survival strategy that erased his story from memory.

Raised by Tradition, Educated by the State, 1924–1941

Vadim Skliar was born on 12 February 1924, in Sakhnovshchyna, then part of Poltava region, Ukraine. His birth was not formally registered until 1937, when it was, inaccurately, entered into the civil registry under the NKVD. Such delays were not uncommon. Across rural Ukraine, administrative breakdown and political disruption left many childhoods unrecorded – acknowledged only when the state demanded it.

In his early years, Vadim lived not with his father, Viktor, but with his grandfather, Ivan Skliar, a psalmist in the local Orthodox parish. It was a household shaped by ritual and rural routine, quietly holding to an older order even as the Soviet state redrew the world around it. Vadim's childhood, like his father's before him, unfolded under pressure: collectivisation, famine, repression. The pace of change was relentless. Survival demanded adaptation.

Unlike his father, who had entered seminary under the Russian Empire, Vadim was educated within the Soviet system. By the 1939–40 academic year, he had completed seven years of study at a secondary school in Bilopillia, Sumy region.[91] He boarded there – a common arrangement for rural children pursuing extended schooling. These institutions were not neutral. Instruction came with ideological training: a deliberate separation from home life, and the steady inculcation of Soviet norms.[92] For children like Vadim, education was not only opportunity. It was reorientation.

---

[91] Bilopillia is a district centre in northeastern Ukraine, historically part of the Kharkiv and Sumy regions. It was home to several mid-level educational institutions by the late 1930s, serving as a boarding hub for students from surrounding rural areas.

[92] Soviet boarding schools, particularly from the 1930s onward, were often used to promote Communist ideology and diminish the role of religion, national identity, and family tradition. See: Fitzpatrick, Sheila. *Education and Social Mobility in the Soviet Union, 1921–1934*. Cambridge: Cambridge University Press, 1979.

By the late 1930s, Soviet classrooms had become instruments of political formation. Ukrainian language and literature were pushed to the margins, especially in higher-track schools, where Russian dominated the curriculum. Lessons opened with slogans. Portraits of Stalin loomed over blackboards. Loyalty to the state was drilled alongside arithmetic. Official textbooks rewrote Ukraine's past, recasting national figures as imperial servants or bourgeois enemies.

Yet within this repressive system, traces of the past endured. Older students whispered Ukrainian verse beyond the teacher's earshot. Grandparents corrected Soviet pronunciations at the dinner table. In rare moments, a sympathetic teacher might insert a folk song into the day's lesson – quiet gestures that signalled the persistence of something older.

Often, these gestures came from women. Soviet schooling enforced ideological conformity, but it also expanded female literacy and brought more women into the profession. Girls like Maria Ivanivna – Vadim's aunt – became teachers, carrying older pedagogical traditions into new frameworks. In quiet resistance, some women educators smuggled folk literature and Ukrainian verse into officially sanctioned lessons.

Vadim's education, shaped by the dogmas of the state, likely bore the fingerprints of such careful interventions. It was imposed from above, yet shadowed by subtler inheritances. It would soon be cut short.

World War II and Forced Labour in Nazi Germany, 1941–1945

The German invasion of the Soviet Union in 1941 altered the course of Vadim's life. Bilopillia, where he had been attending school, was occupied by German forces that October. He appears to have remained there until early 1943. By spring, his stepmother, Evdokiya, had been killed when Soviet bombs struck the village. His father and half-brother fled west. Vadim was left behind.

I cannot know why. Perhaps it was a desperate decision in the chaos of flight. Perhaps there was no decision at all. From here, it does not make sense.[93] But the absence tells its own story. Survival, at a certain point, stops being collective. It fractures. Families, communities – they hold only as long as the pressure allows. After that, survival becomes personal. Not everyone can be carried.

What is certain is that the separation was final. In the years that followed, Vadim searched for his father and brother, but never found them. He was absent from the documents of exile, excluded from the stories that came later. While others crossed borders, Vadim was pulled back into a system that treated his very existence as suspect. His silence was not chosen. It was imposed.

---

[93] Family recollections about this period are conflicting. According to some accounts, Wsewolod wished to wait for Vadim so they could flee together, but the opportunity for escape came suddenly. Vadim may have been away at boarding school or living with his grandfather at the time, though this cannot be confirmed. The decision to flee without him – whether forced by circumstance or made in fear – was never fully explained. That only Wsewolod and Viktor fled, leaving behind every other relative, remains one of the most haunting gaps in the family's postwar story.

On 7 February 1944, Vadim's name surfaced in the registers of Munich's Police Headquarters: a 19-year-old Ukrainian far from home.[94] Registered as "Wladimir", and listed as coming from Stalino (now Donetsk – a city with no known connection to his life), he was one of thousands funnelled through Nazi bureaucracy, his identity reduced to a mis-recorded name and a line in a ledger. The war cared little for accuracy. It cared only for labour.

His sudden appearance in Germany points to a grim reality: he was likely deported as an *Ostarbeiter* – one of more than 2.5 million Ukrainians, mostly young women and men, forced into labour for the Nazi war machine.[95] Transported in overcrowded trains, underfed, uncertain of their fate, these workers faced brutal conditions.

Vadim next appears in a workplace injury report from June 1944. Filed by the Southern German Iron and Steel Professional Association, the record confirms his employment in hazardous industry. Many Ukrainians were sent to such work – physically punishing, poorly provisioned, ruthlessly disciplined. Food was scarce. Illness and injury were routine. Few left records. Fewer still left stories.

---

[94] The *Munich Police Headquarters* functioned as both a local enforcement body and a central node in the management of displaced persons, especially in 1944 – 45. Registration there did not necessarily imply detention – it could also reflect transit processing or workplace assignments under Nazi labour oversight.

[95] 51.1% of civilian foreign workers from the Soviet Union were female (as opposed to a broader average of 33.3%). On the age and gender breakdown of male and female civilian foreign workers, see Herbert, Ulrich. *Hitler's Foreign Workers: Enforced Foreign Labor in Germany Under the Third Reich*. Cambridge: Cambridge University Press, 1997, 462.

Among them was Warwara Burdun, also from Ukraine, born the same year as Vadim. Little is known of her experience. But testimony from Hanna Honchar, deported from Sakhnovshchyna in 1942, offers insight into what Warwara may have endured. She described being rounded up with twenty-six others, handed from local police to German soldiers, and transported by rail to a munitions factory near Hamburg. There, she worked twelve-hour shifts under armed guard, witnessed brutal punishments, and lived in barracks marked by hunger, surveillance, and fear. "*It wasn't honey for us in the camp*", she wrote – a phrase that captures both the understatement and the horror.[96]

In the collapsing months of Nazi Germany, Vadim was employed by Alfred Kunz & Co., an industrial firm still operating between March and April 1945. There, he met Warwara. Their paths crossed in the war's final days, and on 5 April 1945, weeks before Germany's surrender, they married in Munich. Like many such unions, it was not a beginning, but an attempt to hold together something human in the wreckage: no home, no legal status, no certain future – only the need to endure together.

Despite everything, life persisted. Later that year, they welcomed a son, Viktor, named for Vadim's displaced father. Vadim remained

---

[96] Testimony of Anna Romanovna Honchar (née Chernomorets), born 1920 in Nova Mykhailivka, Sakhnovshchyna district, recounts deportation to Germany in 1942 and conditions at the Dynamit Krümmel labour camp near Geesthacht. Though not Warwara's own, her account reflects the experience of many Ukrainian Ostarbeiter from the region. From: Hanna Honchar (née Chornomorets), "*Не мед нам был в лагере...*" in *Спогади-терни. Про моє життя німецьке... Спогади про перебування на примусових роботах у нацистській Німеччині*, ed. H. Hrynchenko and I. Rebrova (Kharkiv: Pravo, 2008), 275–277.

in Munich until at least early 1946, listed as an unskilled labourer, living at Moosacher Straße 82 – an address known to house displaced persons. In the ruins of Nazi Germany, life went on. Stubborn. Unspoken.

Repatriation and Soviet Suspicion, 1946

In 1946, Vadim and Warwara were forcibly repatriated to the Soviet Union – among 2.8 million citizens returned under the Yalta Agreement. Western governments framed it as a homecoming. For many Ukrainians, it was the beginning of a second ordeal.

The Soviet regime treated returnees not as victims, but as suspects. Exposure to life beyond Soviet borders, however brief, was seen as contamination. To have survived abroad was enough to brand someone disloyal.

The process was brutally arbitrary. A returned labourer like Vadim might be asked:

- Why did you not join the partisans while abroad?
- Why did you not commit suicide instead of working for the Germans?
- Who were your supervisors? What did you read? What did you say?

Many were imprisoned, exiled, or sentenced under sweeping laws that criminalised perceived disloyalty. Others were scattered to remote settlements – places where they could be watched, controlled, forgotten. Around 20% of civilian returnees faced imprisonment, exile, or forced conscription, with Ukrainians often targeted more harshly due to nationalist suspicions. Across all returnees, including prisoners of war, that figure rose to an astonishing 42%.[97] Even those not formally punished bore the mark. Internal records flagged them as “formerly repatriated”, restricting access to education, employment, and mobility. The stigma often passed down to their children.[98]

Vadim left no record of arrest or formal exile. But silence was part of the system. What is known is this: he never returned to Sakhnovshchyna. Instead, he resettled in Demyantsy, a small village in the Kyiv region – his wife Warwara’s birthplace. Whether by choice or compulsion is unclear. But the pattern fits. Many repatriated Ukrainians were barred from their former homes, placed instead in rural areas where oversight was easier, and forgetting more complete.

For Vadim, repatriation was no return. It would have been another betrayal – quiet, administrative, absolute. In Ukraine’s long history of forced loyalties, from Pereiaslav, to Poltava, to Yalta, the arc held. The state did not just demand obedience. It demanded forgetting. Returnees rarely spoke of their wartime experiences, fearing surveillance, denunciation, or worse. This silence, now documented by post-Soviet historians, erased a generation’s stories from public memory. Vadim’s absence from the archives is no accident. It is the void left by survival.

---

[97] Zemskov, V. N. "On the Repatriation of Soviet Citizens, 1944–1951." *Istoriya SSSR* [*History of the USSR*], no. 4 (1990).

[98] The Soviet internal passport (*propiska*) system tracked citizens’ residence, employment, and political reliability. Special marks could limit access to housing, education, or travel rights, particularly for those labelled as “former repatriates” or “politically unreliable”.

The scars were administrative and psychological. For many, silence became the only safe response. Even within families, speaking of time abroad carried risk. Disclosure invited suspicion. Most avoided it entirely. The result was an enduring quiet that shaped not only individuals, but generations. Many survivors kept silent well into the 1980s. Their stories faded from view – preserved only in fragments, or not at all. Survival demanded adaptation. Outward conformity masked inward vigilance. Memory became private, if it was kept at all.

Vadim's silence about his time in Germany, and the absence of documentation concerning his repatriation, fits precisely into this pattern. Like countless others, he understood that forgetting was the price of survival. It was also the inheritance he left behind.

Relearning Survival: A Life After Return, 1946–1950

In Demyantsy, Vadim and Warwara built a modest, stable life. But stability came at a cost. Between 1946 and 1947, a new wave of famine swept Soviet Ukraine. Driven by Stalin's relentless grain requisitions and compounded by drought, the crisis claimed hundreds of thousands of lives. In villages like Demyantsy, shelves emptied, fields failed, quotas stripped what remained. The dead were buried quietly – if at all. Soviet authorities denied the famine's existence.

Vadim, likely labouring on a collective farm, bore the weight of this hunger without complaint. Lidia, his daughter, later recalled his guarded silence – a habit forged under the scrutiny of a state that marked returnees like him as suspect. For Vadim, each day was a negotiation: work, comply, survive.

Figure 38: Maria Skliar (left), daughter of Ivan Skliar, and Warwara Burdun (right), 1963. Though dislocation had scattered the family, ties endured. Even in new surroundings, connections held across generations.

But hunger was only part of the shadow. Stalin's regime moved quickly to extinguish any revival of Ukrainian cultural life. Writers were purged, churches re-shuttered, the Ukrainian language driven from public institutions. Though no records survive detailing Vadim's actions, his past as an *Ostarbeiter* marked him for quiet surveillance. Neighbours whispered of deportations. Families like his learned to speak in fragments. Even memories – of faith, resistance, or home – became liabilities. The Soviet demand for forgetting was not only political. It became a way of life.

Vadim's silence became the national condition. Returnees like him were absorbed into the workforce but denied visibility. Internal passports branded them as "repatriated", shrinking futures already curtailed.

In 1948, he and Warwara welcomed a daughter, Lidia. Their children – Viktor and Lidia – grew up far from the displaced persons camps where other Skliars had scattered. They attended Soviet schools, sang Soviet songs.

But the stain of repatriation lingered, casting a shadow over their prospects. Viktor served in the Red Army – the son of forced labourers swallowed by the very system that had once condemned his parents. It was not redemption. It was Soviet normalcy. A normalcy built on silence. And fear. And forgetting.

Figure 39: Lidia and Viktor Skliar, c. 1960s, stand together in Demyantsy. Children of former *Ostarbeiters*, they grew up in a Soviet system that both condemned their parents and claimed their futures.

A World That Did Not Forget, 1950–1985

Vadim lived not only through silence, but through the Soviet Union's long, uneasy aftermath. After Stalin's death in 1953, the regime softened briefly. Ukrainian culture resurfaced in cautious ways. Writers published again. Songs once forbidden returned to public life. But the fear did not lift completely. The children of Vadim carried the weight of his unspoken past into Soviet schools, but they understood its meaning.

Figure 40: Vadim Skliar (left) with his half-brother Vadim Averko (right). Also likely taken in the 1960s.

In the decades that followed, life in Ukraine grew more stable, but no more open. Those who spoke too loudly still disappeared. The Ukrainian language receded from public space. Most families, including Vadim's, kept their heads down. In Demyantsy, he worked, raised his children, and said little. His past remained locked away. Even small memories – of home, of Germany, of hunger – stayed silent.

When reform came in the 1980s, it came too late. Vadim died in 1985, six years before Ukraine's independence. He did not live to see the borders shift or the silence lift. But the life he built – careful, watchful, intact – carried forward something fragile. Memory, however quiet, had not been entirely lost.

Vadim passed away on 30 May 1985, in Demyantsy. Unlike many repatriated Ukrainians who faced imprisonment or lifelong exclusion, he appears to have avoided the worst punishments. He lived, worked, raised a family – not in defiance of repression, but inside its walls. He shaped the only survival left to him—a life that was rural, silent, and undocumented—into his own terms.[99]

In 2010, his daughter Lidia travelled to the United Kingdom to meet her uncle Wsewolod – a gesture of reconnection after decades of silence, distance, and historical rupture. But by then, Wsewolod was seriously ill. Though he had spoken of Vadim throughout his life, when faced with Lidia, he denied having a brother. Whatever memories remained had receded beyond reach; silence now enveloped them both. Lidia left, carrying her father's unspoken story, the weight of a family fractured beyond repair.[100]

* * *

Vadim Skliar's life unfolded between regimes, shaped more by decisions made for him than by acts of choice. His survival was not triumph, but accommodation – a daily negotiation under fear and forgetting. Yet within those confines, he built a family, endured, and carried forward a thread of resilience. Quietly. At cost.

---

[99] In the Soviet Union, "rehabilitation" was rarely granted to repatriated citizens. Many were denied access to university, housing, or party membership well into the 1970s. For Ukrainians, especially those with family connections to nationalist regions or wartime displacement, invisibility often became a survival strategy.

[100] Whether this was a result of illness or a defensive response to a painful rupture remains unclear. The moment underscores the emotional and generational disjuncture that shaped postwar families fractured by war and exile. Recognition, where it once existed, had slipped into silence.

His story mirrors Ukraine's own: a nation forced to navigate erasure, preserving identity through habit when speech became danger. The Holodomor, Soviet censorship, the stain of repatriation – all cast long shadows, silencing millions. Yet in villages like Demyantsy, memory endured. In names, in rituals, in the stubborn will to continue.

Vadim's brother, Wsewolod, followed a different path – fleeing westward in pursuit of survival. Together, their stories reveal Ukraine's fractured heart: one family, divided by history, bound by endurance. Vadim's silence was not surrender. It was strategy. A way to protect what could still be kept.

But as we turn to Wsewolod's journey, the question remains: What does it mean to survive when memory itself becomes the risk?

CHAPTER 10

Youth and Resistance: The Formation of Wsewolod Skliar, 1929–1948

Захочеш – і будеш. В людині, затям,
Лежить невідгадана сила.
Зрослась небезпека з одважним життям,
Як з тілом смертельника крила.

You will, if you wish. Remember this well:
In a human being lies an unguessed power.
Danger and brave life have grown together,
As wings to the body of a condemned man.

– Oleh Olzych[101], from *To the Unknown Soldier*, 1940

[101] Oleh Olzhych (1907–1944), born Oleh Kandyba, was a Ukrainian poet, archaeologist, and nationalist organiser. A member of the Organisation of Ukrainian Nationalists (OUN), his poetry stressed existential heroism and martyrdom. Arrested by the Gestapo for resistance activity, he died under torture in Sachsenhausen. His work remained central to émigré identity and postwar youth mobilisation.

It's hard to imagine what it meant to be fourteen and already certain. Wsewolod was. In the same year – 1943 – he lost his mother to a Soviet bombing; he was writing about the future of the Ukrainian people. At an age when most teenagers are still learning who they are, he was already choosing who to become. It wasn't a performance. It wasn't borrowed rhetoric. It was belief – shaped by war, exile, and the quiet discipline of a generation that had seen too much too early.

I don't want to romanticise that certainty. Some of what he copied into his notebooks I find hard to read now – the absolutes, the creeds, the calls to hatred. But I also understand why it mattered. He wasn't trying to make sense of politics. He was trying to survive it.

And I understand, too, why he might have hated – and feared. He had lived through the Holodomor. He had lost his uncle, and neighbours, to the purges. He had seen the Soviets bomb his village, kill his mother, his aunt, his cousins. I understand the instinct. When the world has tried to erase you, how do you not carry anger? How do you not learn to fear what might come again?

Exile gave him freedom, but it also gave him a burden: to remember what had been destroyed, and to carry it forward. That's what he did – as a young-man who refused, for a time, to let silence win.

* * *

The postwar Ukrainian diaspora was shaped not only by survival, but by the desire to remember – and to resist. For those displaced by war and unable to return under Soviet rule, exile became both refuge and struggle. Across the refugee camps of Germany, and later in Britain, France, North America and beyond, tens of thousands carried with them the trauma of occupation, the memory of lost communities, and the burden of representing a silenced nation abroad.

Wsewolod Victorovych Skliar, born in 1929, was one of them. Uprooted by war, denied return, he lived out the arc shared by many in the Ukrainian émigré generation: from flight and displacement to resettlement and reinvention. But his life did more than mirror that trajectory – it helped define it. Through writing, activism, and cultural preservation, he helped sustain a national identity that totalitarianism sought to erase. His story is one of endurance – and, at first, of refusal: refusal to forget, refusal to assimilate, refusal to accept Ukraine's erasure from history.

Yet Wsewolod's life also illuminates something quieter, and perhaps harder to grasp: what exile felt like. His notebooks and poems chart a world of longing, fragmentation, and reinvention. His silences speak as much as his words. Like many of his generation, he carried the burden of inherited trauma while forging a new existence abroad. His was a life of unremarkable appearance, but remarkable implication: a chef, a father, a husband, a refugee, a writer. A man who did not set out to represent Ukraine abroad, but who, in the very texture of his daily life, came to embody it.

Unlike his brother Vadim – whose path was shaped by enforced return and bureaucratic silence – Wsewolod's life offers a different kind of endurance. His story does not end in triumph. But it begins in resistance. This chapter traces his formation – from a war-torn village to displacement in Germany – not as a hero, but as a man whose daily life embodied a people's refusal to disappear. In the forests of resistance, in the barracks of exile, could a teenager's belief withstand the weight of a nation's loss?

Childhood Under Fire, 1929–1943

Wsewolod Skliar was born on 2 April 1929[102], in Martynova, a small village near Sakhnovshchyna in eastern Ukraine – one of thousands of children born into the uneasy quiet that settled after collectivisation, before war arrived. Two weeks later, on 15 April, he was baptised by Father I. Terlecky – the same priest who had once served alongside Wsewolod's grandfather, Ivan Skliar, in nearby Dar-Nadezhda. Ivan was almost certainly there. The connection between these two parishes – spiritual, familial, geographic – offers a glimpse of the Orthodox networks that still held together community life in Poltava.

Sakhnovshchyna, now in Kharkiv Oblast, was a modest rural settlement, shaped by fear as much as by harvests. Wsewolod was born into its uneasy quiet in 1929 – after collectivisation and *dekulakisation* had already begun to fracture village life, but before the worst of the hunger came. The Holodomor of 1932–33 devastated the grain-producing heart of eastern Ukraine. No records link the Skliars directly to the worst of the famine, but in

[102] The exact year of Wsewolod Skliar's birth is uncertain. He could not recall his birth date, and various documents list conflicting years – 1928, 1929, and 1930. His UK passport states 1928; however, like Viktor's, its details were fabricated to facilitate employment, which suggests 1928 is incorrect. A translation of his baptism certificate from the 1950s records 1929, which, given its independent verification, may be the most accurate. Nevertheless, other records list 1928 and 1930, leaving room for uncertainty regarding his true birth year.

villages like Sakhnovshchyna, trauma didn't need to be witnessed firsthand to leave a mark. It lingered – in strained silences, in the way people talked about the past, in the knowledge that survival had come at a price.

Wsewolod would later describe his early years with a subdued nostalgia.[103] There are few pastoral details, no sentimental recollections of fields or seasons – only the textures of family, repetition, and fear. His home life was built around extended kin, Orthodox rituals, and the quiet presence of dread. He grew up in a world where neighbours vanished, words could get you into trouble, and loyalty to the state was not optional. Soviet authority didn't stop at the village council. It reached into homes, classrooms, thoughts.

His education followed the path set for his generation. While earlier Skliars had trained for the clergy, Wsewolod entered the Soviet school system – designed not simply to teach, but to produce a new kind of citizen. Stalinism shaped him. A parish school had stood in Sakhnovshchyna since the 1890s,[104] but by the 1930s it had been absorbed into the Soviet system. Literacy campaigns, youth groups, cultural clubs – all tools to reshape village life, and with it, identity. Wsewolod probably benefited from the expanded access, but the lessons came wrapped in ideology. Russian replaced Ukrainian in

---

[103] In later reflections (2007), Wsewolod Skliar recalled his childhood home as "39 Klochkovska Street". No official records confirm this address in Sakhnovshchyna, but Klochkovska is the name of a major street in Kharkiv, roughly 90 kilometres away. The name may have been colloquial or misremembered. A 1941 German-issued identity card for Viktor Skliar instead lists "Mainstrasse 51", likely a renamed version of Sakhnovshchyna's main road under occupation.

[104] *Sakhnovshchyna Settlement Council. Historical Note. Accessed March 2025.*

the classroom. Marxist-Leninist slogans replaced prayer. Ukrainian culture, when mentioned at all, was framed as backward, something to leave behind.

And yet, the change was not total. At home, the Skliars spoke Ukrainian and kept their own rhythms of life. These small continuities – language, rituals, songs – were acts of resistance, even if they didn't name them as such. They weren't alone. Across Soviet Ukraine, many rural families kept Ukrainian as the language of the home, quietly preserving what they could while public life became more Russified. In homes like the Skliars', identity didn't endure through open defiance. It endured through the quiet, stubborn repetition of habits that refused to fade. Wsewolod would later reject Russian entirely, refusing to speak it even decades after resettling in the West.

The early 1940s brought a new kind of instability. First the Soviet annexation of western Ukraine, then the Nazi invasion. For a schoolboy in a contested region, war was not an abstraction. It was disruption, dislocation, death. In March 1943, during the Red Army's winter offensive, Wsewolod's mother, Evdokiya, was killed in a Soviet bombing raid. The loss did more than fracture his childhood. It marked a turning point. From that moment, survival was no longer just about the family. It became political.

Six years later, in an autobiographical note, Wsewolod wrote:

"At the age of fourteen, I was already thinking about the future of the Ukrainian people".[105]

These weren't the words of a seasoned exile, but of a boy still trying to find voice. It is hard not to be struck by their clarity, their conviction. But I don't read them as youthful ideology. I read it as grief, turned into purpose. His mother had been killed by the same state that claimed to liberate Ukraine. That trauma didn't drive him inward. It drove him toward defiance. And it leaves us with harder questions: how do you carry a burden you never chose? How does a child learn that exile itself is political?

Wsewolod was not alone. Among the children and teenagers who would later shape the postwar Ukrainian diaspora, many traced their political awakening to a single rupture – a parent's arrest, a bombing, a disappearance. Catastrophe did not always produce ideology. But it did create a need for meaning. For Wsewolod, that meaning took shape in a sense of national responsibility: not inherited, but imposed by loss.

[105] This autobiographical note was written by Wsewolod Skliar in 1949 on the final pages of a personal notebook otherwise devoted to technical instruction. It combines recollection with ideological assertion, echoing the tone and language common among nationalist youth circles of the time. Though declarative in style, the note was not produced for official use and is interpreted in this chapter with attention to both its testimonial and rhetorical character. A full copy is reproduced in *Appendix A: Autobiographical Note*, c. 1949.

The Blackthorn Forest: Defiance Takes Root, 1943–1945

By September 1943, Soviet forces were pressing westward, and the German retreat had begun. For many Ukrainians, this was not liberation, but renewed peril. Stalin's return brought the threat of arrest, deportation, or execution for anyone suspected of disloyalty – including those who had simply survived under German occupation. Among those forced to flee was fourteen-year-old Wsewolod Skliar.

He fled west with his father, crossing into Halychyna – a region where Ukrainian nationalist resistance had taken deep root. In the forests and hills around Sambir and Drohobych, the *Ukrainian Insurgent Army* (*UPA*) was fighting on two fronts: against the Nazis and bracing for the Soviet return. For a young refugee, the journey west was not only physical. It was formative. In this contested landscape, identity became a question of allegiance. Exile became the beginning of political life.

> *"In 1943, we were forced to evacuate from our native land to foreign soil, and to live our lives as God willed. We travelled a great distance from our homeland, turning to our kin in Halychyna. There, I took part alongside my comrades – those known as being from the blackthorn forest. I carried out certain tasks for our people, together with members of the UPA".*

At fourteen, Wsewolod became involved with the UPA in Halychyna. His cautious reference to "tasks" suggests pride—tempered by the weight of memory—and reflects the ambivalence that would later shape his rejection of violence in exile. His mention of the "blackthorn forest"[106] alluded to the hidden world of resistance. Wsewolod was unlikely to have taken up arms, but youth often served in auxiliary roles: as messengers, lookouts, runners. His involvement, however modest, marked an early alignment with the cause of Ukrainian independence.

At the time, the UPA was expanding fast. Founded in 1942 as the armed wing of the *Organisation of Ukrainian Nationalists* (*OUN*), it had launched a full-scale guerrilla war on three fronts: against Nazi occupiers, Soviet forces, and the Polish underground – all seen as threats to Ukrainian self-determination. By mid-1944, the UPA counted up to 40,000 fighters, supported by a dense civilian network.[107] For many, the UPA offered more than resistance. It offered meaning.

That legacy remains deeply contested. Between 1943 and 1945, the UPA and Polish underground forces engaged in brutal interethnic violence, especially in Volhynia and Eastern Galicia. Historians estimate tens of thousands of civilians were killed. For the UPA, these actions were framed as part of a national liberation struggle. They remain a source of lasting moral and political debate.

---

[106] "Blackthorn forest" translates the Ukrainian phrase *терновий ліс*, a poetic euphemism used in postwar nationalist writing to describe partisan life—especially among UPA fighters. The blackthorn shrub (*терен*) appears in Ukrainian folklore and song as a symbol of suffering and endurance. The phrase invoked both hardship and moral clarity in the face of occupation.

[107] *Ukrainian Insurgent Army in the Struggle for Freedom, OPIR*. (2023, July 1). Opir. https://opir.weareukraine.info/ukrainian-insurgent-army-birth-and-death-in-the-struggle-for-freedom/.

Figure 41: UPA partisans from the Ostroh Division in the forests near Surazh, December 1943. The UPA fought on multiple fronts during this period – against Nazi occupation, advancing Soviet forces, and the Polish underground.

Wsewolod's later writings show no attempt to justify this violence. His adult politics leaned toward cultural preservation, not militarism. But in 1943, the forest offered a kind of clarity that civilian life no longer could. For a boy who had lost his mother and his country, it may have felt like the only place left to begin.

By mid-1944, this resistance zone, too, became untenable. With the Red Army encroaching, Wsewolod and his father moved again – this time across the border into Austria. Along the way, they passed through Drohobych and Sambir:

> *"After some time in Halychyna, in the town of Sambir, we were again forced to evacuate – from*

Halychyna this time, as the front approached, bringing with it the terrorists, that is, the Bolsheviks.

We were forced to abandon Ukrainian land and travel to Germany. In Germany, I spent eight months working in a fascist forest, but I did not forget my duty".

Though the details are sparse, his testimony and surviving documents suggest he and his father were transferred between labour camps. He is believed to have worked in Heidenreichstein, most likely in a stone quarry. His certificate from the *Ukrainian Relief Committee*, issued in Gmünd and dated 3 January 1945, confirmed his Ukrainian nationality and authorised travel to Slovakia – offering fragile protection under displaced persons protocols.

IN KRYNICA

3.1.1945
Sparkasse der Stadt Gmünd, N.D.

Bescheinigung

Es wird hiermit bescheinigt, dass Herr /Frau/ . Skljar . . . .
. Wsewolod . . . . ukrainischen Volkszugehörigkeit und griech.
...abstammung ist und sich unter dem Schutz des Ukrainischen Hilfskomitees
in . Krynica . . . . befindet. Mit Genehmigung der zuständigen
Behörden begibt sich der Genannte mit seiner Familie/ . . . . Personen
nach . Slowakei . . . .
Alle militärischen und zivilen Dienststellen werden gebeten, dem Genannten jederzeit Schutz und Hilfe zu gewähren.

KRYNICA

Figure 42: Certificate issued to Wsewolod Skliar by the *Ukrainian Relief Committee* in mid-1944, stamped in Gmünd on 3 January 1945. It confirmed his Ukrainian nationality and authorised travel to Slovakia, providing protection under displaced persons protocols.

By July 1945, father and son had registered as *Displaced Persons* (*DPs*) in Landshut, Bavaria, in the American zone. Wsewolod, still only sixteen, had lived through famine, occupation, forced labour, and war. But his sense of political purpose had hardened, not dimmed:

> *"In 1944, Germany capitulated and I ended up in the American zone.*[108] *On German soil, I was engaged in agitation – above all, agitation among the people so that they would not return to the homeland, but would instead harden themselves with nationalist spirit and steel themselves against the Bolshevik invader-terrorist."*

This was a turning point – a rupture. Wsewolod's identity was forged not in school or scripture, but in flight and resistance. The forests had given him purpose. Exile would test whether he could carry it without losing himself.

His path was not exceptional. Across wartime Europe, a generation of Ukrainian youths were politicised not by manifestos, but by rupture – by movement, hunger, loss, and the hard clarity that trauma creates. Wsewolod's notebooks cast his role in principled terms. But his later writings – quieter, more considered – reflect a man who turned away from violence, from absolutes. His early

[108] There seems to be some confusion in Wsewolod's note with respect to dates. Germany did not capitulate until 1945, and primary records unequivocally show Wsewolod remained in Nazi occupied lands into 1945.

alignment with the nationalist cause was real. But so was the transformation that followed.

Exile's Crucible: Forging Purpose, 1945–1948

In 1945, the collapse of the Nazi regime left millions across Europe in limbo. For many, repatriation was not a return, but a threat. The Soviet Union moved quickly to reassert control over its former territories. But for displaced Ukrainians, especially those from the east, this was not a moment of relief. It was a final rupture. And, for some, a beginning. Exile stripped many of status. But it also opened space – for cultural preservation, for political engagement, for a life built from what had been lost.

Among the displaced was sixteen-year-old Wsewolod Skliar. Together with his father Viktor, he arrived in the American zone of occupied Germany, passing through Displaced Persons camps in Landshut and Bavaria. For many, these camps were places of waiting – liminal spaces between one homeland lost and another never fully granted. But for the young, they became proving grounds. Wsewolod's story was not unique. But it was emblematic. In exile, for a generation of stateless Ukrainians, survival was no longer the only task. The DP camps became the ground from which to construct identity.

This was not idle rhetoric. Within months of arrival, Wsewolod joined the *Ukrainian Committee for Niederbayern-Oberpfalz*, one of dozens of exile institutions created in the aftermath of war. In August 1945, he was issued an identity card in Regensburg and formally registered with the *Ukrainian Committee in Landshut*. In the absence of a state, these bodies offered assistance, coordinated housing, employment, documentation – and shielded DPs from forced return. Many were led by veterans of the nationalist underground or their children. Their purpose was both practical and symbolic: to protect the stateless, and to preserve a nation in absentia.

Wsewolod also joined the *Union of Ukrainian Youth* (*Спілка Української Молоді*, or *SUM*), a nationalist group committed to preserving Ukrainian identity through education and cultural life.[109] In the camps, SUM became a key hub for youth mobilisation and ideological formation. Wsewolod kept his SUM membership patch for life – its sunbeams and oak-leaves a badge of belonging in a world that no longer recognised his homeland.

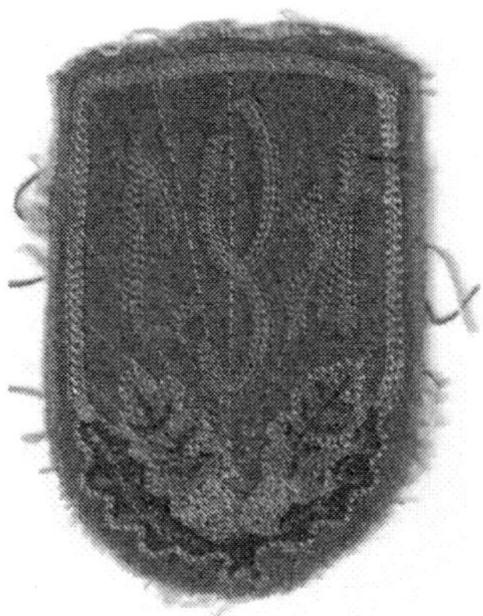

Figure 43 Wsewolod's embroidered patch from the *Union of Ukrainian Youth,* featuring oak leaves and sunrays. These symbols reflected the

[109] Wsewolod's membership card for the SUM identifies him as member 2190, having formally joined 14 September 1947.

organisation's mission to promote cultural resilience and ideological clarity among displaced youth.

Exile did not erase memory. It deepened it. For many Ukrainian DPs, the absence of territory made cultural preservation urgent. Sermons were copied by hand. Political tracts typed on scavenged machines. Wsewolod was not just a recipient of this material – he helped preserve and disseminate it. Among his possessions were wartime speeches from OUN leaders, underground bulletins, and sermons smuggled out of Soviet Ukraine. One, *For Eternal Peace of Their Souls*, mourned the victims of the 1933 Holodomor and condemned the Soviet state for engineering an "artificially prepared" famine. It was both remembrance and indictment. A statement that history, if not reclaimed, would be rewritten.

Among the most striking artefacts is Wsewolod's personal copy of the *Decalogue of the Ukrainian Nationalist* (*Декалог Українського Націоналіста*) – a ten-point creed circulated among partisans, exiles, and camp activists, likely acquired in Sambir.[110] The

[110] *The Decalogue of the Ukrainian Nationalist* was first drafted by Stepan Lenkavskyi in the 1920s and later revised by the *Organisation of Ukrainian Nationalists*. It set out a ten-point code demanding loyalty, sacrifice, and uncompromising devotion to the Ukrainian national cause. Disseminated among interwar nationalists, wartime partisans, and postwar émigré youth, it became a core text of ideological instruction. Some regarded it as a patriotic creed of moral clarity; others, especially in the postwar West, were troubled by its absolutism.
This book does not seek to rehabilitate or denounce the Decalogue. Rather, it presents it as a contextualised record: a document that shaped belief, identity, and action among the young in exile. Its inclusion here reflects how ideology was internalised – not to justify the creed, but to understand the world it created.
See *Appendix C* for a partial transcription, translation, and further commentary on its content.

Decalogue did not speak of policy. It spoke of sacrifice. It demanded readers love Ukraine more than themselves, hate its enemies without compromise, live with honour, obedience, readiness to die. For Wsewolod, this was no relic of wartime. It was a living document – kept alongside his prayer book and nationalist materials.

Yet its legacy was never simple. Composed during total war, the Decalogue's language of purity and hatred reflected a worldview forged in occupation and repression. For some, it became a source of spiritual discipline. For others, its absolutism – especially the call to hate Ukraine's enemies "with hatred and unrelenting struggle" – sat uneasily with postwar efforts at reconciliation.

Even noble ideals, when forged in the crucible of trauma and statelessness, can harden into moral absolutes. The postwar nationalist imagination was shaped by exile, persecution, war – conditions that fostered clarity of purpose, but often narrowed moral scope. That tension remains at the heart of the émigré Ukrainian political tradition, and its legacy.

Wsewolod's later writings reject that absoluteness. He carried forward the Decalogue's call to service and memory, but quietly let go of its most militant imperatives.[111]

The preservation of memory in exile was never neutral. The narratives Ukrainian émigrés preserved foregrounded martyrdom, heroism, sacrifice – but often downplayed internal dissent, interethnic complexity, or moral ambiguity. Those silences shaped

---

[111] For critical discussions of Ukrainian nationalist memory in exile and its contested legacies, see John-Paul Himka, Serhy Yekelchyk, or Andreas Umland.

the community's legacy. They still shape the debates over Ukrainian nationalist memory today.

In this context, nationalism was not just politics. It was survival. It was devotion. Like many exiled Ukrainians, Wsewolod saw Orthodoxy not only as faith, but as culture – one of the few institutions to survive tsarist repression and Soviet annihilation. In 1945, he obtained a prayer book printed for displaced Orthodox believers, its liturgies interspersed with patriotic hymns. For him, faith and national identity were not separate. They were entwined hopes. Both rooted in suffering, both shaped by resistance, both tied to a promise of resurrection – spiritual and political.

Figure 44: Wsewolod's copy of the Decalogue (c. 1943) and a Ukrainian Christmas postcard (1947) made and distributed by the *Ukrainian Insurgent Army*.

By the time he left Ganacker camp in early 1948, Wsewolod was no longer just reacting to history. He had joined a generation shaping it from exile. What had begun in the forests of Halychyna as youthful defiance had become, in the DP camps, a programme of resistance. For thousands like him, these camps were not a pause in history. They were its continuation by other means.

Reading as Resistance

Exile reshaped daily life. But for many Ukrainians in the DP camps, it also redefined what it meant to be free. Without a homeland, they turned to memory. Without institutions, they built them anew – in schools, in youth groups, and above all, in words. Books, poems, and song circulated not as leisure, but as resistance.

In the camps, barracks and makeshift libraries of Bavaria, displaced Ukrainians reconstructed their national identity line by line. Political activism and cultural survival were not separate efforts. They were the same struggle. The same hands that typed leaflets by day copied poetry by candlelight. This, too, was a form of organisation – not of soldiers or votes, but of thought.

Wsewolod Skliar lived inside this world. Outwardly, he turned toward political organising. Inwardly, he found his anchor in literature. For him, as for many in exile, the written word offered both clarity and refuge. Soviet Ukraine had criminalised Ukrainian identity, imprisoned its poets, erased its past. But in the DP camps of Germany, a fragile, unofficial literary network took root. Wsewolod was both a reader and a participant.

In 1947, he compiled a handwritten list of books he had read or hoped to read. He owned only a few, but their titles tell us much: histories of Ukraine, political philosophy, novels, scientific texts. For someone with few possessions, making space for books was not practical. It was ideological.

At the centre of the list was *Zakhar Berkut*, Ivan Franko's historical novel of a 13th-century Carpathian village resisting Mongol invasion. The community survives not by force, but through unity, sacrifice, and discipline – an idealised image of collective resilience that spoke directly to the exile condition. Franko, the blacksmith's son turned national poet, wrote as both a patriot and a critic of injustice. His novel offered young DPs like Wsewolod not just a parable of survival, but a model of civic clarity: a reminder that loss need not mean disappearance.

Equally important was Lesia Ukrainka. Born Larysa Kosach, her work had been banned in Soviet Ukraine but circulated in exile – copied by hand, recited at gatherings, passed from notebook to notebook. Her resistance was moral, not militant. *"I have in my heart that which does not die"*, she wrote. If Franko gave the exile his spine, Ukrainka gave him his composure.

His list also included titles on science and modern technology – including *The Atom and Its Energy*. This eclecticism suggests more than nationalism. It reflects a broader intellectual appetite, a desire to understand the world that now awaited him. The camps were not enclosed spaces. They were staging grounds – for movement, for reinvention, for thought.

Through books, displaced Ukrainians reconnected with a history they had been told to forget. Through poetry, they reasserted their humanity. For Wsewolod, reading was not an escape from loss. It was how he learned to endure it.

Training for a New Life

Survival meant more than shelter or food. It demanded imagination. For those who could not go home – and dared not look back – the future had to be built from what remained. Books gave direction. But it was skills that gave agency. Like language and literature, vocational training became part of a larger task: to rebuild identity in the ruins, one trade – and one page – at a time.

The Allied authorities understood this. From 1945, vocational training became a cornerstone of DP camp policy. Funded by UNRRA and later the IRO, courses sprang up across Bavaria: carpentry, tailoring, radio mechanics, welding, domestic service. For most displaced persons, especially the young, these were not academic diversions. They were lifelines. Stateless, often stripped of qualifications, DPs had to prepare for futures in countries they had never seen. Every certificate earned was a step away from dependency.

Wsewolod Skliar was one of thousands who entered these programmes. By late 1946, at Ganacker DP Camp, he enrolled in multiple tracks. His surviving notebooks document training in three fields: mechanics, electronics, and cooking. In small ledger books, he recorded electrical circuits, resistance tables, safety procedures. In 1947, he passed a hygiene inspection and earned a food-service certificate. That June, at eighteen, he obtained a German driver's licence – proof not only of mobility, but of intent.

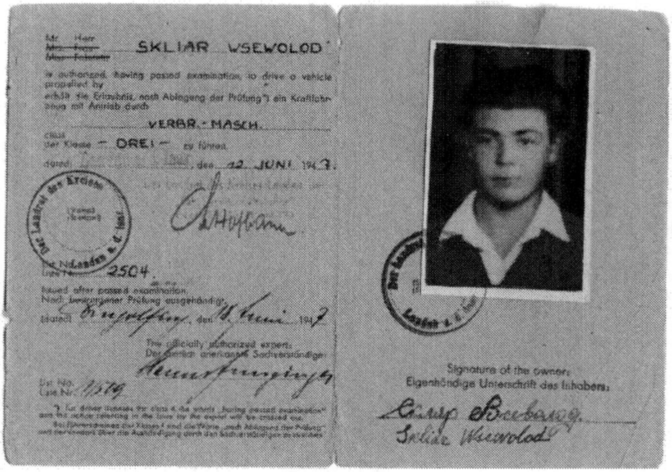
Mr. Herr SKLIAR WSEWOLOD
is authorized, having passed examination, to drive a vehicle propelled by
erhält die Erlaubnis, nach Ablegung der Prüfung*) ein Kraftfahrzeug mit Antrieb durch
VERBR.-MASCH.
class
der Klasse – DREI – zu führen.
dated ..., den 12. JUNI 1947.
2504
Issued after passed examination.
Nach bestandener Prüfung ausgehändigt.
dated ..., den ... 1947
The officially authorized expert:
Der amtlich anerkannte Sachverständige:
List No.
Liste Nr. 1579
Signature of the owner:
Eigenhändige Unterschrift des Inhabers:
Sklia Wsewolod

Figure 45: Wsewolod's German driver's licence, 1947. In the camps, such documents signalled progress – a new foothold after displacement.

The kitchens proved formative. They gave him a trade, but also rhythm and discipline – a structure that would anchor his later life in England. Like many young DPs, he found in labour a form of dignity. It was not just a job. It was a foothold in a world that had tried to expel him.

Yet the deeper shift was philosophical. These courses did not erase the past. But they refused to be governed by it. For young Ukrainians like Wsewolod, learning to cook, weld, or wire a radio was not an abandonment of politics or principle. It was their continuation – by other means. He would not return to Soviet Ukraine. He would not remain stateless. He would not be a ward of history. He would build a life. And he would do it on his own terms.

By early 1948, his application for resettlement had been accepted by the *English Labour Mission*[112]. Like many Ukrainians, he registered through the camp authorities and completed screening by Allied intelligence. He left Ganacker for Hamburg, processed for travel under the European Volunteer Worker scheme. What awaited him was uncertain. But it was a beginning.

* * *

On 12 March 1948, he arrived at the port of Harwich.[113]

He was nineteen. His mother was dead. His homeland was behind barbed wire. But he had his language. And the memory of what had been taken. In the camps of Germany, he had begun to write – and found others like him: exiles who refused to forget, who spoke of Ukraine not as a lost country, but as something carried forward, even when it no longer had borders.

---

[112] A British government recruitment agency established after the Second World War to select displaced persons (DPs) for resettlement in the UK under the European Volunteer Worker (EVW) scheme. Operating from camps across Germany, including Hamburg and Hanover, the Mission prioritised applicants deemed physically fit, skilled, or adaptable to postwar labour demands.

[113] A U.S. Military Government certificate issued in Frankfurt am Main on 17 February 1948 identified Wsewolod Skliar as a 19-year-old Polish-Ukrainian coal miner en-route to England. Lacking any official documents – "lost during the war", as the certificate states – he was authorised to travel on a temporary identity paper in lieu of a passport. The certificate, stamped on his departure (3 March 1948) listed his intended arrival port as Harwich and bears later markings from the Cambridge & District Food Office, indicating his initial processing in eastern England. A photograph attached to the certificate shows him holding an identification number, dressed formally, looking solemn and composed.

He was no longer the boy who fled Poltava. Grief had given him direction. But that direction was not a destination. It was a burden. A duty inherited as much as chosen.

The war had taken his childhood. What remained was not purpose alone, but something quieter, heavier – the task of holding on, of carrying forward a memory that exile could not erase, but could never fully restore.

A Visual Archive of Displacement, 1945–1948

These photographs, taken between 1946 and 1948, were preserved by Wsewolod Skliar throughout his life. Each was given to him in the final years of displacement – during his time in the camps at Eugenbach, Ergolding, and Ganacker – by friends, colleagues, and companions. Some may have been made with his own camera: a battered pre-war Zeiss Ikon BOB 510/2, likely acquired during those years of exile. These photographs, often bearing handwritten inscriptions: brief dedications, messages of friendship, and simple reminders to be remembered. What follows is a visual fragment of that world – quiet testimonies to friendship, resilience, and the fleeting bonds of camp life.

Figure 46 (left): Wsewolod (standing) with a camp companion, Ganacker Camp, 1947 – 48.

Figure 47 (right): Wsewolod and Viktor Skliar outside their barracks, Ganacker Camp, Bavaria, 1948. Taken shortly before their emigration to England, this rare portrait captures father and son in matching suits and ties.

Figure 48: Wsewolod Skliar (top left) with carpentry workshop colleagues, Ergolding Camp, 16 January 1946. Inscribed: *"In long remembrance to V.S. from Vasya, Henia, Volodia, and Vitya – friends from the carpentry workshop".*

Figure 49 (left): Marusia Slyvka with child, Ganacker Camp, 3 December 1947. *"To my acquaintance Wsewolod Skliar, during our time in Ganacker Camp".*

Figure 50 (right): Wsewolod Skliar (right) with two friends and a young child outside Ganacker barracks, c. 1947. This photograph captures a quieter, more intimate moment in camp life. No dedication survives, but the men's pocket squares and jackets suggest it was a special occasion.

Figure 51 : Romik Hanna, Ganacker Camp, 9 February 1948. Given to Wsewolod with the words: *"I give my photograph as an unforgettable remembrance"*.

Figure 52: Group portrait from Ganacker Displaced Persons Camp, Bavaria, 12 February 1947. Dedicated on the reverse to Wsewolod Skliar by Anton Rybalko, Petro Ratii, and Mykola Haiie: *"A memory forever, during the time of our stay in Germany"*.

CHAPTER 11

Silence as Legacy: Wsewolod Skliar in Postwar Britain, 1948–1954

Скажи мині правду, мій добрий козаче,
Що діяти серцю, як серце болить?
Як важко застогне, як гірко заплаче,
Як дуже без щастя воно защемить?

Tell me the truth, my good Cossack:
What should the heart do when it aches?
When it groans with sorrow, weeps bitterly –
When it throbs for want of happiness?

– Oleksandr Afanasiev-Chuzhbyinsky[114],
from *What Was on My Heart*, 1855

[114] Oleksandr Afanasiiev-Chuzhbyinsky (1816–1875) was a Ukrainian and Russian-language writer, folklorist, and memoirist born in Hlukhiv, then part of the Russian Empire. Though better known for prose sketches and ethnographic writing, his lyrical

The war was over, but exile had only just begun. For Wsewolod Skliar and tens of thousands like him, resettlement in Britain marked not safety, but suspension. Their nations had been erased, their status undefined. In the absence of home, they built memory. In the absence of rights, they built routines. And in the absence of sovereignty, they built Ukraine – imagined, organised, and sustained from afar.

When I began drafting this chapter, I assumed it would be the easiest. I knew Wsewolod. I had seen him. Spoken to him. There were photographs, letters, records. His daughters are still alive. Unlike so many others in this book, he left behind traces I could follow. I wanted to tell his story. But it turned out to be the hardest chapter to write.

Not because the sources were thin – although many were. And not because the events were dramatic – they weren't. It was difficult because the man himself, the one I thought I knew, kept slipping away, the closer I looked. I expected to find a story of transition: from war to peace, from displacement to rootedness, from political fervour to domestic life. But what I found was something quieter, more ambiguous. He lived. He worked. He endured. And in doing so, he left behind almost nothing – except for everything.

The deeper challenge, though, was not just personal. It was historical. I struggled to understand what this life – a life spent mostly outside Ukraine, mostly in kitchens, mostly silent – could tell us about Ukraine's history. Wsewolod didn't write a memoir.

---

poetry – often Cossack-themed – explored loss, restlessness, and romantic nationalism. His verse contributed to the emotional register of 19th-century Ukrainian identity, particularly in exile and elegy.

He didn't found an organisation. He rarely spoke of the war, and never returned home. His was not the kind of story historians tend to centre.

And yet it is precisely in these margins – in the quiet, in the repetition – that something essential remains. Because Wsewolod's life is not separate from the story of Ukraine. It is what happened when history moved elsewhere. When the borders shifted, and the slogans faded, and survival took a different form. It is the life of a man shaped by war, by loss, by ideology – and then shaped again by family, by work, by habit.

What follows is not a narrative of transformation. There is no dramatic pivot, no moment of reinvention. There is, instead, a slow reconstitution. A life held together by language, by memory, by structure. A legacy not declared, but practiced – daily, quietly, without spectacle.

Arrival in Exile, 1948–1950

Wsewolod arrived in Britain 12 March 1948, one of over 80,000 European Volunteer Workers recruited to help rebuild a country still emerging from war.[115] Most were from Eastern Europe. Few had come by choice. Stateless and unprotected, they were assigned unfamiliar jobs, subject to movement restrictions, and required to report to police. Each step was conditional. Alien registration

---

[115] *European Volunteer Workers* (*EVWs*) were recruited from postwar DP camps to fill labour shortages in the UK. Though formally "volunteers," they were assigned to specific jobs and hostels under state control, often with no pathway to permanent residence. Data on EVWs sourced from: The National Archives (UK). *Colonial Office Working Party on the Recruitment of West Indians for United Kingdom Industries*. August 12, 2009. Accessed March 2025.

booklets tracked their movements.[116] Every change of work or residence required official approval. It was, in effect, a second displacement – this time administered in paperwork.

And yet, from the earliest records and diary entries, it's clear Wsewolod was not simply adapting. He was already mobilising. Amid labour placements and hostel beds, between train journeys and night shifts, he set about rebuilding a version of the country he had lost. These were deliberate acts of conviction – attempts to assert identity, continuity, and political presence in the absence of a homeland.

Wsewolod's first weeks were spent at West Wratting Camp in Cambridgeshire, where he was processed alongside other young men from the Ukrainian diaspora. He noted little in his diary beyond a walk with his friend Anton and the hunger that followed. "*Came back like a 'wolf'*", he wrote.[117] There is no sense of drama in those early entries. Just fatigue, hunger, and a quiet acclimatisation to new limits.[118]

---

[116] The *Aliens Order of 1914* imposed strict registration and movement controls on foreign nationals in Britain. Though wartime in origin, it remained in force after 1945 and governed the lives of EVWs like Wsewolod Skliar. Under its rules, displaced persons and European Volunteer Workers were required to register with the police and obtain government permission for any change in residence or employment.

[117] The original Ukrainian of this diary entry, along with the others cited in this chapter, can be found in *Appendix A: Selected Diary Excerpts*.

[118] Wsewolod had known Anton Rybalko from Ganacker DP camp in Bavaria. Their re-encounter in Britain reflects the broader continuity of refugee social networks across resettlement.

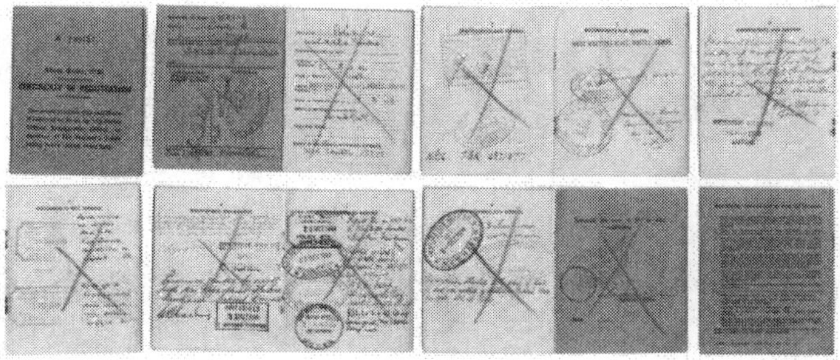

Figure 53: Wsewolod Skliar's *Alien Registration Certificate*, issued in March 1948 – evidence of a life administered through paperwork, where exile was recorded before it was recognised.

By week's end, he was placed at the British Portland Cement factory in Sundon, working alongside another Ukrainian, Mr Vasylovych. The labour – unloading stone from freight wagons – was intense and unfamiliar. "*I didn't do anything*", he wrote, "*only struggled desperately with the work, but it felt frightening and eerie*". On 28 March, he added: "*I was too late. I couldn't manage to remove the last [load] from the wagon, so Vasylovych had to support me*". It was far from the civic or intellectual contribution he had once imagined. Reflecting later, he described this as "*the first beginnings in English work*" – a life that went on, he wrote, "*filled only with work – no real success to speak of*".

His alien registration card records postings in Brighton and Chichester, including a period clearing unexploded ordnance.[119]

[119] Between 1948 and 1951, Wsewolod Skliar moved repeatedly between hostels, military camps, and temporary lodgings across southern England – a pattern shared by many *European Volunteer Workers*. His known locations include Leighton Buzzard,

The work was gruelling, the routines numbing, and the future uncertain. And yet something else persisted beneath the exhaustion: a refusal to let meaning vanish with displacement. If he could not fight for Ukraine with weapons or policy, he would do it with memory, with language, with culture. That belief didn't disappear in exile. It adapted.

Rebuilding Ukraine from Afar, 1950–1954

Beneath the surface of this enforced mobility, another life was taking shape. He joined the *Association of Ukrainians in Great Britain* (*AUGB*), contributed to émigré publications, and organised cultural events. In 1949, he wrote: *"I organised a drama circle specifically for the advancement of culture and the elevation of the Ukrainian spirit"*. He copied scripts by hand, recruited a cast, and kept the project going even as others fell away.

Billingshurst, Luton, Site 4 near Chichester, Chichester, Mundham, West Wratting (Cambridgeshire), Newhaven, Folkestone, Sevenoaks, Dover, Swingate, Shorncliffe, Woolwich, London, Leicester, and Victoria. Longer placements included the *WSCAEC* Hostel in Chichester (1 December 1948 – 31 October 1949) and the War Department EVW Camp at The Fort, Newhaven (1 November 1949 – 1 July 1951). These movements reflect the instability of the period: EVWs were often relocated with little notice, sent where labour was needed, and housed in accommodation that was rarely permanent.

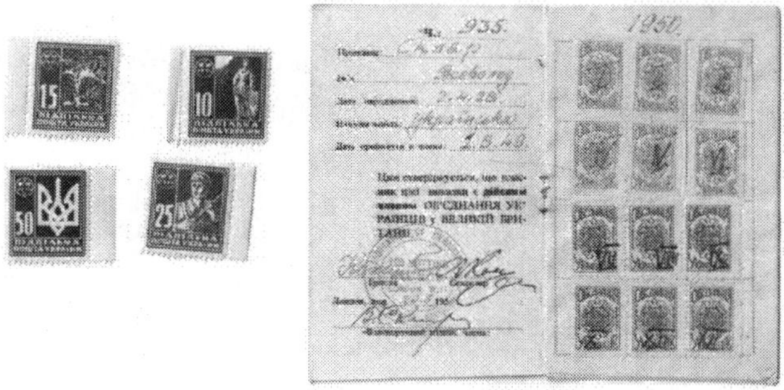

Figure 54: Wsewolod Skliar's membership booklet for the *Association of Ukrainians in Great Britain (right)*, stamped through 1950, records small but regular contributions. Alongside, symbolic stamps issued by nationalist groups (left) offered a different kind of currency – part receipt, part reminder.

He also contributed financially. Membership booklets from the time show regular donations to Ukrainian nationalist organisations, including the *Organisation of Ukrainian Nationalists* (*OUN*). Stamped receipts and symbolic postage marked these contributions – tokens of loyalty to a state that no longer existed.

But loyalty was more than financial. In the years that followed, what had begun in the camps as preservation evolved into interpretation, myth, and, at times, reinvention. Across the émigré press, in leaflets and circulars preserved in Wsewolod's collection – many linked to OUN and UPA networks – wartime loss was reimagined as national sacrifice. Some narratives cast defeat as a seed of future resurrection and spiritual rebirth. Others fused mourning with militancy. In one striking example, OUN-B[120] publications from the early 1950s

---

[120] OUN-B refers to the Banderite wing of the *Organisation of Ukrainian Nationalists*, led by Stepan Bandera after a 1940 split. More militant than the rival Melnyk faction

invoked Babyn Yar – the ravine where tens of thousands of Jews were massacred by Nazi forces – as a symbolic site of Ukrainian nationalist martyrdom, layering their own commemorations onto a place of shared and contested trauma. [121]

Such rhetoric, often declarative and mournful, offered exiles what one could call a moral architecture: a way to transform exile into purpose, loss into legacy. It was less a reckoning than a reaffirmation – a mythic continuity in place of a fractured present.

In that atmosphere of mourning and mobilisation, political commitment became one of the few available anchors. Wsewolod was among those who took up that work – speaking at *Federation* events in the early 1950s and contributing to émigré publications.

Yet the strain showed. His diaries reveal moments of emotional fatigue and disillusionment with the fractious nature of the diaspora. In 1953, he wrote: "*In England, there are over seven Ukrainian parties, and each of them conducts politics in its own*

(OUN-M), it advocated for Ukrainian statehood through revolutionary means and became closely associated with the Ukrainian Insurgent Army during and after the Second World War.

[121] Examples of such rhetoric, preserved in Wsewolod Skliar's personal collection of wartime and early post-war materials, include a 1952 OUN-B leaflet titled *Холодний Бабин Яр* (*Cold Babyn Yar*), which commemorates the execution of the OUN "*Kyiv group*" by Nazi forces and frames Babyn Yar—more widely known as a Holocaust site—as a symbol of nationalist martyrdom. An undated UPA pamphlet, *За що бореться Українська Повстанча Армія (УПА)?* (*What Is the Ukrainian Insurgent Army Fighting For?*), presents the UPA's armed struggle against both Nazi Germany and Soviet Bolshevism in heroic terms of national liberation. A further document, an excerpt from the *Statute of the Organisation of Ukrainian Nationalists (Banderites)*, outlines OUN-B's revolutionary goals and ideological code. These texts illustrate how postwar émigré circles crafted a moral framework that mythologised loss, legitimised resistance, and upheld a vision of national continuity.

way... these very parties bitterly quarrelled into even smaller splinter groups, and this leads to complete anarchy! Every time, one hears various quarrels, insults... it leads to serious troubles". His frustration was not rare. Across the diaspora, ideological passion often gave way to exhaustion. Organisations thrived. Cultural groups met. Fundraisers circulated stamps and pamphlets. But no unified vision prevailed. Memory was preserved through coexistence, as opposed to consensus.[122]

Figure 55: Wsewolod Skliar speaking at a Ukrainian political gathering in Britain, c.1950. His public activism in the 1950s reflected the diaspora's struggle to reconcile nationalist ideals with exile's constraints.

To invest so much in a cause – to give your time, your money, your voice – only to watch it splinter around you. The speeches and

[122] The postwar Ukrainian diaspora was not ideologically unified. Major divisions existed between those aligned with the *Organisation of Ukrainian Nationalists* (and its various wings), supporters of the *Ukrainian People's Republic in Exile*, and more apolitical cultural groups. These fault lines shaped émigré politics throughout the Cold War and remain the subject of ongoing historical debate.

fundraisers continued, but I imagine the effort began to feel heavier. Not because he stopped believing, but because belief alone was no longer enough. His diary is full of energy in these years, but it is not a steady energy. At times, it reads like an attempt to hold things together – in politics, in language, in self. At others, it barely holds at all. The lines grow more crowded, the frustration more raw. Commitment offered structure, but it also exposed the cracks. And I think some part of him began to break under the weight of trying to make it matter.

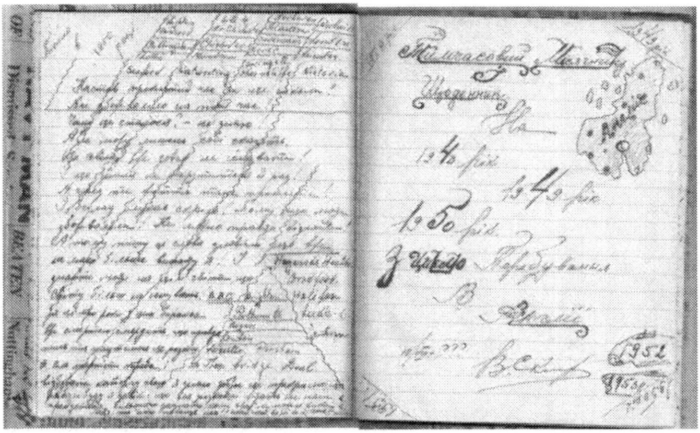

Figure 56: Pages from Wsewolod Skliar's diary, dated 1950. Part personal record, part psychological map, they show not only a list of towns across England but the agitated scrawl of a young man adrift. Between locations and years, his pen loops and crowds the page – less a narrative than an outpouring. The visual disorder reflects the emotional state behind the words: restlessness, fatigue, and the attempt to impose structure on a dislocated life.

Frustration ran through his diary entries – not just political disappointment, but personal anguish, fatigue, and disorientation. His writing, at times, became almost unbearable to read: a litany of doubt, of a, of a young man trying to find shape in a world that had been stripped of meaning. In one entry from 1950, he writes:

> *"The damned time has come, like never before! Everything went mad in that moment! Why is this happening? – I don't know! And I can't even tell myself that the world has long ceased to exist! This earth cannot turn even once! Because of this life – so cursed! And chaos weeps everywhere! Because people have gone mad. Justice could not be found".*

I don't know what prompted this. There's no accompanying explanation, no reference to events or people. But it doesn't feel abstract. It feels like a plea of desperation. And reading it now, across time and language, I want to answer it. To say something. But of course I can't. Maybe he found his own answer – in family, in politics, in work, in the structure that came later. Or maybe the writing itself was the answer: not a solution, but a release. A way to speak when nothing else could hold the weight.

Life in Britain offered small anchors. In Newhaven's Fort Sussex by 1950, Wsewolod balanced work with attempts at normalcy. The years prior had been consumed by study, his diary noting, "*The years 1948–49 were dedicated to studying English. Day and night, sitting at my desk with books, I paid no attention to the fact that I was young*". Language was a lifeline, though it isolated him. "*Spending nearly a full year in Mundham, I didn't even get to know any kind of Miss – all because I was studying English*", he wrote, a fleeting connection to a teacher never blossoming. By February 1950, he was in Folkestone, exploring the town and seeking connection at a local club, where he met an Englishwoman. "*February passes, with no romance in sight*", he noted, a hint of longing beneath his practicality.

Social moments brought glimmers of joy, though they were often solitary. Wsewolod's friend from Germany, A. Rybalko, struggled to adapt, his mind unravelling under exile's weight. "*Back in 1948, I had a best friend from Germany – A. Rybalko – who, because of various thoughts and anxieties, lost his mind*", Wsewolod recalled. Rybalko's visions of "*bombs, angels, and so on*" haunted their evenings, a stark reminder of the war they'd fled. Yet Wsewolod pressed on, holding onto his Ukrainian roots through language and memory. These early years, marked by quiet study and fleeting encounters, showed a young man carving out space for connection amidst the dislocation of exile.

By the early 1950s, another shift had begun. Wsewolod enrolled in evening classes at Hammersmith Technical College for Women – one of the few institutions that accepted male DPs. There, he trained in catering.[123] Many displaced persons had arrived as doctors, engineers, teachers. But in postwar Britain, qualifications didn't travel. Kitchens, fields, and factories became the way forward.[124]

Most Ukrainians were directed into agriculture or manual labour. But Wsewolod already knew kitchens – from Germany, from the hostels. It was a narrow path: long hours, hygiene exams, kitchen

---

[123] In 1951, Wsewolod enrolled in evening courses at Hammersmith Technical College for Women – an unusual choice, but one of the few institutions accepting male DPs. He completed a City & Guilds qualification in basic catering, studying nutrition, hygiene, and commercial food preparation. For a young man who had grown up amid war and flight, the classroom was a quiet victory. He subsequently completed a diploma over three years.

[124] In 1950 over half of Ukrainian male EVWs were assigned to farming. Women were steered into textiles and domestic service. Data from: Krawec, Roman. "European Voluntary Workers." *Ukrainians in the UK*. Accessed March 2025.

drills. But it offered something rare: predictability. An avenue forward.

He began work at St. Charles Hospital in Ladbroke Grove, first as a kitchen assistant, later as a cook. He moved into a shared house with his father in Paddington, whom he now supported. Their lives were shaped by shift patterns, communal living, and the quiet demands of postwar London[125]. He still attended diaspora meetings, but less often. He still gave, but less visibly. Slowly, the sharp edges of political engagement gave way to something steadier.

In 1954, after more than a year at St. Charles, Wsewolod left. There had been a disagreement with the head of the kitchen – details are sparse – but his diary captures the moment with typical understatement: *"As for me – I don't play with fate, whether it turns out good or bad"*. He said goodbye to the staff. *"Some didn't believe I was leaving after thirteen months"*, he wrote. *"But later, you'll come to understand it was deserved"*. The next day, he planned to visit a new kitchen – an American one. *"What I'll end up doing"*, he added, *"in the results to come, it will become clear"*.

[125] The house, 270 Gloucester Terrace, was owned by Adrian Kohut (1914–1979), a prominent émigré figure who later chaired the Federation of Ukrainians in Great Britain (1953–1956). Though not a Ukrainian enclave, the property's ownership placed Wsewolod and Viktor within the broader orbit of organised civic life in exile. Despite Kohut's public standing, his relationship with the family was, at times, strained; during Julia's hospital stay following the birth of her first child, she was unexpectedly evicted from the property.

Figure 57: Chef Wsewolod Skliar, photographed on 12 August 1954 while working at the U.S. Air Force Officers' Club in South Ruislip.

That kitchen turned out to be the U.S. Air Force Officers' Club in Ruislip. The work came with formality, stability, and a salaried wage. It suited him. He was precise, attentive, and respected by his supervisors. The pay was modest, but the job was stable. It gave him a place to stand.[126]

As I trace these years – his first six in Britain – I see a man searching not just for stability, but for purpose. And I think he found it, at least for a time. Not in ease or comfort, but in structure, in contribution, in control. The ideals he carried from Ukraine hadn't faded; they had been threaded into the routines of daily life. Drama circles, nationalist meetings, the discipline of the kitchen – they

[126] Wsewolod's pay at the U.S. Air Force Officers' Club was £9 per week – modest by contemporary standards, but significantly more stable than previous placements.

were all, in their way, expressions of the same conviction: that his life in exile could still be shaped by meaning.

In trauma literature, there is a concept of inward turn – when the external world becomes too unstable, and a person begins to rebuild from within. I think Wsewolod was somewhere along that path. The intensity was still there. The political fire hadn't gone out. But it had found new containers: work, repetition, precision. Silence hadn't taken hold yet – but I can see it forming. The outlines were beginning to show.

* * *

By 1954, Wsewolod's fight for Ukraine had woven itself into Britain's rhythms – drama circles, speeches, kitchen shifts. Yet beneath this public struggle, a quieter defiance persisted. In hostel rooms, late at night, he turned to an old notebook. There, in careful script, he preserved poems – verses once learned by heart, now copied by hand. Folk songs. Soldier's ballads. Nationalist laments. None were his own, yet each line tethered him to a homeland slipping from view.

These pages, unknown to all, echoed a lineage of Ukrainian poetry long threatened by silence – a tradition passed across generations, often in secret, and sometimes at great cost. As his days filled with work and purpose, his nights became a quiet refusal: to forget, to yield, to let language vanish. If the world no longer asked for his voice, he wrote anyway. Not to be heard. But to remember.

CHAPTER 12
A Chorus of Echoes: Wsewolod Skliar and the Poetry of Witness,

І дивно: я і я. Тоді й тепер. Що є спільного? – Абсолютно нічого. А проте це ж таки я, той самий...

"And strangely: I and I. Then and now. What is shared? – Absolutely nothing. And yet, it is still me, the same..."

– Mykhailo Yalovy[127] alias Iulian Shpol, from *The Golden Foxes*, 1928

---

[127] Mykhailo Yalovy (1895–1937), also known by the pseudonym Iulian Shpol, was a poet, prose writer, and editor associated with the Executed Renaissance. A leader in Ukraine's literary avant-garde, he was arrested during Stalin's purges and shot at Sandarmokh.

The suitcase, a silent repository of a life upended, held many fragments of Wsewolod Skliar's past. Yet, nestled among official papers and worn identity cards, one notebook contained something very unexpected: pages filled with Ukrainian poems in his unmistakable, careful script.

The careful man I had known in silence seemed a world away from the emotion in those lines – love, exile, defiance. It was easy to want to believe these were his own compositions, a secret testament to the turmoil of his youth.

The reality was more complex. He hadn't written them. Or not all of them. Some were copied, others recorded – verses remembered, overheard, or passed between voices. A few may have been his own.

With dedicated investigation, I could trace the lineage of verses by Lesia Ukrainka, whose fierce hope defied despair; lines from Volodymyr Sosiura, whose lyricism captured the soul of Ukraine; and even melodies attributed to Yaroslav Barnych, whose songs became popular during the struggles for independence. Interspersed were much older Cossack *dumy* and laments, finding new resonance in a modern exile. Many other entries remained unattributed, their specific origins perhaps lost to the informal pathways of oral tradition or the fragmented archives of a displaced people – or, perhaps, even written by Wsewolod.

What was most striking were the variations. Many of the poems and songs recorded in Wsewolod's notebook differed, sometimes subtly, sometimes significantly, from their more formally published counterparts. This suggests a deeply personal and organic process of preservation. He may have been writing them down from memory, the lines shaped by the cadences he recalled from childhood or from

DP camp barracks and émigré gatherings. Perhaps he copied them from other aging, handwritten notebooks passed from hand to hand, themselves vessels of an evolving tradition. Or maybe, in the quiet solitude of his English hostel rooms, after long shifts in unfamiliar kitchens, the act of writing became a form of internal dialogue, where the remembered words of others intertwined with the contours of his own experience. Each page, filled with that careful, deliberate script, was more than just a collection of verses; it was an act of devotion.

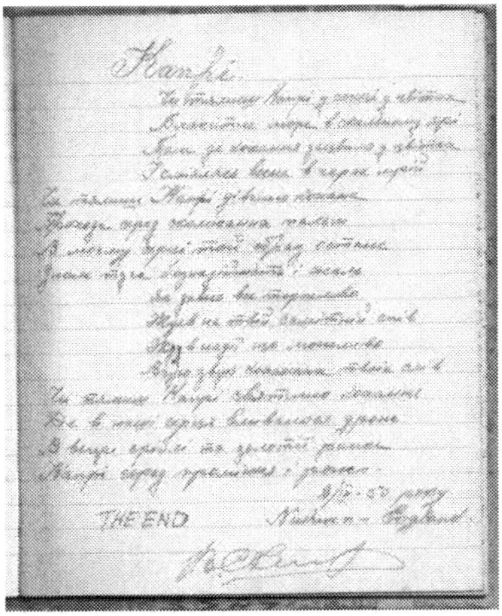
Капрі.

THE END

Figure 58: A typical page from Wsewolod Skliar's notebook, featuring the handwritten poem 'Kapri' – provenance unknown – dated Newhaven, England, April 2, 1950 and signed by Wsewolod. The notebook's worn pages, filled with careful script, reflect widespread cultural preservation by emigrants.

This painstaking work of recording was not merely a pastime. It was imbued with a sense of purpose, a connection to a homeland that was, by then, physically inaccessible but emotionally omnipresent.

In a diary entry from 1949, penned during his early, unsettling years in Britain, he articulated this drive:

> *"This diary is not being written for journalism, but only for my own interest, so that in the future I might return to it, when I am home again... I write about my experiences in England, and also about daily life, its sorrows and thoughts about my native land, about my dear Ukraine".*[128]

Like many Ukrainian emigrants in the United Kingdom, even in exile, he imagined return. And in copying these verses, a glimmer of that return remained.

A Carried Tradition

Wsewolod's impulse to record and safeguard cultural fragments was far from unique; it was a defining characteristic of the Ukrainian diaspora, and indeed, a recurring pattern in Ukrainian history whenever its culture faced suppression. Across the devastated landscapes of postwar Europe, this act of literary preservation became a cornerstone of survival and identity.

Under Nazi rule, Ostarbeiters – forced labourers, many of them Ukrainian – composed verses that documented loss, exile, and the struggle to retain humanity. In displaced persons camps, poetry was copied by hand and passed between beds. In exile communities, banned histories were printed in basements. Newspapers

---

[128] This excerpt is drawn from Wsewolod Skliar's handwritten diary. For the full transcription and editorial note on orthography and interpretation, see *Appendix A: Foreword to Diary (1951, Britain)*.

flourished.[129] Émigré networks grew, sustained by letters, shared books, and reproduced verse.

Wsewolod himself was part of these networks, maintaining contact with figures like Mykola Francuzenko, a fellow Ukrainian writer who would later broadcast for Radio Liberty and Voice of America, a friendship likely forged in the shared experiences of the 1940s and sustained through letters for decades.

To write, to copy, to circulate Ukrainian literature, especially poetry, under such circumstances, was an act laden with meaning. It was a quiet but determined refusal of erasure. One recorded these words because one remembered, and in the political landscape of the mid-20th century, for a Ukrainian, remembering itself was a dangerous, often politically charged, act.

This instinct to preserve, to make words a vessel of national endurance, had deep historical roots. In the mid-19th century, Taras Shevchenko, Ukraine's poet and a figure of almost sacred national importance, composed much of his most powerful work while under strict tsarist surveillance and during his harsh exile. His poems, though banned by imperial censors and deemed inflammatory, were smuggled across the vast Russian Empire, copied by hand, memorised by illiterate villagers, and whispered in secret gatherings from one generation to the next. Shevchenko's

---

[129] Ukrainian diaspora presses after the war played a critical role in sustaining cultural memory and political identity. Among the most influential were the Shevchenko Scientific Society (Paris and New York), which preserved banned scholarship and historical studies, and the Association of Ukrainian Writers Abroad (Munich and later New York), which published literature censored inside Soviet Ukraine. Other major hubs included the Ukrainian Free Academy of Sciences (Munich) and editorial groups in Buenos Aires and Toronto, which issued exile newspapers, poetry, and memoirs throughout the Cold War period.

words outlived the regimes that sought to silence them, becoming a testament to the indomitable spirit of a people. For him, and for countless Ukrainians who followed, poetry was not mere artistry or performance; it was a fundamental tool of survival, a spiritual lifeline in the face of oppression.

Yet, this very lineage of poetic witness had faced an almost unimaginable assault in the decades immediately preceding Wsewolod's exile. The Ukrainian poets who had followed Shevchenko's path, who had experienced the brief, brilliant cultural renaissance of the 1920s, found themselves targeted with horrific ferocity by Stalin's regime. They were not writing in secret from exile; they were systematically hunted, arrested, and ultimately, in many cases, buried in the mass graves of the gulag or the killing fields of places like Sandarmokh. Their names were expunged from literary histories, their books removed from libraries, their words cut brutally short. This was the fate of the "Executed Renaissance."

The Generation That Was Erased

In 1933, a Ukrainian poet named Mykhailo Yalovy was arrested and disappeared into the Soviet prison system. His name was excised from public memory. His work was banned. His family was left in silence.

Yalovy was born in 1895 in Dar-Nadezhda; the very same Poltava village where Wsewolod Skliar's grandfather, Ivan, served as a psalmist, and where Wsewolod's father, Viktor, spent his formative years. Yalovy, the son of a parish clerk, and Viktor, the son of the psalmist, born only four years apart, would have inhabited the same small rural world. It is almost inconceivable that their families, so closely tied to the local church and community, did not know one another. They might have attended the same village school, heard the same church bells. Yalovy became a writer, a voice of the revolution's early promise before its descent into tyranny; Viktor became a bookkeeper, a man of ledgers and quiet conformity. Their paths diverged significantly in belief and fortune, but they were rooted in the same soil.

When a figure like Yalovy vanished, his absence would not have gone unnoticed. In places like Dar-Nadezhda, official erasure rarely succeeded in creating complete forgetfulness; rather, it left behind a haunting, unspoken shape, a void around which life cautiously reconfigured itself.

Did Viktor speak of it? Did young Wsewolod, only four at the time, hear his name murmured – or deliberately left out? We cannot know. But decades later, living in English exile, Wsewolod meticulously preserved verses that seemed to carry the imprint of the very silence that had enveloped the Executed Renaissance.

One poem in the notebook, dated February 1950, does not name Yalovy. But it grieves with the same cadence:

У в'язниці

Сидить Катя у в'язниці
Стала біла як стіна
І склонила свою головоньку
Покотилася слеза

Сидить Катя у в'язниці
Зазирає край вікна
Всі дівчата без неї гуляють
Їй на серці тяженько

In Prison

Katya sits alone in prison,
Pale and still, like a wall.
She bows her tender little head
One quiet tear begins to fall.

Katya sits alone in prison,
She gazes out the window's frame.
All the girls are out there walking

	But her heart is not the same.
Прощай Харків прощай Київ *Прощай Дубенская тюрьма* *Прощай, прощай любая матінко* *Бо Катюру бує нема*	Farewell, Kharkiv. Farewell, Kyiv. Farewell, Dubno prison. Farewell, farewell, dearest mother For Katya is no more.
Бує замучили Катюру *Ці проклятії кати* *Бує не вернеться Катя з тюрьми,* *Любая матінко не жди!*	They tortured Katya to the end, Those cursed executioners. She will not return from prison Dearest mother, do not wait.
2/15-50p. Newhaven-England	February 15, 1950. Newhaven-England

Figure 59: Signed by Wsewolod Skliar, the poem reflects on Soviet-era atrocities, including at Dubno Prison[130] in 1941. While the authorship is uncertain, the piece exemplifies the themes of loss and repression prevalent in Ukrainian exile literature.

The poem ends with execution. Katya, tortured, does not return. The language is plain, almost childlike. But the implication is clear: a quiet act of witness to unspeakable atrocities.

In the 1920s, Ukraine experienced a brief cultural flowering. Under the Soviet policy of *korenizatsiya* – "indigenisation" – Ukrainian-language schools, universities and publishing houses proliferated. Theatres staged bold new plays. Journals filled with experimental

[130] In June 1941, as Germany invaded, Soviet NKVD units executed hundreds of political prisoners across Ukraine. At Dubno, detainees were shot or mutilated before the retreat. These killings became symbols of Soviet repression in émigré memory.

prose and poetry. Kyiv, though historically the spiritual heart, saw Kharkiv designated as the Soviet Ukrainian capital. A generation of writers seized the opportunity to reimagine Ukrainian identity as a vibrant, modern, literary, experimental European culture.

It was not to last. By the 1930s, cultural expression – especially expressions of national consciousness – was treated as treason. Over 250 Ukrainian writers were repressed. Some were sent to the gulag. Others were executed. Entire literary movements, artistic schools, and intellectual circles were dismantled, their members vanishing from public life, their works banned and destroyed.

Figure 60: Members of VAPLITE, Kharkiv, 1926. Several pictured were executed during Stalin's purges, including Mykola Kulish, Oleksa Slisarenko, Mike Johansen, and Hryhoriy Epik. Their fates would come to define the trauma remembered as the Executed Renaissance.

Among those lost were Mykola Zerov, whose classical forms were deemed elitist; Mykola Kulish, who reinvented Ukrainian drama; Les Kurbas, who transformed its theatre. Most were shot at

Sandarmokh – a forested gulag site in Karelia – and dumped into mass graves. Yalovy was one of them. He had led the writers' group VAPLITE – the Free Academy of Proletarian Literature – whose members had once dreamed of a culturally autonomous Ukraine. They were buried in Karelia's cold forest soil, and in censorship and enforced forgetting. Their disappearance came first in life, and then in memory.

The term *Rozstriliane Vidrodzhennia* – the Executed Renaissance – came later. But the wound it described was immediate; and deep. It was known in villages like Dar-Nadezhda. It was known by sons who left and never returned. And decades later, this unspoken trauma was known by a man in British exile, quietly preserving poems in the margins of his working life.

Aftermath and Echo

By the mid-1950s, Wsewolod's copying slowed.[131] Life in Britain absorbed him – kitchen work, resettlement schemes, the birth of his daughters. His notebooks grew sparse. But the suitcase remained: folded pages, soft with wear, tucked beneath pay slips and ration books.

He never spoke of the poems he had copied – not to his wife nor his children. They were not performed, not shared, not typed up for any wider audience. They remained a deeply personal testament.

[131] A single later-written poem has been identified, dating from 1970, on a typewritten document, but covered with handwritten Ukrainian verse – an acrostic poem spelling out *UKRAINA*.

But the record itself, the physical act of having preserved these words, endured.

In 1997, more than fifty years after Yalovy's execution, a group of Russian and Ukrainian researchers uncovered a mass grave at Sandarmokh – a pine forest in Karelia where thousands of prisoners of the *Great Terror* had been executed and buried in secret. Among the dead were poets, playwrights, linguists, teachers: members of Ukraine's cultural avant-garde who had simply vanished from the historical record. For decades, their fate had been rumour. Now, it had a place. And names. Kulish. Kurbas. Yalovy. Their bones returned to public memory.

Wsewolod never saw this reckoning. He died in 2011, years before the memorial plaques were raised. But in his notebooks, a different form of memory persisted – not of names, but of griefs too heavy to discard.

A Quiet Canon

What does it mean to write for no one? Wsewolod's notebook offers no definitive answer. It was not crafted for readers. It was not shaped by literary ambition. But perhaps that is the point. His verses belong to a different kind of canon – not official, not curated, but carried. A literature of survival. Words kept not to be read, but not to be lost.

In the Ukrainian diaspora, one phrase appears again and again: "*Ne zabud*" – never forget. But forgetting is not a single act. It is erosion. And against that erosion, people like Wsewolod did not build monuments. They preserved.

Not in manifestos. Not in anthologies. But in silence – in shared rooms, between children's bedtimes. For him, poetry was not performance. It was shelter. A way to hold something from his past intact when everything else had been dismantled.

And he was not alone. Across Ukraine and its exiled communities, others wrote and preserved too – in Crimean Tatar, Yiddish, Polish. Few meant for their words to last. And yet, some did.

And they still do. Today's Ukrainian exiles, scattered once more by war, write and preserve for many of the same reasons Wsewolod did: not to be heard, but to remain. Language becomes the last claim. A record that survival happened – even when the world looks away.

* * *

After his death, the suitcase was opened. The notebooks were found. Transcribed. Translated. They sit now in drawers, in folders, in scanned PDFs on quiet desktops. They are not studied. They are not taught. But they remain.

A quiet echo, perhaps, of another voice once heard in Dar-Nadezhda – long since silenced.

They remain because someone once chose to write. Not to be published. Not to be praised. But to refuse silence.

That, perhaps, is what the Executed Renaissance left behind: an instinct, a tradition, a reflex – which still imprints strongly on Ukrainian identity today. To write. To record. To say: *I was here. I am here.*

The writing ended. The work of living did not. The next chapter follows that life, through its actions and motions.

CHAPTER 13

From Slogan to Silence: The Settling of a Life, 1954–1964

Хлопчик понурився, видно, втомився –
Праця заїла в дитини життя...
Погляд байдужий на чімсь зупинився...
Одіж обірвана, висить шмаття.

The boy slumped, plainly exhausted –
Labour had chewed through his childhood.
His indifferent gaze landed somewhere...
His torn clothing hung in tatters.

– Hanna Suprunenko[132], from *In the Village*, 1908

---

[132] Hanna Suprunenko (born Halyna Ivanivna Steletskaya, 19th century–c. 1927) was a Ukrainian poet and educator from Luhny in Poltava province. Her work spans political verse, lyric introspection, and social observation, often combining folk rhythms with a commitment to justice, love, and emotional resilience. A village schoolteacher by training, she later studied in Moscow and worked in public education following the 1917 revolution. Her poetry appeared in *Zoria*, *Rada*, and *Ukrainska Muza*, and reflects both the material hardship and emotional force of rural Ukrainian life in the early 20th century.

If the first six years of exile were about return, the next ten were not. Something shifts in Wsewolod in 1954 – not all at once, gradually. He stops writing poetry. The diary falls silent. The slogans that once filled his notebooks are completely replaced by menus and recipes. A life once structured around a vision for Ukraine begins to settle into the reality of Britain.

The change begins, oddly, with something that looks like momentum. In the summer of 1954, he attends a seminar in France – political in purpose, nationalist in tone. It's the kind of event he would have relished a few years earlier. But it's not politics he comes back with. It's Julia.

Born in France to Ukrainian émigré parents, Julia Davidenko had grown up in a world shaped by continuity more than rupture. In their letters, she was affectionate, candid, insistently Ukrainian. Their marriage that autumn was both a love story and an act of logistics: pay slips, paperwork, formal approval. Like much of postwar life, it was deeply personal, and shaped by bureaucracy.

Julia's presence altered more than Wsewolod's romantic life. She brought with her a different relationship to Ukraine – less ideological, more domestic; shaped by continuity, not rupture. Her Ukraine lived in lullabies, embroidery, and meals, not in manifestos or meetings. She too had inherited absence, but expressed it through gesture rather than declaration.

They marry that autumn, and everything begins to contract – inwards, domestically, and permanently. His oldest daughter is born. He takes a job at a seaside hotel in Eastbourne. His second daughter is born. Ukrainian is still spoken at home, but the outward-facing life retreats. The writing stops. The meetings dwindle. Conviction softens. What emerges in its place is the quiet, steady architecture of British routine.

That, I think, is where the shift begins. But it isn't until the family returns to London – a few years later, quieter, more settled – that the idea of return seems to vanish. There's no speech, no statement. Just the soft erosion of possibility. A rented flat. A steady job. A church not attended. The Cold War performance may have been a final echo, but by the time he's back in London, the silence has taken hold. What was once imagined as temporary has become the shape of a life.

* * *

The seminar was held at the École de Vésines in Châlette-sur-Loing, France a modest campus outside Montargis, organised by *Ukrainian National Unity* (*UNÉ*).[133] The gathering brought together displaced Ukrainians from across Western Europe for a programme of civic instruction, ideological training, and postwar coordination. He had attended similar meetings before – but this time, the event that marked him most was personal.

[133] The event in question was the Second Course of Civic Action, organised by the diaspora network Ukrainian National Unity (UNÉ).

Figure 61: Julia Davidenko (centre, second row) with her sister at the 7th Congress of the Ukrainian National Union (UNÉ), early 1950s. Her presence reflects the civic roles women played in diaspora life.

Julia was there – poised, sharp-witted, quietly assured. She already moved fluently within the rituals of diaspora life. Their connection was immediate, and decisive.

Their courtship unfolded largely through letters – dozens survive, exchanged between London and Arras, written in Ukrainian. In the displaced world of the émigré community, letter-writing was more than communication; it was orientation, and often, confession. Wsewolod's diary, by contrast, captured the facts with characteristic reserve: *"After returning to London...I decided to write a letter to Yuliya and propose marriage to her, and she agreed!"* His letters to her were different – unguarded, at times intensely emotional. *"My heart gives me no peace... I love you... I fear you do not believe me"*. Another closed simply: *"I am yours forever. Love, Wsewolod"*.[134]

Figure 62: Wsewolod Skliar and Julia, married at Arras in France, 13 November 1954. Like many displaced couples, they began their married life far from home, with paperwork.

They married in November, over two days and two ceremonies – first a civil registration, then a church wedding in Arras, France. It was love, and logistics: to bring Julia to Britain, Wsewolod had to submit pay slips, references, and confirmation of lodgings. Even in marriage, paperwork shaped the path.

Soon after, in the Spring of 1955, their oldest daughter, Catherina Juliette, was born. This was shortly followed by a move to Seaford on England's south coast.[135] Wsewolod had taken a position at the

---

[134] See *Appendix A: Letter from Wsewolod to Julia, August 1954* for an illustrative transcribed and translated letter.

[135] The couple moved from 270 Gloucester Terrace, London, to Basement Flat, 4 The Esplanade, Seaford, Sussex.

Hotel Norfolk in Eastbourne. The work was seasonal and unglamorous. At times, he travelled to other towns for short-term kitchen placements, but the job offered a foothold – a rhythm to replace the flux of earlier years.

I've often wondered what they were thinking. To move to Seaford with a newborn, into a basement flat at 4 The Esplanade – it sounds bleak now, and I suspect it felt bleaker then. Wsewolod had spent time on the coast during his Displaced Person years, much of it in temporary camps. Maybe he thought Julia would like the sea air. Maybe he associated it with something stable, or at least familiar. Or maybe it was simply where the job was. But whatever he hoped for, Seaford doesn't feel like a success. Not a failure, exactly – just a place that doesn't last.

Their second daughter, Nina Anna Evedokia was born in 1956.

By the late 1950s, the outward signs of resistance had mostly disappeared. The meetings had stopped. The writing had stopped. The idea of return hadn't been rejected – but it no longer directed his days. He remained emotionally distant – dutiful, present, largely silent. He brought food home from kitchens but rarely cooked. The stories he once wrote stayed locked in notebooks. "*He said he couldn't remember anything*", his daughters recalled. "*I don't remember*", he would say.[136]

---

[136] This was unlikely to be literal amnesia. Among men of Wsewolod's generation, such statements often masked deliberate silence. Across the Ukrainian diaspora, many who had survived war, occupation, or Soviet repression avoided discussing the past – not from forgetfulness, but from fear, trauma, or a belief that such memories had no safe or

But if speech was limited, language remained. Ukrainian was spoken at home, alongside French. He taught his daughters from childhood, and later his oldest grandson. With other grandchildren, he would begin every exchange in Ukrainian – offering quiet corrections, waiting for replies. It was not performance. It was cultural insistence. A private act of continuity, not longing.[137]

This was survival, shaped by the expectations of his generation. In postwar Britain, discretion was a kind of dignity. Emotion was private. Presence was enough. He worked hard, paid taxes, lived quietly. And still, his identity held – carried in language and memory. Across the diaspora, especially among working-class men, ideology receded behind labour. Silence often served as both defence and discipline: a way to manage vulnerability in unfamiliar systems. Historians of exile have noted how masculine reticence became, for many, a quiet scaffolding of endurance.

The fervour of belief gave way to the obligations of work. The family marked rituals – baptisms, holidays – but he was disengaged.

---

useful place in postwar life. This pattern of reticence was common in oral histories of displaced persons, particularly those who had experienced loss, complicity, or shame. Silence became a survival strategy.

According to his daughter Nina, the silence at home was partly protective: "*As children we were told not to talk about what went on in the family, the war, and history. I think this was through fear of being arrested and sent back to prison. A sense of betrayal and distrust*". This persisted through the 1960s. For many displaced persons, silence became not only a coping strategy, but a form of resistance in itself.

[137] According to his daughter Nina, Wsewolod retained a deep attachment to Ukrainian language and culture throughout the 1960s. He refused to listen to non-Ukrainian music and deeply resented the fact that his daughters were taught Russian instead of Ukrainian at school. He tried to pass Ukrainian on to his grandchildren too – gently but insistently.

In exile, memory no longer required declaration – only the discipline of continuation. In this, Wsewolod was typical. He worked long hours, raised his daughters, and rarely spoke of Ukraine – not out of betrayal, but because the country he had once imagined no longer matched the place that emerged.

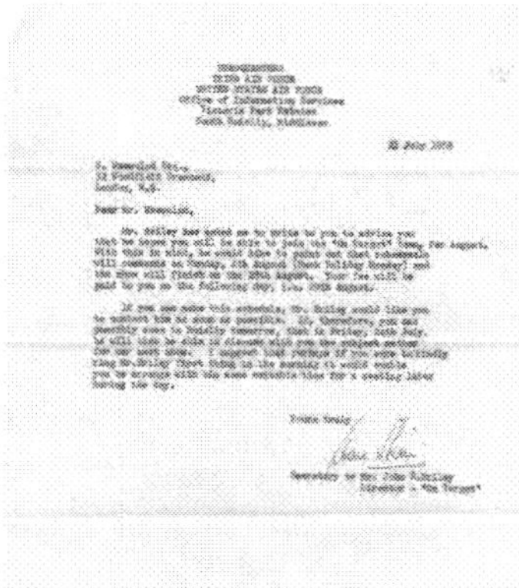

Figure 63: Letter to Wsewolod Skliar from the U.S. Air Force Office of Information Services, dated 23 July 1958, inviting him to join the Cold War programme *On Target*. The project used émigré testimony to counter Soviet narratives.

In 1958, he received a letter from the U.S. Air Force Information Services inviting him to join "On Target", a Cold War orientation team that staged reenactments of Soviet atrocities and resistance.[138]

[138] The programme, titled On Target, was a Cold War propaganda initiative organised by the U.S. Air Force Information Services. It brought together émigrés from across Eastern Europe to deliver rehearsed testimony about Soviet repression, often framed through dramatic reconstructions. Wsewolod was first contacted about it in 1956, but did not formally take part until 1958. His point of contact was John Briley, then a junior officer in the U.S. Information Services and later the Oscar-winning screenwriter

It was a performance – carefully scripted, ideologically useful. He agreed. He rehearsed. He took part. Then, he returned home. There is no diary entry. No reflection. Just the invitation, folded neatly among menus and ration cards. A final gesture toward a cause that had once shaped him, and now merely shadowed him. Not with renewed conviction, but perhaps out of duty, or reflex, or simply the expectation that he should.

That same year, the family returned to London. Soon after, Wsewolod began work at the Columbia Club near Lancaster Gate – a formal American venue hosting NATO officers and diplomats. In its kitchens, he found what he had not yet had: continuity. The Club's hierarchy and discretion suited him. He asked for little, and delivered consistently.

In 1964, his father Viktor died. Wsewolod arranged the funeral. He hosted members of the Ukrainian émigré community. He stood beside the grave. And then he drank. More than was typical. Family say something in him shifted that day. Whatever he had carried in silence – duty, expectation, memory – seemed to turn inward. The idea of return, if it had ever lingered, faded completely.

What remained was habit. Work. Language. Presence. And silence.

---

of Gandhi. These orientation programmes were staged for Allied troops and were intended to bolster anti-Soviet sentiment. Within émigré circles, participation was viewed ambivalently: for some, it was a necessary form of witness; for others, it blurred the line between testimony and propaganda. Wsewolod's own views remain unknown. He left no reflection or commentary. Just the letter.

CHAPTER 14
The Quiet That Remains

Так, я буду крізь сльози сміятись,
Серед лиха співати пісні,
Без надії таки сподіватись,
Жити буду! Геть думи сумні!

Yes, I will laugh despite my tears,
I'll sing out songs amidst my misfortunes,
I'll have hope despite all odds,
I will live! Away, sad thoughts!

– Lesia Ukrainka, from *Contra Spem Spero*[139], 1890

---

[139] *Contra spem spero* ("*Hope Against Hope*") is Lesia Ukrainka's 1890 declaration of perseverance in the face of despair. Written when she was 19 and already battling tuberculosis, the poem reclaims vitality through paradox: *"I will laugh through my tears... I will live!"* It became one of the most beloved texts in the Ukrainian canon – a secular hymn of refusal, often invoked in contexts of exile, illness, and resistance.

The suitcase was never meant to be opened.

Inside, there were no revelations, no final answers, no explanations neatly written to solve mysteries. Instead, there were fragments: recipes scrawled hastily on yellowed paper, identity cards carefully tucked away, scraps of poetry written secretly, and faded photographs, their edges worn from handling. Small things, easy to overlook. Yet each one was heavy with silence.

This book began with questions: what did it mean to be Ukrainian when Ukraine did not exist? What does it mean to pass on a heritage you were never allowed to name? What does it mean to survive in silence? For Wsewolod Skliar, the silence was neither weakness nor surrender – it was a strategy. In exile, he learned to live quietly, passing down his heritage through subtle rituals, whispered phrases, and careful gestures.

This silence was not uniquely his. It stretched far beyond a single family, woven into the fabric of Ukrainian survival itself through tumultuous centuries. Viktor Skliar knew it first, carrying the unspeakable memory of famine and the stark choices of war and displacement. He gave Wsewolod a history often without words, a language that existed mostly between lines. In turn, Wsewolod passed this quiet inheritance forward, to those who would follow, embedding it in the way he lived, the way he remembered, the way he ultimately withheld.

But silence exacted its own toll. Each generation inherited not only resilience but distance, preservation alongside uncertainty. Did silence protect, or did it obscure? Did it shelter or separate? These were questions left unanswered, wounds quietly passed on. Perhaps that is always the cost of survival: to carry forward the unseen burdens, to navigate history without maps.

For generations, Ukrainians lived at the edges of their own story, forced into silence by external powers, preserving an alternative remembrance – told through repetition and gestures. Each small act of cultural preservation, each whispered story, each carefully kept tradition became an assertion against erasure: *we are still here.*

The world, for long stretches, seemed not to notice this quiet endurance, often overlooking the nation struggling beneath the weight of empires. Yet, the need for Ukraine's story to be heard, for its identity to be recognised, has never faded. The resilience forged in those long years of silence – through famine, war, repression, and exile – created a deep wellspring of strength. It taught that survival does not always announce itself loudly. Often it hides in the smallest acts, repeated carefully, insistently, quietly.

Wsewolod never lived to see a time when Ukraine's voice would resonate with such global urgency. But his quiet inheritance, the legacy of endurance he embodied, remains a poignant testament to the spirit of a people who have long understood that memory, even when unspoken, is a powerful force. His life, understated and cautious, reflects a truth fundamental to the Ukrainian experience: that the fight for identity is often a quiet, internal battle before it becomes an external one.

This is what remains from the Skliar family's journey: fragments deliberately preserved, silences meaningfully kept, acts quietly repeated. Discipline, not weakness. A profound form of survival; not surrender. The suitcase, now open, reveals not just the story of one family, but the enduring human need to hold onto meaning when history seeks to strip it away.

What remains is the quiet – and in understanding it, a way of hearing what was once, and often still must be, unsaid.

Слава Україні. Героям слава.

Figure 64: Wsewolod Skliar and his wife Julia, toasting at their daughter's wedding, Cliveden, England, 1989.

Коли умру, життя скінчиться
Коли в могилу спатиму ляжу
Тоді кохать мене не треба
Кохай тепер, коли живу.

When I die, life will end.
When I lie down in the grave to sleep,
Then love for me is not needed –
Love me now, while I live.

– Ukrainian Folk Song, transcribed by Wsewolod Skliar, from *Мені Шістнайцять*, 1950[140]

[140] This quatrain comes from a Ukrainian folk song often titled "*In the Autumn Garden*" or "*I Am Sixteen*". Though widely popularised in the 1950s and 1960s, Wsewolod Skliar's 1950 transcription predates formal publication, suggesting it circulated earlier in oral tradition.

EPILOGUE

A Life Remembered: Wsewolod Skliar, 1964–2011

І мене в сем'ї великій,
В сем'ї вольній, новій,
Не забудьте пом'янути
Незлим тихим словом.

And me – in the great family,
Of the newly born free –
With a quiet word, and without any spite,
Remember me.

– Taras Shevchenko, from *Zapovit*[141], 1845

---

[141] Taras Shevchenko's poem *Zapovit* (*Testament*, 1845) is one of Ukraine's most iconic texts. Written in the final years of serfdom, it links personal mortality to collective freedom, urging remembrance "with a quiet word" in the family of the free. Recited at funerals and protests alike, it remains a national hymn of dignity and defiance.

By 1964, the archive begins to fade. The notebooks fall silent. The meetings end. And what I know of Wsewolod becomes less about documents, and more about memory. These years do not yield easily to narrative. They are composed instead of rhythms – the repetition of gesture, the accumulation of habits, the way a life unfolds when it is no longer waiting to begin.

The family moved to Princethorpe House that year: a high-rise council flat in Westbourne Park, London. For Wsewolod, it was the first permanent home he had known since childhood. The building stood among rows of postwar estates – concrete, unadorned, quietly anonymous. Inside, however, it marked a threshold: from impermanence to rootedness. From exile to endurance.

There were few objects on display. The walls were bare. But in drawers, cupboards, and boxes, memory remained. The suitcase – locked, heavy, unopened – sat in a corner for decades. It was not from his arrival in exile, but from his early married years. Still, it became the vessel of everything withheld. Near it, a battered wallet: Viktor's. Inside, identity papers, conscription slips, the passport of his wife. Preserved but never explained. These were not heirlooms. They were residues – kept not to honour the past, but to contain it. And in their silence, they spoke.

Council housing offered shelter but not ease. The Skliars lived among Irish labourers, Jamaican nurses, Maltese dockers – lives side by side, not always together. English was spoken outside. Ukrainian and French, at home. Wsewolod, never quite at ease in English, still called it "*the language of the kitchen*".

Figure 65: Princethorpe House, Westbourne Park, London, 1960s – the Skliars' first permanent home in exile, a concrete symbol of rootedness amid displacement.

Each summer, from the late 1950s to early 1970s, the family travelled to Arras to visit Julia's relatives. These returns offered continuity – not to Ukraine, but to family, to rhythm, to place. In France, Wsewolod joined meals, played cards, smoked, drank beer. He did the same in London – present but reserved, always slightly apart.

It was in the kitchens that he worked – first at the Columbia Club, later at The Londonderry, and finally The Howard Hotel, where he rose to executive chef.[142] His menus survive. They read now like

[142] In the early 1970s, as the U.S. government prepared to wind down its operations at the Columbia Club, Wsewolod was offered a relocation and employment package to move to the United States – an unusual opportunity for a non-citizen hospitality

quiet ledgers of labour: printed cards listing Crème Velour, Délice de Sole Palace, roasted game. The medals he later received – from an employer he respected – acknowledged that work, not as spectacle, but as service – rare formal recognition for a displaced Ukrainian, and one he quietly cherished.[143] He wore his uniform with formality and pride.[144]

Figure 66: Staff ID card for Wsewolod Skliar at The Howard Hotel in London, where he began as First Sous Chef.

---

worker. For many émigrés, such an offer would have represented both professional advancement and geopolitical alignment. But Wsewolod declined. London had become home. His reasons, though never formally recorded, appear rooted in responsibility: to Julia, to their daughters, and to the life he had carefully built since 1948.

[143] Wsewolod Skliar was awarded both Silver and Gold Service medals by the U.S. government in recognition of his work. These civilian awards, though rarely given to hospitality staff, were occasionally used to honour individuals whose professionalism supported American diplomatic or military institutions abroad.

[144] Nina, Wsewolod's younger daughter, recalled: "*He was very proud of his job and his achievements, but wanted us to go further. Not that he found it demeaning. He was a very proud, humble man*".

His daughter Catherina recalled him as present but distant through these years. He visited regularly, brought food, discouraged her from entering catering. Affection, when it surfaced, took the form of care, not speech. Once, he served her at his restaurant – a moment of quiet pride.

When I hear stories of those years, what comes to me first are not events, but textures. The quiet of his flat. The preciseness of his flat-cap, suit, and tie. The way he shuffled a deck of cards before dealing. He played belote[145], always with precision. No instruction, no explanation – only the game, passed down from Julia's French-Ukrainian family. Watching him, I understood that connection did not require speech. It required presence, rhythm, care.

* * *

He did not speak of the past. Not of his mother, killed in 1943. Not of the underground. Not of what it meant to flee. "I don't remember", he would say, and I came to understand that this was not forgetting, but protection.

Then the suitcase.

[145] *Belote* is a popular French card game, traditionally played by four players in teams of two. It combines elements of trick-taking and strategy and is widely played in France and francophone communities. For émigré families like the Skliars, it became part of domestic ritual – a quiet continuity linking generations.

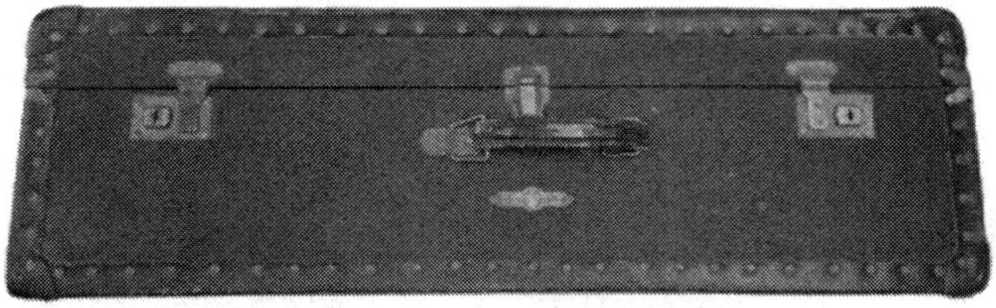

Figure 67: Wsewolod and Julia Skliar's suitcase, c.1954. Stored out of sight, it remained locked for decades; present, but never opened.

It lived in a cupboard, behind boxes and bric-a-brac – entirely inaccessible. No one opened it. No one was allowed. Its silence was part of the house. Books remained – the few he had brought with him – but the past did not decorate the walls. No icons. No photographs. No trace of the village, or the war, or the years in flight. The past did not vanish. It was stored.

When they fled Soviet Ukraine during the war, Wsewolod and Viktor brought a cart filled with what they thought might sustain them – tools, icons, household items. In Transnistria, the cart's contents were taken. The physical remnants of their past – clothing, books, photographs – were stripped away. What remained was what they could recover, barter for, rebuild.

By the time Wsewolod left Ganacker Displaced Persons Camp in 1947, his world fit on a single export list. A form recorded thirty-six items: one pair of shoes, one pair of boots, three undershirts, a handbag, a heater, seven books, two pairs of trousers, and a suitcase to contain it all. No keepsakes. No icons. No photographs. The purpose was bureaucratic. Its effect, poetic: a life reduced to clothing, paper, silence.

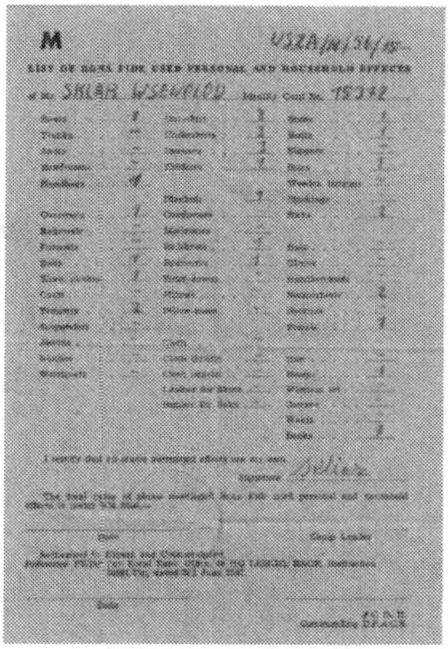
M

LIST OF BONA FIDE USED PERSONAL AND HOUSEHOLD EFFECTS

SKLIAR WSEWOLOD

Figure 68: Wsewolod Skliar's inventory of personal belongings, Ganacker Displaced Person Camp, 1947. This form recorded his total possessions: thirty-six items, including clothing, bedding, and a suitcase – his life reduced to essentials

There were other objects, too. A wallet – his father's – filled with conscription papers and his wife's passport. It was never spoken of. But it was kept.

These were not souvenirs. They were remnants of rupture. What memory could not carry aloud, it carried in fragments – preserved, resisted, deferred.

* * *

Julia's presence was different. She transmitted memory not through objects, but through repetition: a lullaby hummed, clothes embroidered, *varenyky*[146] made by hand. Memory surfaced not as lesson, but as cadence.

Figure 69: Julia Davidenko (centre-right) with siblings and friends in traditional Ukrainian clothing, c. 1950. The embroidered *vyshyvanky* reflect identity enacted through gesture and repetition.

In postwar France, she took part in diaspora life – dancing in cultural troupes, writing for émigré publications, attending civic events organised by groups like the Ukrainian National Union (UNÉ). They were forms of belonging, performed through presence.

After marrying Wsewolod, Julia withdrew from diaspora politics. In France, she had danced in cultural troupes, attended civic events, written for émigré publications. But in London, that world

[146] *Varenyky* are stuffed dumplings, often filled with potato, cheese, or fruit, and are a staple of Ukrainian cuisine – commonly prepared during holidays or family gatherings.

receded. The distance from her community, the demands of motherhood, the weight of a new language – all shifted her focus. French became the dominant tongue at home, but Ukrainian endured: in song, in ritual, in the quiet rhythm of family life. Her daughters remembered what she did more than what she explained. She did not restore a lost world. She acknowledged its rupture – and continued anyway.

* * *

In 1978, Wsewolod applied for British citizenship. He had resisted it for years – not because he rejected Britain, but because he had not meant to stay. But the years passed. Ukraine remained out of reach. The application marked no new allegiance, only an acceptance: that return would not come. His first passport listed him as "Sous Chef de Cuisine". It gave him movement, not resolution.

When Ukraine gained independence in 1991, he said nothing. For his daughters, that silence was striking. The man who had once devoted himself to national liberation seemed unmoved. But it was not indifference. It was estrangement – from a homeland whose political reality no longer resembled the imagined one he had carried.

He retired in 1999. There was a party at the hotel. Photographs were taken. A clock and a gold watch were presented. He smiled, briefly. Then he returned to routine.

Retirement unsettled him. Without the structure of the kitchen, he grew quiet, even more so than before. He walked. He visited. He watched. I remember him helping my mother with chores; sitting at the table, with a single beer. Catherina recalled short, functional phone calls, quiet visits, and familiar gestures – offering help, then waiting to be directed. The past remained untouched. He was present, but never open..

He died in 2011, after a brief illness. No great farewell. No final story. Only a quiet funeral, humanist and conventional, held in a London venue with no trace of Ukraine. No incense. No hymns. Just the soft murmur of English words and the presence of family. His daughters' quiet tears seemed to echo the silence he had kept – not empty, but dense. A life, folded inward, held without display.

Even his final words to Julia – "*You were the best thing that happened to me*", followed by something like "*It's time to live*" or "*Enjoy the rest of your life*" – were brief. But they were not empty. They were the full extent of what could be said after a lifetime of unspoken things.

* * *

When I began writing this book, I thought I was looking for what he had hidden. But the longer I worked, the more I came to see that what he left was not absence – it was form. A way of carrying memory that did not rely on narrative. A way of surviving without explaining survival.

Wsewolod never returned to Ukraine. But Ukraine did not leave him. It lived in his posture, his language, the way he waited for someone to get the words right. It lived in what he kept in drawers. In the recipes he copied. In the suitcase he never unlocked.

Today, another generation of Ukrainians is being scattered across the world by war. Some will return. Others will not. Their memories, too, will not always be written in books or speeches. They will survive, as Wsewolod's did, in quiet acts: in the careful folding of a document, the maintenance of a tradition, the passing of a language across continents. Continuity sustained not through proclamation, but through presence.

This is not a story of redemption. It is a record of quiet fidelity. He endured. He worked. He loved, in his way. And when the past was too heavy to carry in words, he carried it in silence.

That, in the end, was enough.

* * *

I didn't plan to write this book. I only meant to open a suitcase. But once I saw what was inside – not stories, not answers, but silence, carefully kept – I realised I couldn't turn away. I wrote it because I had to. I wanted to confront what it means to be Ukrainian when you're several generations removed, when the language is half-forgotten and the geography abstract, yet something still pulls. What I found wasn't a single truth or a clean inheritance. I found absence – but not emptiness. Silence, yes, but not apathy. What was passed down was not grief, exactly. It was a way of carrying history without showing its weight. And I needed to understand that. Not to claim it, not to resolve it – but to listen to what was never said, and to ask why it still echoes.

AFTERWORD

The Unquiet Echo: From Maidan's Hope to War's Defiance, 2011–2025

Wsewolod Skliar departed in 2011, taking with him his universe of silences. He left behind photographs, a few books, official papers charting a life of displacement, and a notebook filled with Ukrainian poems – some copied, some remembered, none previously known to his family. And, of course, the suitcase. For years after his passing, it sat in my grandmother Julia's flat, then eventually came to me – a silent, locked testament to everything unsaid, a physical manifestation of the "quiet that remains." It was never meant to be opened. But history, relentless and brutal, has a way of prying open even the most carefully guarded legacies. As the decade after Wsewolod's death unfolded, Ukraine, the homeland he carried within him yet never returned to, began to scream its existence to a world that had long preferred not to listen. The silences he embodied, the silences of generations of Skliars before him, became not just a personal quest but an urgent echo of a nation's fight to have its story heard.

The quietude of Wsewolod's later years, his retreat from the fervent nationalism of his youth into the contained world of his London kitchen, seemed a world away from the events that convulsed Ukraine just a few years after his death. In the winter of 2013–2014, Kyiv's Maidan Nezalezhnosti – Independence Square – erupted. A revolution born of refusal, a generation's defiant stand against a president steering the nation back into Russia's suffocating embrace. Where Wsewolod's generation had whispered their hopes in clandestine meetings or Displaced Person camp barracks, this new generation roared. They draped themselves in blue and yellow, sang the anthem with open fervour unimaginable for much of the 20th century, and demanded dignity.

Watching Maidan, I thought of Viktor Skliar, Wsewolod's father, who fought briefly for an independent Ukraine in 1919 before the Red Army crushed his dreams. I thought of Wsewolod himself, a fourteen-year-old in the *blackthorn forest* of Halychyna, carrying out tasks for the UPA, already *thinking about the future of the Ukrainian people*. The spirit was the same, but the expression profoundly different. The young faces on Maidan, imbued with a hope that seemed almost reckless, were not whispering. They built barricades, braved Berkut batons, sniper bullets. The "Heavenly Hundred" became new martyrs, their sacrifice a stark testament to the enduring price of asserting Ukrainian identity against a tide of erasure. This was not Ivan Skliar's quiet endurance, nor Wsewolod's strategic silence in exile. This was a public, costly, unequivocal reclamation of voice.

The Kremlin's response was swift and brutal, a chilling echo of past imperial transgressions. In March 2014, Russia annexed Crimea, a blatant land grab orchestrated under the guise of protecting Russian speakers, a narrative eerily similar to justifications used for centuries to undermine Ukrainian sovereignty. Shortly thereafter, war erupted in Ukraine's eastern Donbas region, fuelled by Russian operatives, funding, and forces. A profound sense of historical recurrence settled in; it was as if the old fears had returned, the same betrayals merely dressed in new slogans. Wsewolod, who had so deeply resented the imposition of the Russian language on his daughters in British schools, who refused to speak it himself, would have seen this not merely as a political manoeuvre but as a deeply personal and historical assault.

For eight years, the war simmered, a bleeding wound on Ukraine's eastern flank. The world expressed concern but largely looked away, deeming it a regional squabble in a part of Europe "too often overlooked." For Ukrainians, both at home and in the diaspora, these years were a reckoning. Diaspora families like ours, descendants of those who had fled Soviet terror or Nazi occupation, found themselves thrust into new roles – fundraising, advocating, explaining to a largely indifferent West the existential nature of the threat. The quiet networks of cultural preservation Wsewolod had once nurtured became support lines for a country under siege. The stories of the Holodomor, Soviet repression, the struggle for independence – once the bedrock of the Skliar family – were no longer just history; they were urgent warnings.

Then came February 24, 2022. The silence of a European dawn shattered by the roar of Russian missiles and tanks crossing sovereign borders. The "special military operation," as the Kremlin called it, aimed to subjugate Ukraine, eradicate its identity, end its story as an independent nation. The brutality shocked the world, yet for those who knew Ukrainian history, who had grown up with inherited traumas like the Skliars, there was a horrifying familiarity.

The images that flooded screens – civilians huddled in metro stations, refugees streaming westward, cities pulverised into rubble – were a devastating replay of the 20th-century horrors that shaped my family. I thought of Evdokiya, Wsewolod's mother, killed by a Soviet bomb in 1943, and of countless families mourning today. I thought of Viktor and young Wsewolod fleeing Sakhnovshchyna, losing everything to robbers in Transnistria, and the millions of Ukrainians in 2022 forced to flee with only what they could carry. The Holodomor, which taught Viktor and others the state's brutal use of hunger, echoed in Russia's blockades and attacks on grain infrastructure, threatening global food security.

Yet, alongside the devastation, something remarkable happened. Ukraine, so often defined by suffering and silence, fought back with courage and unity that astonished the world. The quiet resilience of generations of Skliars – Ivan enduring under tsar and Soviet rule, Viktor adapting through famine and war, Wsewolod preserving language and memory in exile – was now magnified and weaponised. Citizens became warriors, teachers took up arms, artists documented atrocities. The Ukrainian language, which Wsewolod had fiercely guarded, became an emblem of defiance – heard in presidential addresses, trench songs, messages scrawled on captured tanks.

The "quiet that remains" took on new meaning. No longer just about the unspoken, the suitcase histories. It became the quiet determination in a soldier's eyes, the hum of a generator in a darkened city, prayers whispered in ruined churches. And the world, finally, began to listen. Ukraine was no longer a footnote or "borderland"; it was the frontline of a global struggle for democracy and self-determination.

Yet, even as Ukraine fights for its future on the global stage, the long shadow of past traumas lingers in quieter ways. Villages like Sakhnovshchyna – once marked by famine, repression, and endurance – now face a slower, more insidious disappearance. Houses stand hollowed, fields lie untilled, and the young no longer stay. But not everything has vanished. A handful of women in the community continue to bake the *korovai* – a ceremonial bread once shared at weddings, now sent to soldiers on the front – it remains a gesture of care and continuity. This is not the silence of survival, nor of censorship, but of absence – the quiet that follows when history recedes and no one remains to speak. Another kind of quiet – not willed, but abandoned – that remains.

As I delved deeper into the Skliar archive, transcribing Wsewolod's copies of poems and diary entries, the urgency of his once-private words felt amplified by daily headlines. His copied poem, "The Train Departed," with its lines, "Death walks among us in the transports / Bullets terrifyingly whistle above us," seemed to speak directly to Ukrainians fleeing war-torn regions in 2022. His call to "Remember her with great kindness... And rebuild her crosses – Do not let your wrath be dulled by the Muscovites... This is your duty – Nationalist!" – once confined to émigré circles, now felt like a national rallying cry.

As of May 2025, the war grinds on. The cost – in lives, infrastructure, trauma – is immeasurable. The future remains uncertain. But the attempt to erase Ukraine has failed. Instead, it has galvanised a national identity more unified than perhaps ever before. The fragments of memory, traditions, the language Wsewolod and Julia passed down are now part of a vast, collective assertion of identity.

The suitcase is open now. Its contents – the photographs, the folded documents, the worn notebooks – are no longer just the relics of one family's brutal century. They are part of a larger testament. They speak to the endurance of a people told they do not, or should not, exist – yet who continue with unwavering defiance. The silence Wsewolod embraced was perhaps his way of protecting a memory too precious or painful to expose to a world not ready to hear it. Today, his descendants, and those of countless Ukrainian families, face a different imperative: to speak, to record, to ensure these stories are not forgotten – that the "quiet" is understood not as absence, but as the deep pause before a nation reclaims its voice.

The Skliar family's journey, from the Cossack heartlands of Poltava to the refugee camps of Germany and the council estates of London, is a testament to survival. But it is also a prelude. The quiet work of preserving identity, of carrying memory through generations of oppression, laid the foundation for the unquiet defiance the world witnesses today. The final lines of this book, written before the invasion, now resonate with even greater, more painful, and more hopeful power:

Слава Україні. Героям слава.

The fight continues. The story is still being written. And the quiet, now infused with the roar of resilience, remains.

Note on Method and Sources

This book draws on a wide range of sources – archival, oral, personal, and published. Its foundation lies in primary materials: church records, refugee documents, family papers, and official files. These were supplemented by oral testimony, private collections, and selected historical and theoretical works. Together, they form a partial but resonant record of one family's passage through the broader history of Ukraine.

Archival material includes parish registers from the Poltava, Kharkiv, and Cherkasy regions, clergy appointment books, and civil registry entries – used to reconstruct the lives of early Skliar ancestors. Soviet-era documents – including employment records, internal passports, and military files – provide insight into survival under Stalinist rule and wartime occupation. Refugee registration cards, transit permits, and postwar records from the International Tracing Service (ITS) in Bad Arolsen document the displacement of Viktor and Wsewolod Skliar.

The personal archive of Wsewolod and Julia Skliar – letters, photographs, poems, menus, and bureaucratic paperwork – forms the emotional and documentary core of the book. A separate cache of over forty letters exchanged between them in the early 1950s was transcribed and translated by the author. Additional oral testimony from Wsewolod's descendants (recorded 2007–2025), and materials shared by Lidia Skliar, helped expand the record of life in exile.

The personal archive of Wsewolod and Julia Skliar – letters, photographs, handwritten poems, menus, and bureaucratic forms – forms the emotional and documentary core of the book. A separate cache of over forty letters exchanged between Wsewolod and Julia in the early 1950s was transcribed and translated by the author. Additional oral testimony from Wsewolod's descendants (recorded 2007–2025), and photographs and materials shared by Lidia Skliar, further expanded the record of life in exile.

Where gaps exist, published and digital resources were consulted to establish broader context. These include digitised clerical publications, diaspora newspapers, and key works of Ukrainian history, memory studies, and displacement. Online platforms – such as the Encyclopaedia of Ukraine, FamilySearch, and institutional archives – were used to verify names, dates, and terminology.

Dates reflect the best available evidence. Where precise records do not exist, years are given conservatively. Approximate dates are marked with qualifiers (e.g. *c.*, *about*, *likely*), and no specific date is included unless confirmed by documentation or consistent testimony.

This is not a comprehensive account. It is shaped by the fragmentary nature of the surviving archive, and by the silences left behind. Where no documents remain, memory and fragment are treated as evidence in their own right. In such cases, silence is not absence, but structure – and part of what this book seeks to interpret.

Selected Further Reading

The following English-language books helped shape my understanding of Ukraine's history, memory, and diaspora — and may offer readers a deeper path into the themes explored here.

History and Testimony

- Serhii Plokhy, *The Gates of Europe: A History of Ukraine* (Penguin, 2015) – a sweeping, accessible introduction to Ukraine's historical arc
- Orest Subtelny, *Ukraine: A History*, Fourth Edition (University of Toronto Press, 2009) – a classic account, especially strong on early and Soviet-era Ukraine
- Yaroslav Hrytsak, *Ukraine: The Forging of a Nation* (Hurst, 2023) – a bold, thematic reinterpretation of Ukrainian identity
- Anna Reid, *Borderland: A Journey Through the History of Ukraine* (Orion, 1997) – a journalist's vivid travelogue through Ukraine's layered past
- Anne Applebaum, *Red Famine: Stalin's War on Ukraine* (Allen Lane, 2017) – a Pulitzer Prize-winning account of the Holodomor, combining archival research and moral urgency
- Timothy Snyder, *Bloodlands: Europe Between Hitler and Stalin* (Bodley Head, 2010) – essential reading on mass violence across Nazi- and Soviet-occupied lands
- Catherine Merridale, *Ivan's War: Life and Death in the Red Army, 1939–1945* (Faber, 2005) – explores the human toll of war from inside the Soviet ranks

- Nicholas Bethell, *The Last Secret* (André Deutsch, 1974) – on the forced repatriation of displaced Soviet citizens after WWII
- Artem Chapeye, *Ordinary People Don't Carry Machine Guns: Thoughts on War*, trans. Zenia Tompkins (Seven Stories Press UK, 2025) – a contemporary voice from Ukraine's current war, balancing irony and resistance

Literature

- Taras Shevchenko, Kobzar, trans. Peter Fedynsky (Glagoslav Publications, 2013) – foundational poetry of Ukrainian nationhood, grief, and defiance
- Ivan Franko, Zakhar Berkut, trans. Theodosia Boresky (Independently published, 2022) – a historical novella of 13th-century Carpathian resistance
- Josef Wallmannsberger (ed.), Executing a Renaissance: The Poetological Nation of Ukraine (ibidem Press / Columbia UP, 2024) – essays on cultural revival under repression, engaging Ukraine's "Executed Renaissance" past and present
- Mark Andryczyk (ed.), The White Chalk of Days: The Contemporary Ukrainian Literature Series Anthology (Academic Studies Press, 2017) – a showcase of post-independence literary voices
- Lyuba Yakimchuk, Apricots of Donbas (Lost Horse Press, 2021) – powerful poems on war, exile, and fragile belonging

Theory

- Miroslav Hroch, *Social Preconditions of National Revival in Europe: A Comparative Analysis of the Social Composition of Patriotic Groups among the Smaller European Nations, 2nd ed.* (Columbia University Press, 2000) – a foundational study outlining the "three stages" model of national movements: cultural interest (Phase A), patriotic mobilisation (Phase B), and mass political nationalism (Phase C). Hroch's framework has proven especially influential in interpreting the trajectory of Ukrainian nation-building.
- Marianne Hirsch, The Generation of Postmemory (Columbia University Press, 2012) – on inherited trauma and the memory work of descendants
- Svetlana Boym, The Future of Nostalgia (Basic Books, 2001) – a philosophical meditation on longing, memory, and exile

APPENDIX A
Personal Writings of Wsewolod Skliar

This appendix presents selected excerpts from Wsewolod Skliar's handwritten Ukrainian-language diaries, as referenced in the main chapters. Each entry is shown in two columns: the left contains an English translation; the right presents the original Ukrainian transcription.

These source manuscripts were composed in cursive Ukrainian and are aged and unevenly legible, often featuring crossing-out, variant orthography, and informal or inconsistent punctuation. Certain letter forms – especially ч, ш, and щ – appear variably, and some words admit multiple plausible readings. Every effort has been made to preserve the originals as faithfully as possible. However, minor ambiguities remain, and the texts should not be treated as fully regularised editions. Nonstandard and archaic spellings have been retained to reflect the manuscript's character.

All transcriptions and translations are by the author.

APPENDIX A

Autobiographical Note, c. 1949

Я син одної культурної сім'ї, жив і виховувся під советським режимом, але дуже українського батька, виховав сина в дусі українського націоналіста. Я мавши 14 років думав про майбутність українського народу.

I am the son of a cultured family. I lived and was raised under the Soviet regime, but by a deeply Ukrainian father who brought up his son in the spirit of Ukrainian nationalism. At the age of fourteen, I was already thinking about the future of the Ukrainian people.

В 1943 р. ми мусіли евакуюватись з своєї рідної землі на чужу землю і так проводити своє життя як прикаже Бог, але переїхали дуже велику віддаль від своєї землі, подались до своїх рідних братів в Галичину і там я брав участь з своїми хлопцями, так званими з тернового лісу. Виконавши деякі завдання для свого народу, в місці з членами УПА.

In 1943, we were forced to evacuate from our native land to foreign soil, and to live our lives as God willed. We travelled a great distance from our homeland, turning to our kin in Halychyna. There, I took part alongside my comrades – those known as being from the blackthorn forest. I carried out certain tasks for our people, together with members of the UPA.

Проживши деякий час в Галичині в місті Самбір, мусіли евакуватись. З Галичини, бо приближався фронт терористів, тобто більшовиків, і мусіли кинути українську землю і їхати до Німеччини.

After some time in Halychyna, in the town of Sambir, we were again forced to evacuate – from Halychyna this time, as the front approached, bringing with it the terrorists, that is, the Bolsheviks. We were forced to abandon Ukrainian land and travel to Germany.

В Німеччині пробувши вісім місяців працюючи в фашистському лісі, али не забував про свій обов'язок. В 1944 р. Німеччина капітулювали і я попав до Американської зони в німецькій землі я займався агітацією а головне то агітацією нарід щоб не їхав до батьківщини, а гартувався націоналістичними духам і гартував себе проти загарбника-терориста большивика, і багато погодилося на мою пропозицію, ам деяка частина людий плювали в вічі, говориш що більш достойні бути в С.С., а особливо молодь.

In Germany, I spent eight months working in a fascist forest, but I did not forget my duty. In 1944, Germany capitulated and I ended up in the American zone. On German soil, I was engaged in agitation – above all, agitation among the people so that they would not return to the homeland, but would instead harden themselves with nationalist spirit and steel themselves against the Bolshevik invader-terrorist. Many accepted my proposal, but a certain portion of the people spat in my face, you say –

[claiming] they were more worthy of being in the S.S.[147], especially the youth.

Тепер знаходжуся на терені Англії і також займаюся нац. справами і допомагаю всім своїм братам чим тільки можу, організував драм-гурток спеціально для підвищення культури і підвищення українського духа.

I am now living in England, where I continue to work in national affairs and assist my brothers however I can. I organised a drama circle specifically for the advancement of culture and the elevation of the Ukrainian spirit.

Так я б сказав що я маю м тепер близько двадцяти років і думаю що те що я зробив в 14 роках тоє для мене тепер дуже й дуже цінним але то вже пройши, але не забуте й думаю що тепер я буду робити більше як я робив ще зовсім молодим і буду дбати о визволенілі українського народу.

So I would say that I now have about twenty years behind me, and I believe that what I accomplished at the age of fourteen remains for me deeply meaningful. That has already passed, but it is not forgotten. I believe that now I will do even more than I did when I was still very young – and I will continue to care for the liberation of the Ukrainian people.

[147] "S.S." here could refer to the 14th Waffen-SS Division (Galician Division), formed in 1943 and composed primarily of Ukrainian volunteers. The speaker's tone suggests disapproval of those who joined this formation rather than aligning with the Ukrainian Insurgent Army.

APPENDIX A

Н.О.У. В.С.

N.O.U. W.S.[148]

Selected Diary Excerpts

Foreword to Diary

Перед Слово.

Foreword.

Цей щоденник пишиться не для публіцистики а лишень для свого власного інтересу, що на майбутнє прийдеться повернутися додому і буду мати що згадати, але в мі ж класі пишу переживання в Англіі; а також щоденне життя, прикрості та думки про свій рідний край, про свою Неньау Україну.

This diary is not being written for journalism, but only for my own interest, so that in the future I might return to it, when I am home again and want something to remember – even from my school days. I write about my experiences in England, and also about daily life, its sorrows and thoughts about my native land, about my dear Ukraine.

Не забувай про рідний край
Не забувай про свою рідну
землю. А все згадай й добрами
У славі, честі й оповится.

Never forget your native land
Never forget your beloved soil
Recall it all, and through good
deeds. It shall be wrapped in
glory and honour.

[148] N.O.U. – Likely a non-standard or reversed rendering of "ОУН" (the Organisation of Ukrainian Nationalists), or a personal shorthand. "W.S." refers to the author, Wsewolod Skliar.

APPENDIX A

<table>
<tr><td>Чужиня – 1951 – Англія</td><td>Stranger – 1951 – Britain</td></tr>
<tr><td>Згадай їй добром великим…
За всі століття, що пройшли –
І зобудовуй Її хрестожи –
Не дай гні тилити москалям…
Постав навколо великі горе!!
Це Твій обов'язок –
Націоналіст!

Англія</td><td>Remember her with great
kindness…
For all the centuries that have
passed –
And rebuild her crosses –
Do not let your wrath be dulled
by the
Muscovites…
Surround her with great sorrow!!
This is your duty – Nationalist!

England</td></tr>
</table>

Note: While the foreword is dated 1951, the diary covers the years 1948-1955, suggesting it was written several years after the diary was started. It contains several nonstandard or poetic constructions.

<table>
<tr><td>16/III–48: пішов з другом Рибалькою Антоном на прогулку і прийшов як "вовк" голодний. Ліг спати.</td><td>16 March 1948: Went with my friend, Rybalko Anton, for a walk and came back like a 'wolf', hungry. Lied down to sleep.</td></tr>
<tr><td>26/III–48 р: Врано в 7 год. поїхав до праці; не перший день не робив нічого, ишень одчайдушновався з оботою, але було страшно й моторошно.</td><td>26 March 1948: In the morning at 7 o'clock I went to work; on the first day I didn't do anything, only struggled desperately with the work, but it felt frightening and eerie.</td></tr>
</table>

28/III – 48. Поставили мене скидати камінь з вагонів разом з п. В. Васильовичем, і коли кінчалась робота то я був пізній, так що не міг вже вивезти останнього ва [illegible] ои з вагона, що прийшлось В. В. підтримувати мене.

28 March 1948: They set me to unloading stone from the wagons together with Mr V. Vasylovych, and when the work was finishing, I was too late, so I couldn't manage to remove the last [illegible] from the wagon, so V. V. had to support me.

Extended Diary Entry following 28 March 1948:

Це перші початки на англійській роботі. І так продовжується моє життя тільким зацікавленні працею, жадних життєвих успіхів не багу.

These were my first beginnings in English work. And so my life went on, filled only with work – no real success to speak of.

Вже за два місяці ознайомився з українським громадянством, починаю розвертати свої справи. На третій місяць житвя в Англії я почав думати за драм-гурток і доетавши пєси почав переписувати ролі. Коли ролі були переписані, треба було знайти людей, котріб могли вгастувати в драм-гур.

After just two months, I'd grown familiar with Ukrainian "citizenship", and began to sort out my affairs. In the third month of living in England, I began thinking about forming a drama group, and having received a play, I began copying out the roles. Once the roles were copied, we had to find people who could take part in the group.

Але нарешті про кінці претього місяця я зібрав 12 осіб і почали розучувати ролі.

By the end of the third month, I had gathered twelve people and we began rehearsals.

Довго не прийшлося вчитись, бо пєса була маленька і за місяць часу ми її поставили. Маючи при боці гарний драм-гурт, я не звертаго уваги на наяік трудноці, а все старався поширати його та щоб поставити якусь одширнішу пєсу чи драму. Але довго не прийшлося – там з [illegible] цем було тяжко.

We didn't have to study long – the play was short, and within a month we had staged it. With a strong drama group at my side, I didn't focus on the difficulties, and always tried to expand it to stage a more substantial play or drama. But I didn't stay long – things became difficult there.

З Німеччини мене розлучили з друзями, з яким місці був в іншому, так що не хотілося ставати п'єси над цим. Я поїхав до іншого фабрику (Mundham – Chichester), де й проживав до жовтня місяця. Й в 1948 р. в кінці – де т. С.У.Б. – де й був до 1949 р.

I was separated from my friends when I left Germany and sent to another place, so it no longer felt worthwhile to keep putting on plays. I went to another factory (Mundham – Chichester), where I lived until October. And at the end of 1948, I returned to the AUGB (С.У.Б.), where I stayed until 1949.

APPENDIX A

1948 – 49 pp. в мене були посвячені для вивчення Англійської мови. День і ніч сидючи кело книжок не звертаючи уваги на те, що молодий і час прийшов саме трбе підти розвижитись.

The years 1948 – 49 were dedicated to studying English. Day and night, sitting at my desk with books, I paid no attention to the fact that I was young, and that it was really time to go out and grow.

Ще в 1948 р. мав найліпшого друга з Німеччини – А. Рибалко, котрий з різних думок і переживань з'їхав з глузду, правда йому помогиа біблія, що спершу забміснувся був так, що коли виходив вечорам, то йому привиджувалися якісь бом, англи і т.п.

Back in 1948, I had a best friend from Germany – A. Rybalko – who, because of various thoughts and anxieties, lost his mind. The Bible did help him, though: at first, he was so unsettled that when he went out in the evenings, he would see visions – bombs, angels, and so on.

Перебуваючи майже цілий рік в Mundham, я не познайомився навідь з якою не будь Miss, завдяки тому, що виучував англійську мову.

Spending nearly a full year in Mundham, I didn't even get to know any kind of Miss – all because I was studying English.

APPENDIX A

Struck-through Diary page, approximately 1950:

Настав проклятий час, як ще ніколи! Усе збожеволіло для той час! Чому це стається? – не знаю! А не можу лишень собі сказати, що світу вже довго не існувало! У цю земля не обкрутитися й раз! А через це життя таке проклят!

The damned time has come, like never before! Everything went mad in that moment! Why is this happening? – I don't know! And I can't even tell myself that the world has long ceased to exist! This earth cannot turn even once! Because of this life – so cursed!

І безлад бідкає скрізь! Тому що люди збожеволіли! Не можло праву віднайти!

And chaos weeps everywhere! Because people have gone mad. Justice could not be found.

Note: the original text continues beyond this point.

Лютий 50: в новому місті побуту ознайомлюся з місцевістею і завіду ю до клубу, де й знайомлюся з одною англійкою і так проходе лютий жадного понюблення не видко.

February 1950: In the new town, I'm settling in with the local area and I drop by the club, where I meet an Englishwoman – and so February passes, with no romance in sight.

20/VII/52. Прийшов той, час що мусив покинути роботу в госпіталі (St. Charles). Як звичайно, о 6-ііі год. ранку пішов до праці, де й виникло не порозуміння з завідувачем кухні. Але для мене жануної долі взагалі не граю чи буде добре чи зле. О 1-ш год. Закінчив роботу [?] попрощявся з дівчатами, а також з усім шнафом кухні. Правда, де хто не вірив що лишаю роботу після 13и місяців але пізніше удосто віришся. Отже тепер приход цілковития зміня і не знаю, як воно буде далі.

20 July 1952. The time came when I had to leave my job at the hospital (St. Charles). As usual, at six o'clock in the morning I went to work, where a misunderstanding arose with the head of the kitchen. But as for me – I don't play with fate, whether it turns out good or bad. At one o'clock I finished work [?], said goodbye to the girls, and also to the whole kitchen staff. Honestly, there were some who didn't believe I was leaving the job after thirteen months – but later, you'll come to understand it was deserved. So now comes a complete change, and I don't know how things will go from here.

Завтря думаю їхати подивитися на працю та, намерио, заступити працювати (при американській кухні). Що буду то за успіхи далі буде видно.

Tomorrow I'm planning to go and look at a job, and, I intend, to start working (in the American kitchen). What I'll end up doing – in the results to come, it will become clear.

APPENDIX A

Extended Diary Entry following 28 March 1948:

В Англії знахадиться понад сім українських партій, і кожна з них веде політику по-своєму. Партії, котрі числяться: ОУН, ОУН(р), УНДС, УГРДП, ОДВУ та інші.

In England, there are more than seven Ukrainian political parties, each pursuing its own agenda. The main ones include: OUN, OUN(r), UNDS, UHRDP, ODWU, and others.

Бо ціж партії горозко мовялися ще на дрібніші партійки, і то виходить ціла анархія! Кожного разу можна почути різні сварки, образи і павідь, доходить до великих речей. зовсім не хочу задлачувати, малех партій з, тоі причиш що іх, і тому в кількох партійних може належати за тиж.

But even these parties have splintered into smaller factions, and the result is total anarchy! Every time, you hear arguments, insults, and sharp retorts – it escalates into major confrontations. I absolutely do not want to get entangled in this, even a little, because there are so many of them that someone could end up belonging to several parties in a single week.

Note: This diary entry continues, but only the beginning has been transcribed and translated here. The remaining section continues with a description of meetings and political debate.

APPENDIX A

Letter from Wsewolod to Julia, August 1954

W. SKLIAR.
270, Gloucester Terrace
London, W. 2.
England.

11.8.54.

Моя Кохана Юля!

Отримавши від Вас листа спішу дати Вам відповіть, а рівночасно дякую! Мені ніколи не приходило на думку, а також і на розум, що я можу так виглядати як Ви кажете: „самолюбний чоловік до певної міри я можу призняти Вам рацію, а з другої сторони, ні! Бо в той час я був перемучений і ніколи не досипав, а тому і я так виглядав. А з рештою Ви сама переконалися який я є „самолюб" !?

W. SKLIAR.
270, Gloucester Terrace
London, W. 2.
England.

August 11, 1954.

My Beloved Yulia!

Having received your letter, I hasten to reply and, at the same time, to thank you! It never occurred to me, nor did it enter my mind, that I could appear as you say: "a self-loving man." To a certain extent, I can accept your reasoning, but on the other hand, no! Because at that time I was exhausted and never got enough sleep, and that's why I looked that way. As for the rest, you yourself have seen what kind of "self-lover" I truly am!?

В дійсності ця „маленька [?] перегородина нам шлях, але аж великих труднощів вона нам не приносить. Бо на протязі чотирьох, п'яти тижднів ми могли б бачитися з Вами в Лондоні. Ще не отримуючи від Вас листа - я вже не офіційно, але особисто почав робити заходи щоб стягнути Вас до Лондону.

In reality, this "little [?]" may partition our path, but it doesn't cause us any great difficulties. Because for four or five weeks, we could have been seeing each other in London. Even before receiving your letter, I had already begun, unofficially but personally, to make arrangements to bring you to London.

Що торкається Вашої родини, то Ви маєте вияснили амсолютну рацію, щоб я побачив їх, а вони мене, але тут стає велика проблема, що я не зможу приїхати до Франції аж до наступного року, а це є дуже і дуже довгий час для нас! Я вірю в те, що Ваші родичі нічого не будуть мати, проти того щоб ми побралися. А пізніше ми б могли разом поїхати до Ваших Родичів і відвідати їх.

Regarding your family, you have grasped the absolute truth of the matter: I should see them, and they me. But a big problem arises here: I won't be able to come to France until next year, and that is a very, very long time for us! I believe that your relatives will have no objections to us getting married. And later, we could travel together to visit your relatives.

Мені вирунула думка, що може Ви, а також Ваші родичі подумали над тим: „хто він і, що він за один є”? На це я можу лишень в декількох словах подати Вам свою характеристику, а також Моєї родини ([?] мого тата, бо мама залишилася забитою в 1943 р.).

A thought occurred to me: perhaps you, and your relatives too, have wondered: "Who is he, and what kind of person is he?" In response, I can only offer a brief character sketch of myself and my family (particularly concerning my father, as my mother was killed in 1943).

Що торкається моєї особи, то я лишень можу сказати те: Ви Юля особисто мене бачили і могли оцінити мене, (я себе ніколи не оцінюю, а також дуже рідко можу оповідати сам про себе, „що я знаю, то я нічого не знаю, слова Скурата,) але можу сказати що маю трохи освіти, а також свій фах, це наразі мій такий висновок. (А як що схочете знати більше, то я зможу написати повностю все.)

As for myself, I can only say this: Yulia, you saw me personally and could form your own judgment. (I never judge myself, and I also very rarely speak about myself – "what I know is that I know nothing," as Skurat said.) But I can say that I have some education and also my profession; that, for now, is my assessment. (And if you wish to know more, I can write everything in full.)

Мій Тато походить з родини священника, а також сам закінчив Духовну Семінарію, людина є старша, а також дуже логідна.

My father comes from a family of priests and also graduated from the Theological Seminary himself. He is an older man, and also very logical.

APPENDIX A

Дорога Юля – вірьте мені, що Ви [?] не будете, бо я люблю Вас, а коли я люблю, то це не є лиш фантазія, це є завершення моя мрія і велике досягнення моеї докприни.

Dear Yulia – believe me, nothing untoward will happen to you, because I love you. And when I love, it is not just a fantasy; it is the culmination of my dream and the great fulfilment of my principles.

Вірю, що Ви зрозумієте мене, так як я зрозумів Вас. Прийміть щирі побажання від мене а також мого Тата. Ви і Ваша родина.

I believe that you will understand me, just as I have understood you. Please accept sincere wishes from me and also from my father, for you and your entire family.

Вибачте мені, але я все ж [?] хотів би мати відповідь на попереднє моє питання - білими днями думаю за Вас і все дужче і дужче кохаю Вас.

Forgive me, but I still very much would like to have an answer to my previous question. Through bright days, I think of you, and I love you more and more, stronger and stronger.

Остаюся на віки Ваш Коханий

I remain forever yours, Your Beloved,

Всеволод

Wsewolod

PS. Передає щире побажання "your brother".

P.S. He sends sincere wishes to "your brother."

Цілую Вас безліч раз В. Скляр	Kissing you countless times, W. Skliar.

Note: This 1954 personal letter from Wsewolod, writing from London to Yulia, is composed in an emotionally expressive and informal style. It features frequent deviations from standard Ukrainian, including non-standard phonetic spellings, morphological variations, and grammatical constructions typical of conversational speech. While the broader context often makes Wsewolod's intent clear, a precise interpretation of every nuance is not always possible. Nonetheless, the letter vividly conveys his deep affection and underlying anxieties.

APPENDIX B

Soviet Directive on Grain Procurement – Kharkiv Region, 1932

This directive, issued in November 1932 by the Bureau of the Kharkiv Regional Committee of the Communist Party of Ukraine, targeted the districts of Sakhnovshchyna and Balakliia for failing to meet grain procurement quotas. It ordered sweeping punitive measures, including the suspension of supplies, arrests, party expulsions, and the deployment of mobile courts. Quoted in Chapter 6 it offers a stark illustration of the mechanisms of state terror during the Holodomor. The original record can be consulted at *State Archives of Kharkiv Region*.

English Translation:

STRICTLY CONFIDENTIAL

Communist Party (Bolsheviks) of Ukraine
Kharkiv Regional Committee of the CP(B)U

On the Course of Grain Procurement in Sakhnovshchyna and Balakliia Districts

1. In order to achieve a decisive breakthrough in grain procurement by mobilising the party organisations of the Sakhnovshchyna and Balakliia districts to accomplish the combat task – breaking the sabotage of procurement organised by kulak elements, eliminating resistance from certain village communists who had become de facto agents of sabotage,

and implementing on-site effective measures for carrying out the decisions of the Central Committee (30 October) and the Regional Committee (1 November) – dispatch the following commissions:

To Sakhnovshchyna district:

1. Hvozdishko /authorised by the Regional Committee/,
2. Shterna,
3. Slynko,
4. Demidov /authorised by the Regional GPU/.

To Balakliia district:

1. Sodin /authorised by the Regional Committee/,
2. Nikonenko,
3. Chernikov,
4. Kazimirskiy /authorised by the Regional GPU/.
5. Grant the commissions full authority, depending on the local situation, to take the following measures alongside mass mobilisation:

2.

a) Identify communists in villages and collectives who have acted as agents of sabotage, expel them from the party, and bring them to trial as traitors to the working class and collective peasantry.
b) Immediately halt the issuance of goods to those failing to deliver grain, whether collectivised or individual farmers.
c) Suspend all types of credit to kolkhozes that are demonstrably non-compliant with the grain plan, and hold chairmen and leadership boards legally accountable.
d) Remove goods from villages and kolkhozes that fail to meet quotas, and redirect these to those delivering grain to the state.
e) Prosecute individual farmers who wilfully default on their grain obligations according to existing laws.
f) Purge kolkhozes sabotaging grain delivery of all hostile and alien

elements; kulaks identified as organisers or inspirers of sabotage are to be detained by the GPU.

3. To ensure ruthless punishment of bread thieves and criminal elements embedded in kolkhoz leaderships, dispatch travelling sessions of the Oblast Court to these same districts under the law on the protection of socialist property:

a) To Sakhnovshchyna district under the chairmanship of Comrade Belyaev,
b) To Balakliia district under the chairmanship of Comrade Haylit.

These court sessions are to review all grain procurement cases and conclude no fewer than ten trials within five days, with verdicts published in the press.

The commissions and travelling courts are to arrive in the districts no later than 9 November 1932.

Transcription (original Ukrainian):

ЦІЛКОМ ТАЄМНО
КОМУНІСТИЧНА ПАРТІЯ (БІЛЬШОВИКІВ) УКРАЇНИ
ХАРКІВСЬКИЙ ОБЛАСКОМ КП(б)У

О ходе хлебозаготовок в Сахновщанском и Балаклеевском районах

1. Для создания решительного перелома в ходе хлебозаготовок мобилизации парторганизации Сахновщанского и Балаклеевского районов на решение боевой задачи – сломить саботаж хлебозаготовок, организованный кулацкими элементами, уничтожить сопротивление хлебозаготовкам со стороны части сельских коммунистов, ставших фактическими проводниками саботажа, и принятия на месте эффективных мер для реализации решения ЦК от 30/Х и Обкома от 1/XI, командировать:

В Сахновщанский район комиссию в составе т.т.

1. ГВОЗДИШКОГО /уполномоченный Обкома/,
2. ШТЕРНА,

3. СЛИНЬКА,

4. ДЕМИДОВА /уполномоченный Обл. ГПУ/.

В Балаклеевский район в составе т.т.

1. СОДИНА /уполномоченный Обкома/,

2. НІКОНЕНКО,

3. ЧЕРНИКОВА,

4. КАЗИМИРСКОГО /уполномоченный Обл. ГПУ/.

5. Дать комиссиям полномочия в зависимости от обстановки на месте, наряду с развертыванием массовой работы, принять следующие меры:

2.

а) Выявить коммунистов в селах и колхозах, ставших фактически проводниками саботажа хлебозаготовок, исключить их из рядов партии и предать суду, как предателей интересов рабочего класса и колхозного крестьянства.
б) Немедленно прекратить отпуск товаров нездатчикам хлеба, как колхозникам, так и единоличникам.
в) Прекратить всякого рода кредитование явно недобросовестных колхозов, которые не выполняют плана хлебозаготовок, а председателей правлений привлекать к ответственности.
г) Вывезти товары из сел и колхозов, невыполняющих план хлебозаготовок, перебросив эти товары в села и колхозы, сдающие хлеб государству.
д) Индивидуальников, злостно невыполняющих обязательства, не сдающих законтрактованный хлеб, не выполняющих плана хлебозаготовок, привлекать к ответственности согласно существующим законам.
е) Очистить колхозы, саботирующие хлебозаготовки, от всякого рода чуждых и враждебных элементов, а кулацкие элементы – организаторов и вдохновителей саботажа хлебозаготовок – изъять органами ГПУ.

3. Для беспощадной борьбы с расхитителями хлеба и преступными элементами, засевшими в правлениях отдельных колхозов, на основе

закона об охране общественной /социалистической/ собственности, направить в эти же районы выездные сессии Облсуда:

а) в Сахновщанский район под председательством т. БЕЛЯЕВА,
б) в Балаклеевский район под председательством т. ГАЙЛИТА.

Этим сессиям рассмотреть все дела о хлебозаготовках и в пятидневный срок рассмотреть не менее чем по 10 дел с опубликованием приговоров в печати.

Обязать комиссии и выездные сессии выездного суда выехать в районы не позже 9/XI-32 г.

APPENDIX C

Decalogue of a Ukrainian Nationalist, c. 1943-1945

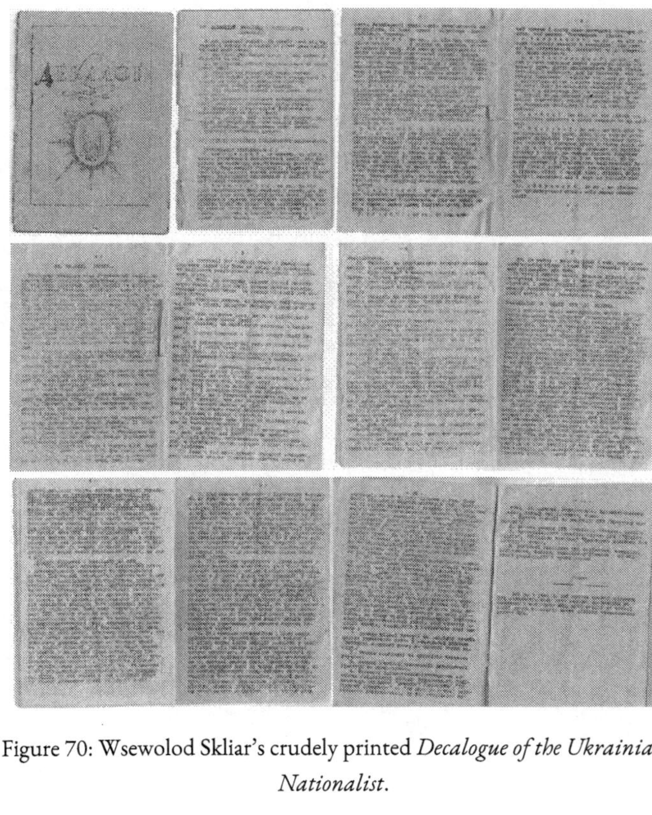

Figure 70: Wsewolod Skliar's crudely printed *Decalogue of the Ukrainian Nationalist.*

APPENDIX C

The following document – comprising the *Decalogue of the Ukrainian Nationalist*, the *Twelve Traits of Character*, and the *Forty-Four Rules for Life* – is presented here not as an endorsement but as a historical record. Its inclusion reflects the role such texts played in the ideological formation of many young Ukrainians in exile during and after the Second World War, including Wsewolod Skliar. Drafted in the interwar and wartime years and circulated among members and sympathisers of the Organisation of Ukrainian Nationalists (OUN), this material exhorts loyalty, sacrifice, and absolute commitment to the nationalist cause. While it was interpreted by some émigrés as a creed of moral clarity, others – especially in the postwar West – regarded its call to hatred and martyrdom with deep unease.

This book does not seek to rehabilitate or condemn the ideological content. Rather, it aims to document how belief systems shaped individual lives and communal memory under conditions of displacement and statelessness. The moral absolutism of the Decalogue – including its exhortation to "*with hatred and unrelenting struggle... confront the enemies of your Nation*" – must be understood in the context of wartime occupation, trauma, and exile, which narrowed political options and sharpened ideological fervour.

Wsewolod's personal retention of these texts into his adult life suggests they remained symbolically important. Yet his later writings show a marked turn away from militancy. While he maintained a strong sense of duty and cultural guardianship, there is no evidence that he upheld or acted upon the Decalogue's more extreme imperatives. What follows, then, is reproduced as a primary source of historical significance – a document that shaped a generation, and whose legacy remains contested.

APPENDIX C

Note on Provenance

Wsewolod's copy of the OUN Decalogue, can be firmly dated to pre-1948 on the basis it was stored with his papers brought from Germany to Britain in 1948. Textual and visual evidence points to a more specific range of 1943–1945. The document's content, including references to the "Ukrainian Revolutionary Army" (UPA, formed 1942), aligns with OUN-B's wartime ideology under Stepan Bandera, particularly during the UPA's peak resistance against Soviet and Nazi forces in Halychyna. The cover's Tryzub emblem and serif typography, typical of OUN-B underground presses in occupied Ukraine, further support this dating, reflecting wartime printing constraints. While a precise date is unavailable due to the absence of a printer's mark, the Decalogue's likely provenance is an OUN-B press in Halychyna, possibly Lviv, distributed to UPA recruits like Wsewolod Skliar in Sambir. This assessment is based on historical context and the document's physical condition, which shows wear consistent with wartime use and subsequent exile.

ДЕКАЛОҐ	DECALOGUE
10 ЗАПОВІДЕЙ УКРАЇНЦЯ - НАЦІОНАЛІСТА	10 COMMANDMENTS OF THE UKRAINIAN NATIONALIST
Я дух одвічної стихії, що зберіг тебе від татарської потопи й поставив на грані двох світів творити нове життя.	I am the spirit of an eternal force that preserved You through the Tatar deluge and placed You at the border of two worlds to create new life.

APPENDIX C

1. Здобудеш Українську Державу або згинеш у боротьбі за Неї.
2. Не дозволиш нікому сплямити слави ні честі Твоєї Нації.
3. Пам'ятай про Великі Дні наших змагань.
4. Будь гордий з того, що Ти є спадкоємець боротьби за славу Володимирового Тризуба.
5. Пімсти смерть Великих Лицарів.
6. Про справу не говори з ким можна, лише з ким треба.
7. Не завагаєшся виконати найнебезпечнішого чину, якщо цього вимагатиме добро справи.
8. Ненавистю й безоглядною боротьбою прийматимеш ворогів Твоєї Нації.
9. Ані просьби, ані грозьби, ні тортури, ні смерть не приневолять тебе зрадити тайни.

1. You shall establish the Ukrainian State or perish in the struggle for it.
2. You shall not allow anyone to defile the glory or honour of your Nation.
3. Remember the Great Days of our struggle.
4. Be proud that you are the heir to the fight for the glory of Volodymyr's Trident.
5. Avenge the deaths of the Great Knights.
6. Do not speak of the cause with those you may, only with those you must.
7. You shall not hesitate to carry out the most dangerous act, if the good of the cause demands it.
8. With hatred and unrelenting struggle, you shall confront the enemies of your Nation.
9. No pleas, nor entreaties, nor torture, nor death shall compel you to betray secrets.

10. Змагатимеш до поширення сили, багатства й простору Української Держави.

10. You shall strive to expand the power, wealth, and territory of the Ukrainian State.

12 ПРИКМЕТ ХАРАКТЕРУ УКРАЇНСЬКОГО НАЦІОНАЛІСТА

12 TRAITS OF CHARACTER OF A UKRAINIAN NATIONALIST

Український націоналіст є:

1. всеготовий, це значить, що він є вояком Української Революційної Армії. Він бореться на великому, всеобіймаючому фронті Української Національної Революції, віддаючи всі свої сили, готовий кожної хвилини віддати й своє життя. Український націоналіст є завжди в повній боєвій готовости.

A Ukrainian nationalist is:

1. Ever ready - that is, he is a soldier of the Ukrainian Revolutionary Army. He fights on the broad, all-encompassing front of the Ukrainian National Revolution, giving his all, ready at any moment to give even his life. The Ukrainian nationalist is always in full combat readiness.

2. б е з к о р и с н и й , це зн., що він Ідею Українського Націоналізму й службу для Неї ставить вище всіх скарбів світа цього. Для Неї проміняє з радістю можливість спокійного та вигідного життя на тверду долю жовніраборця, теплу хату на окопи чи тюрму. Щастя шукає і знаходить в радости з боротьби й перемоги в почуванні служби Великій, Святій Справі. Лише в щасті Української Нації щастя українського націоналіста. Її воля, слава й могутність - його найбільше бажання.

3. ч е с н и й , це зн., що він ім'я націоналіста носить гідно й ніколи не сплямить ніяким нечесним вчинком. Він завжди придержується високих вимог націоналістичної моралі. Мораль опортуністичного світу родить і плекає безділля, страх, фаризейство, вигоди й угоди. Мораль націоналіста, це мораль нового світу, світу чину й боротьби. Вона є основою чинного й чистого мов хрусталь, характеру націоналіста, Лицаря-Революціонера.

2. Selfless - that is, he places the Idea of Ukrainian Nationalism and service to it above all the treasures of this world. For it, he gladly exchanges a peaceful and comfortable life for the hard fate of a soldier-struggler, a warm home for trenches or prison. He seeks happiness and finds it in the joy of struggle and victory, in the experience of service to the Great and Holy Cause. Only in serving the Ukrainian Nation does the nationalist find himself. Her will, glory, and power - these are his greatest desires.

3. Honest - that is, he bears the name of a nationalist with dignity and never defiles it with any dishonourable deed. He always upholds the high standards of nationalist morality. The morality of the opportunistic world breeds and nurtures idleness, fear, hypocrisy, comfort and compromise. The morality of the nationalist is the morality of a new world - a world of action and struggle. It is the foundation of the active and crystalline character of the nationalist, the Knight-Revolutionary.

4. к а р н и й , це зн., що він безоглядно підпорядкований і вірний аж до смерти Ідеї Українського Націоналізму, Організації Українських Націоналістів і провідникам. Кожний приказ для нього святий. Він знає, що карність це основа організації й сили, а анархія це руїна. Тому завжди піддержує авторітет Проводу Української Нації з Вождем Українського Народу на чолі.

4. Disciplined - that is, he is absolutely subordinate and faithful unto death to the Idea of Ukrainian Nationalism, the Organisation of Ukrainian Nationalists, and its leaders. Every command is sacred to him. He knows that discipline is the foundation of organisation and strength, while anarchy is ruin. Therefore, he always upholds the authority of the Leadership of the Ukrainian Nation with the Leader of the Ukrainian People at its head.

5. а к т и в н и й і п і д п р и є м ч и в и й , це зн., що він бореться всіми силами використовуючи всі можливості, кожну хвилину для добра Великої Справи - Української Національної Революції. Він не знає безділля. В нього за думкою й словом іде чин, мов за блискавкою грім. Бо життя це рух, боротьба, а спокій це застій і холодна смерть. Кожну ідею, організацію чи людину оцінює по ділах, а не словах. Пасивність - це прикмета рабства. Пасивності раба протиставляє творчу ініціативу й напружену активність борця-провідника.

5. Active and enterprising - that is, he fights with all his strength, using every opportunity, every moment, for the good of the Great Cause - the Ukrainian National Revolution. He does not know idleness. With him, action follows thought and word as thunder follows lightning. For life is motion and struggle; stillness is stagnation and cold death. He judges every idea, organisation, or person by deeds, not words. Passivity is the trait of slavery. Against passivity, he pits creative initiative and the tense activity of the fighter-leader.

6. в і д в а ж н и й , це зн., що він завжди відважно й неустрашимо протиставляється всім перешкодам і небезпекам. Він не знає, що то є страх. Заяча вдача боягуза-труса йому чужа і гидка.

7. р і ш у ч и й , це зн., що він кожний приказ і кожну свою постанову виконує рішучо, без вагань. Постановив - зробив.

8. в и т р е в а л и й , це зн., що він завжди бореться завзято й витревало. Він знає, що без витревалости, доведеної аж до впертості, нема перемоги.

9. з р і в н о в а ж е н и й , це зн., що він у всіх випадках життя задержує повну рівновагу духа. Життя націоналіста повне трудів, перешкод і небезпек. Щоб їх побороти, щоб опанувати положення й зібрати всі сили до удару у відповідне місце - треба насамперед опанувати себе.

6. Courageous - that is, he always boldly and fearlessly confronts all obstacles and dangers. He does not know what fear is. The rabbit-hearted nature of a coward is foreign and repulsive to him.

7. Decisive - that is, he executes every command and his own resolutions firmly, without hesitation. What he resolves, he carries out.

8. Persistent - that is, he always fights with determination and endurance. He knows that without persistence - carried to the point of stubbornness - there can be no victory.

9. Balanced - that is, he maintains complete composure in all circumstances of life. The life of a nationalist is full of toil, obstacles, and danger. To overcome them, to assess the situation, to gather strength for a strike at the right place - one must first master oneself.

Тому український націоналіст у підземеллі й в отвертому бою, в окопах і в тюрмі, в тріюмфі чи на ступнях шибениці, завжди однаково спокійний, гордий і усміхнений. Вміє по лицарськи побіджати і вміє по геройськи вмирати.

That is why the Ukrainian nationalist - whether in the underground or in open battle, in trenches or in prison, in triumph or on the steps of the gallows - is always equally calm, proud, and smiling. He knows how to win with knightly honour, and how to die heroically.

10. точний, це зн., що він завжди придержується точности в житті включно аж до дрібниць.

10. Precise - that is, he always adheres to precision in life, even in the smallest details.

11. здоровий, це зн., що він хоче бути здоровим. Він хоче, щоби ціле молоде українське покоління було здорове. Україна потребує сильних і здорових духом і тілом синів. Тому сам в міру можливости вправляє та поширює руханку і спорт, не нищить свойого здоровля вживанням отруй /не пє і не курить/, ні гулящим життям.

11. Healthy - that is, he wants to be healthy. He wants the entire young Ukrainian generation to be healthy. Ukraine needs sons strong and healthy in body and spirit. Therefore, he himself, as far as possible, practises and promotes exercise and sport, does not destroy his health with poisons (he neither drinks nor smokes), nor with a debauched life.

В українського націоналіста Велика Ідея в серці, вогонь революційного духа в грудях, міцні й гнучкі мязи, сталеві нерви, бистрий соколиний зір і слух та твердий пястук.

A Ukrainian nationalist has the Great Idea in his heart, the fire of revolutionary spirit in his chest, firm and supple muscles, steel nerves, sharp falcon-like eyesight and hearing, and a strong fist.

12. обережний, це зн., що він завжди придержується строго всіх засоад конспірації.	12. Cautious - that is, he always strictly observes all the principles of secrecy.

Following the Ten Commandments and the Twelve Traits, the document continues with a detailed section entitled *"Rules for Life"* (*Правила Життя*), which lays out the ideological, moral, and practical foundations of Ukrainian nationalist existence – including forty-four rules members must follow. This section is aimed in particular at members and candidates of the Organisation of Ukrainian Nationalists (OUN). It begins with a sweeping declaration of the Ukrainian nation's eternal mission to rise from historical defeat and lead a spiritual and political renewal through the creation of a sovereign Ukrainian state. Past failures in the national struggle are reframed as a call to action, with the reader urged to cast off the remnants of a colonised past and embrace a life of revolutionary service and total devotion.

The text places a strong emphasis on personal discipline and moral integrity. Nationalists are commanded to live by the principles previously outlined in the Decalogue and the Twelve Traits: self-discipline, courage, loyalty, and discretion. These values are to be demonstrated through everyday behaviour and lifelong readiness for sacrifice. The ideal nationalist avoids indulgence, maintains physical and moral purity, and interprets hardship not as misfortune but as proof of inner strength and devotion. Service to the nation is elevated to a spiritual calling, and reverence is accorded to the memory of those who died in its defence – the so-called "Great Knights". The text insists that each act must be performed as if it were to be remembered forever.

Beginning on page 7, the document turns to a section titled *"To OUN Candidates: For Your Knowledge"*, offering an intensive briefing for new or aspiring members. This portion articulates the OUN's self-conception as heir to Ukraine's revolutionary tradition and the vanguard of its future independence. The organisation is described as both the guardian of the past and the organiser of a reborn national order. As such, it requires from its members not only belief, but discipline, secrecy, and constant action.

The document lays out five categories in which every candidate must excel: moral, physical, social, professional, and political. Morally, the candidate must be blameless – honest, temperate, patriotic, and self-sacrificing. Physically, he must be strong and prepared to endure hardship in clandestine or military conditions. Socially, he must lead by example and win the respect of his community. Professionally, he must be diligent and competent, contributing his skills to the nationalist cause. Politically, he must be literate in Ukraine's history, geopolitics, and ideological enemies – above all, communism, and international socialism – not to debate them, but to resist and defeat them.

The final pages list the knowledge expected of every candidate. This includes fluency in Ukrainian history and geography, awareness of cultural heritage, and a thorough grasp of the movement's canon – including the Decalogue, the Twelve Traits, and the Forty-Four Rules for Life. Candidates must also understand the structure and programme of the OUN and be familiar with key ideological terms and enemies. The document concludes with an emphatic statement: only those who meet these exacting standards – moral, intellectual, and physical – may truly call themselves members of the OUN.

APPENDIX D
Image Credits

Every effort has been made to trace copyright holders. Where original authors or rights holders could not be identified, such materials are reproduced in good faith for educational and historical purposes. The author will be pleased to rectify any omissions in future editions.

This table lists credited external images used as figures in the manuscript – primarily artworks, maps, and archival photographs. All unlisted figures in this book – photographs, letters, documents, and objects – are drawn from the author's personal or family archive.

All listed images are, to the best of our knowledge, either in the public domain or made available under Creative Commons licences that permit reproduction. Each is reproduced with appropriate attribution to its original institution or repository. Descriptions reflect the image's historical context or its interpretive role within the surrounding narrative.

Figure	Description	Source
1	Map of central regions of the Ukrainian SSR (1939)	From *Bolshoi Sovietskii Atlas Mira*, Vol. II. Moscow: Glavnoe Upravlenie Geodezii i Kartografii pri SNK SSSR, 1939. Published by the Chief Administration of Geodesy and Cartography under the Council of

		People's Commissars of the USSR. Adapted for this publication.
4	Photograph of Virgin Orans mosaic	Unknown Author. Google Arts & Culture. Wikimedia Commons.
5	*Terra Cosaccorum* (*Land of the Cossacks*)	University of Alberta, Chrysant & Leslie Dmytruk Collection of Maps of Ukraine & Eastern Europe. Published by archive.org.
6	*Peasant Family* by Taras Shevchenko, (1843)	National Museum Taras Shevchenko, Kyiv. Wikimedia Commons.
7	*Reply of the Zaporozhian Cossacks to Sultan Mehmed IV*, sketch by Ilya Repin (1893)	Kharkiv Art Museum *(Харківський художній музей*).
8	*The Intercession* (1739 – 41), painted for the Church of the Intercession in Sulymivka, Poltava	National Art Museum of Ukraine (NAMU), Kyiv, Ukraine. Wikimedia Commons.
10	Postcard depicting rural life in Poltava guberniya, probably late 19th century	From the collection of Volodymyr Koziuk. Published by Euromaidan Press.
11	*Zemstvo Members Having Lunch* by Grigorij Myasoyedov (1872)	Tretyakov Gallery, Moscow. Published by the Yorck Project. Wikimedia Commons.
12	*Church of St. Helena. Chapel of the Church of the Holy Sepulchre* by Vasily Polenov (1882)	Tretyakov Gallery, Moscow. Wikimedia Commons.

14	Ethnographic map of Ukrainian-inhabited territory (1915)	Leibniz Institute for East and Southeast European Studies. Wikimedia Commons.
15	Postcard showing Sakhnovshchyna (c. 1900)	Unknown.
16	Photograph of Ukrainian women from the Poltava region (c. 1914)	Unknown Author. Wikimedia Commons.
17	Photograph of The Destruction of St. Michael's Golden-Domed Monastery, Kyiv (1935–1937)	Unknown Author. From: *Вечерський В. В. Втрачені об'єкти архітектурної спадщини України*. – К.: НДІТІАМ, 2002. Wikimedia Commons.
18	Photograph of Trinity Church in Opishnya (1920)	Unknown Author. From: *Encyclopaedia*, Vol. 12: *Religion and the Church*. Poltava: "Poltava Writer", 2009. Wikimedia Commons..
20	Postcard showing Poltava Seminary (c. 1905)	Unknown Author. Wikimedia Commons.
23	Photograph of a *korovai* from Sakhnovshchyna – a traditional Ukrainian ceremonial bread, recognised as part of Ukraine's intangible cultural heritage (2022)	Original photograph by the Kharkiv Regional Military Administration. Image cropped and resized for this publication. Licensed under Creative Commons Attribution 4.0 International (CC BY 4.0). Licence available at: https://creativecommons.org/licenses/by/4.0/. Wikimedia Commons.
24	*Bread Is Our Strength* propaganda poster by Дмитрий Стахиевич Моор (1931)	From The Sergio Grigorian Collection of Soviet Political Posters, at Red-Avantgarde. Wikimedia Commons.

25	*Black Square (Black Suprematic Square)* by Kazimir Malevich (1915)	Tretyakov Gallery, Moscow. Wikimedia Commons.
26	Postcard marking 15th Anniversary of the Holodomor (1948)	Ukrainian Youth Association. From: Morgan Williams, *Holodomor through the eyes of Ukrainian artists*; U.S. – Ukraine Business Council. Wikimedia Commons.
30	Photograph of Soviet SU-2 flight crew and ground personnel (c. 1942)	Unknown Author. Wikimedia Commons.
33	Map of Nazi Occupied Europe September 1943	Original map created by Wikimedia Commons user "Female bodybuilder enthusiast". Image adapted for this publication. Licensed under Creative Commons Attribution-Share Alike 3.0 Unported (CC BY-SA 3.0). Licence available at: https://creativecommons.org/licenses/by-sa/3.0/. Wikimedia Commons.
35	Photograph of Displaced Persons camp, Wittlich, Germany (1945)	From: *History of the Fifteenth United States Army. 21 August 1944 to 11 July 1945*, U.S. Army Command and General Staff College, 100 Stimson Ave, Fort Leavenworth, Kansas (USA), 13 December 1946. Wikimedia Commons
41	Photograph of UPA partisans (c. 1943-1947)	Unknown Author. Published by: The Center for Liberation Movement Studies. Wikimedia Commons.
60	Photograph of members of Vaplite (c. 1926)	Unknown Author. Wikimedia Commons.

Acknowledgements

Above all, this book is a testament to those whose stories it contains. I owe my deepest gratitude to the generations of my family and the countless Ukrainians whose quiet resilience, endurance, and sacrifices form its very heart. Though many of their voices were silenced or lost, some of their stories have finally found space here. I hope they do not judge me too harshly.

I must particularly thank my aunt, Nina, who first motivated me to begin writing and generously reviewed early drafts, offering clarity, insight, and encouragement when I most needed them.

Thanks are also due to my mother, Catherina, to whom I am indebted for carrying forward her Ukrainian identity and whose memories helped illuminate key details

Finally, special thanks to my partner, Peishan. Although she has not yet read this manuscript – and remains slightly bemused by my dedication to it – her patience and support throughout the writing process has been invaluable.

About the Author

With family origins in central Ukraine, Ben Skliar-Ward writes about the intersections of history, memory, and identity. His work focuses on the quieter currents of the past: how families navigate political rupture, how belief and habit persist under pressure, and how silence becomes its own form of legacy.

The Quiet That Remains is his first book. It traces the broad arc of Ukrainian history through the lives of his Ukrainian relatives across famine, war, and exile – not through heroic narrative, but through fragments, contradictions, and what remains when history passes over the ordinary. His approach combines archival research with a careful attention to what is missing, withheld, or only half-remembered.

Ben lives in London and works in financial crime prevention.

Printed in Dunstable, United Kingdom

79345246R00167